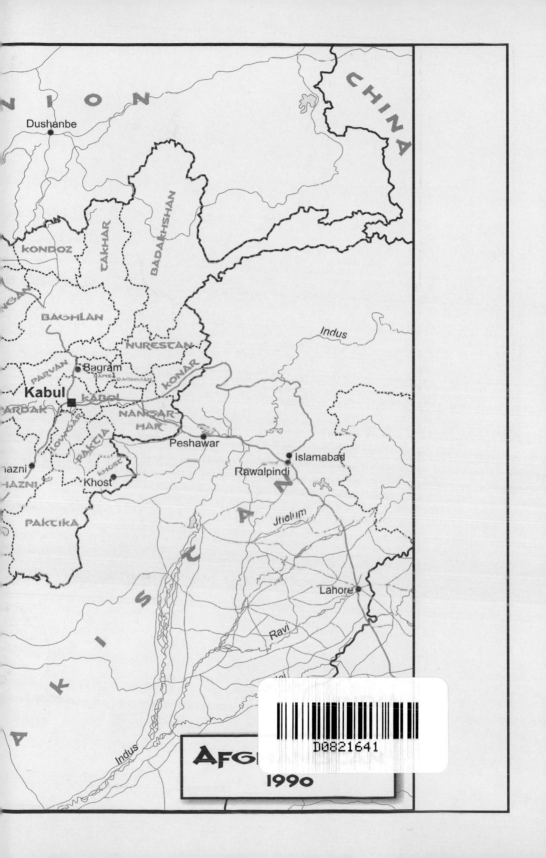

CHINA

N I O N

Dushanbe

KONDOZ

TAKHAR

BADAKHSHAN

BAGHLAN

Indus

NURESTAN

PARVAN

Bagram

KONAR

Kabul

KABOL

WARDAK

NANGAR

HAR

LOWGAR

PAKTIA

Peshawar

KHOST

Islamabad

ghazni

Rawalpindi

GHAZNI

Khost

PAKTIKA

Jhelum

Lahore

Ravi

Indus

AFG

1990

D0821641

BREEDING GROUND

ALSO BY DEEPAK TRIPATHI

Overcoming the Bush Legacy in Iraq and Afghanistan

Sri Lanka's Foreign Policy Dilemmas

RELATED TITLES FROM POTOMAC BOOKS, INC.

The Other War: Winning and Losing in Afghanistan
—Amb. Ronald E. Neumann (Ret.)

After the Taliban: Nation-Building in Afghanistan
—Amb. James F. Dobbins

How We Missed the Story: Osama bin Laden, the Taliban, and the Hijacking of Afghanistan (U.S. Institute of Peace)
—Roy Gutman

BREEDING GROUND

Afghanistan and the Origins of Islamist Terrorism

DEEPAK TRIPATHI

FOREWORD BY RICHARD FALK

Potomac Books, Inc.
Washington, D.C.

Library of Congress Cataloging-in-Publication Data
Tripathi, Deepak.
  Breeding ground : Afghanistan and the origins of Islamic terrorism / Deepak Tripathi ; foreword by Richard Falk. — 1st ed.
      p. cm.
  Includes bibliographical references and index.
  ISBN 978-1-59797-530-8 (hardcover : alk. paper)
  1. Afghanistan—History—Soviet occupation, 1979-1989. 2. Afghanistan—Politics and government—1973-1989. 3. Afghanistan—Politics and government—1989-2001. 4. Afghanistan—Politics and government—2001- 5. Communism—Afghanistan—History. 6. Anti-communist movements—Afghanistan—History. 7. Islam and politics—Afghanistan—History. 8. Terrorism—Religious aspects—Islam—History. 9. Terrorism—Afghanistan—History—20th century. 10. Terrorism—Afghanistan—History—21st century. I. Title.
  DS371.2.T74 2010
  958.104—dc22

                                                                    2010037450

Printed in the United States of America on acid-free paper that meets the American National Standards Institute Z39-48 Standard.

Potomac Books, Inc.
22841 Quicksilver Drive
Dulles, Virginia 20166

First Edition

10 9 8 7 6 5 4 3 2 1

For Madhu

CONTENTS

Foreword	ix
Preface	xvii
Acknowledgments	xxv
Note on Style and Spellings	xxvii
Glossary	xxix

1.	THE CONCEPT OF TERROR	1
2.	CULTURE OF VIOLENCE	17
3.	AFGHANISTAN IN THE COLD WAR	21
4.	AFGHANISTAN UNDER COMMUNISM	31
5.	TOWARD DISINTEGRATION	39
6.	THE SECOND COMMUNIST COUP	47
7.	LET BATTLE COMMENCE	59
8.	THE REAGAN OFFENSIVE	67
9.	CONSEQUENCES OF THE U.S.-SOVIET WAR	77
10.	THE FINAL DAYS OF COMMUNISM	87
11.	THE REMAKING OF THE POST-SOVIET WORLD	97
12.	THE RISE OF THE TALIBAN	107
13.	DIALECTICS OF THE AFGHAN CONFLICT	117
14.	THE NATURE OF AL QAEDA	127
15.	CONCLUSION	135

Afterword	143
Appendices	153
Notes	171
Bibliography	203
Index	217
About the Author	224

FOREWORD

A fghanistan remains an unsolved political riddle for current intervenors; it first seductively tempts political actors to make ceaseless efforts to find the solution, and then disappoints and frustrates those who succumb to the temptation. The latest in a long array of promises to bring stability and justice to Afghanistan is a renewed escalation of engagement by the United States. For whatever reason, President Obama staked his global security credentials on switching counterinsurgency horses: promising to jump off in Iraq, while committing to mount more firmly in Afghanistan in what he has misleadingly called "a war of necessity." Unfortunately, with the passage of time, it seems like one more example of a liberal American political figure's futile attempt to convince the national security establishment, political conservatives, Republicans, and the Pentagon/ CIA bureaucracy that he is militarist enough in foreign policy to be a trustworthy custodian of the country's vital interests. John F. Kennedy, Lyndon B. Johnson, and, to a much lesser extent, Bill Clinton, all impaled themselves on this petard of seeking credibility with the domestic military-industrial complex, not only at great cost to their political reputation and to America's global leadership role, but also, most significantly, with the results of casualties at home and massive death, displacement, and destruction for the society at the scene of the conflict.

Is there any reason to suppose that the Afghan riddle is now any riper for solution by way of a ramped-up counterinsurgency strategy under the aegis of American leadership? Actually, recent developments mainly lend credence to the opposite assessment, which supports the view that the ineffectuality of the externally imposed pro-Washington government in Kabul is being increasingly outmaneuvered and undermined by a wily, revived version of the Taliban—a Taliban reinforced by a series of Islamist and other resistance militias that pose an increasing challenge to the US/NATO forces. Even the severely compromised Karzai leadership, which owes its very existence to the United States intervention shortly after September 11, feels compelled to publicly complain about the unacceptability of recent American military tactics that are producing large numbers of Afghan (and Pakistani) civilian casualties from missiles fired by drone Predators at what were supposed to be al Qaeda and Taliban targets. Such drone attacks have led to increasingly strident protests in Afghanistan against the U.S.-led NATO operations, and have further eroded the legitimacy of the Karzai government, which was permanently discredited by the fraudulent electoral process that most ambiguously confirmed Karzai's mandate in mid-2009.

The stakes of the United States of finally getting Afghanistan "right" are very high, primarily for the Afghan people, who have for decades borne the brunt of suffering and dislocation resulting from a punishing sequence of foreign interventions that have sundered the delicate social fabric of a country consisting of multiple ethnicities and a variety of related tribal, clan, and regional—yet rarely national—loyalties. These results have been disastrous for the country, first during the harshly imposed decade of Soviet Communism beginning in 1978 and then later, when an extreme form of political Islam rose up in resistance to the Soviet presence. The resistance was strongly backed and armed by such external actors as Pakistan, China, and the United States, and eventually triumphed over internal competitors vying for control of the country. This set of developments resulted in a tragic instance of blowback that produced several cycles of violent chaos within Afghanistan and has made the political outcome of a moderate, stable, competent, unified, humane, and secular Afghan governance as distant as ever. Such a dynamic of violence and corruption has continued for almost forty years and seems likely to gather an intensifying fury in response to the prospect of the escalating intervention that embodies the Obama approach.

The impact of the persisting Afghanistan War on Pakistan, and the region, should not be overlooked. The strategic stakes are high. There is a likelihood that existing rampant anti-Americanism in Pakistan will intensify further in response to any expanded American military commitment, reinforced by cross-border attacks on suspected Taliban and al Qaeda sanctuaries in Pakistan. In the background, of course, is the risk of an extremist takeover of the Pakistani governing process, encouraging terrorists to seek access to nuclear weapons and increasing the possibility of a regional war between two nuclear weapons states. The Afghan stakes in demilitarizing the American role are great, but because of the Pakistan dimension, the regional and global dangers of a heightened counterinsurgency in Afghanistan are even greater.

Unfortunately the United States seems to be embarking on yet another experiment in counterinsurgency doctrine and practice conducted with severe consequences for a third-world nation. In Vietnam the United States had total military dominance and yet lost the war, suggesting limits to the relevance of military power in shaping political outcomes. It is worth recalling a paradigmatic conversation between an American counterinsurgency specialist and his Vietnamese counterpart at the end of the Vietnam War:

Col. Summers: You know you never defeated us on the battlefield.
Col. Tu: That is true but irrelevant.

Absorbing the lessons of this irrelevance would help reorient thinking about what to do in Afghanistan. But there is great resistance to learning such lessons, not least from the governmental and market forces that Dwight Eisenhower had famously warned about in his farewell address more than a half century ago—the aforementioned military-industrial complex that exerts almost total control over policy formation and debate with respect to issues of war and peace. It needs to be understood that this military-industrial complex, with growing media support and a network of Washington Beltway think tanks, has been successfully solidifying its influence over the course of these last five decades, receiving an enormous boost in the form of the September 11 attacks. American militarism now is underwritten by a shockingly excessive budget that approximates the amount spent by the rest of the world combined, possesses several hundred foreign military bases in more than sixty countries, has navies in all five major oceans, and has embarked on a variety of projects to ensure military dominance in space. This set of circumstances has a deterministic impact, making it nearly impossible for American political leaders, and much of the public, to think outside the militarist box when it comes to shaping policy for Afghanistan. What should be surprising is that despite this enormous investment in military technology and interventionary diplomacy, the U.S. government and the American people have never felt more vulnerable than at any other point in the nation's history.

After the failure in Vietnam the American military leadership did initially try to regroup by shaping a new consensus, which was put forward in a form that became known as the Weinberger/Powell doctrine. The essential message of these reformulations of grand strategy was that the United States should never again get involved in a war unless it could bring overwhelming force to bear on its adversary and enjoy the strong backing of American society for the war effort. These two preconditions for future intervention were thought to take into account the main deficiencies of the American counterinsurgency approach as applied in Vietnam—namely, not bringing sufficiently overwhelming force to bear and failing to maintain the support and optimism of the American public as casualties mounted. From the mid-1970s on, this overall reluctance by the United States to pursue interventionary goals by overt military means was labeled the Vietnam Syndrome. Each American president since Vietnam has bemoaned these limitations on foreign policy, but it was not until 1991, when George H. W. Bush's first words after winning the Gulf War were "[w]e have finally kicked the Vietnam Syndrome," that military intervention began to get back its good name in the Washington think tanks and the earlier lessons of the Vietnam defeat were forgotten. Of course, the elder Bush's exaltation meant that the United States, with its ultra-modern military machine and the absence of an inhibiting draft of middle-class Americans, believed it could now fight and win wars quickly anywhere on the planet and, what is more, without significant American casualties, drain on resources, or high-profile protest at home. This revived militarist triumphalism was reinforced by the Kosovo War in 1999 when the NATO operation achieved its aims from the air without losing a single combat soldier, giving rise to the celebratory claim that American military superiority had reached such technological heights that future wars would be fought with zero casualties. From such a giddy perspective, there seemed little reason to exert much restraint on the projection of American power around the world.

This renewed, yet always misguided, confidence in the political potency of military superiority was influential in fashioning a mindlessly militarist overreaction to the September 11 attacks. Afghanistan became the first theater of operations for a neoconservative grand strategy built around the September 11 provocation and given grandiose names such as the "global war on terror" and the "long war." As with Kuwait and Kosovo in the 1990s, American dominance in conventional war-fighting capabilities produced lightning results in Afghanistan with few American casualties and seemed to effortlessly remove from power the abusive and extremist Taliban regime and to disrupt al Qaeda operations, causing survivors to flee across the border. The Afghanistan War was touted at the time as a "near perfect war" by such Washington policy wonks as Michael O'Hanlon. This kind of thinking reached its theatrical apogee on May 1, 2003, when George W. Bush spoke of the successful invasion of Iraq from the deck of an American aircraft carrier while the infamous banner proclaiming "Mission Accomplished" waved gently in the afternoon breeze and the sun sank symbolically behind the American leader.

But then a second awakening started to cloud this rose-tinted outlook of the new generation of Washington warriors and war planners. The post-battlefield occupation of Iraq unleashed an unexpectedly fierce national resistance, making it a much more costly and menacing phase of the war than had been expected. More disturbingly, while Iraq claimed center stage, the supposed quick fix in Afghanistan began to unravel, presaging a geopolitical disaster in the making, but remaining only a sideshow for the Bush II presidency. As many analysts noted, the neoconservative grand strategy that had been developed prior to September 11 awaited some political pretext to justify a military attack on Iraq. This was conceived as the first step in an ambitious plan to politically restructure the entire Middle East, and thereby secure military bases and Gulf oil supplies for the West, while contributing to long-term security for Israel.

From this perspective of grand strategy, Afghanistan was indeed a sideshow, and that it was treated as such exhibited the priorities of the neoconservatives. The entire mobilizing emphasis on al Qaeda and the war on terror was not what it seemed and claimed to be. Rather, it was largely designed to establish a mandate for taking full global advantage of what was hailed as a "unipolar moment" following the Soviet collapse. The main objective was to establish a global security system to be administered from Washington and anchored in effective political control of the Middle East. It was to be the first empire of truly global scope sustained by a capitalist global marketplace and reinforced by the supposedly omnipotent military power of the United States. Instead of an easy victory in Iraq, the American leadership in 2009 became saddled with a new "Iraq Syndrome," as well as the urgent need to cope with an economic meltdown of global proportions, intensified by a declining dollar, high unemployment rate, and rising fiscal and trade deficits.

As the Iraq War consumed American energies, resources, and political will, the supposed gains of the 2001 Afghanistan intervention began to disappear. At the same time, second comings of both the Taliban and al Qaeda in Afghanistan seemed almost inevitable. What is worse, this latest rendering of the struggle for the future of Afghanistan is further complicated and fraught with risk because the Afghan destiny is now so closely intertwined with that of Pakistan. This raises the nightmare fear of an extremist takeover in Islamabad, access by extremist non-state actors to weapons of mass destruction, and the alarming prospect of a regional nuclear war between India and Pakistan.

From this complex and disturbing vantage point, Deepak Tripathi's wonderfully lucid telling of the Afghanistan story is both timely and illuminating. It convincingly counters the tendency of the counterinsurgency specialists to focus their attention on ahistorical abstractions about military tactics and weaponry while largely ignoring the societal context and ethnic complexities wherein this particular conflict is situated. Tripathi incisively narrates the several generations of recent Afghan conflict and turmoil, and calls our attention to several crucial features of the Afghan reality often disregarded by past foreign intervenors: the crucial ethnic dimensions; the presence of the tolerant and moderate Hanafi version of Islam, traditionally exerting an impressively unifying effect during times of national crisis; and the long history of effective and heroic resistance to a series of foreign interventions in Afghanistan that became possible due to the temporary suspension of chronic internal tribal and religious rivalries. Tripathi's multidimensional assessment helps us understand that it will take far more than a refurbished counterinsurgency doctrine to turn the tide in Afghanistan and avoid having one more American leader sink into an Asian quicksand at great cost to himself, and even greater cost to the Afghan people and potentially to the entire region.

Beyond providing a clear-sighted, nonideological assessment of the overall situation in Afghanistan, including its regional setting, Tripathi brilliantly depicts the manner by which the cumulative effects of foreign intervention have generated "a culture of violence" in the country. This disquieting conclusion is further exacerbated by the ethos of terrorism that has been adopted by all participants in the conflict and that constantly blurs the boundaries between warfare and massacre. Overall, Tripathi is warning foreign intervenors, in this case the United States and Pakistan, to stop placing their bets on violence and militarism and turn toward developmental assistance, making creative use of traditional Afghan modalities of conflict resolution and reconciliation. It may seem doubtful that such a drastic and belated turnabout is politically feasible, but at the very least Tripathi shows us convincingly why it is necessary if catastrophe is to be avoided.

Tripathi ends this masterful account of the tangled web of chaos and violence—now menacingly engulfing Pakistan as well as Afghanistan—by calling on the United States to play its vital role at a time when the need for stability has never been greater. The essence of this call is to foster a switch in Afghanistan from military strong-arm tactics to an approach centered on development, internal reconciliation, and social, political, and economic reconstruction that relies on indigenous creativity and tradition. Even if such a sea change in the American role miraculously took place it would take some time to determine whether Taliban forbearance could be achieved. Tripathi advocates a similar kind of reorientation of the American approach in Pakistan: a demilitarization of economic assistance and the use of diplomatic and economic leverage to induce the Pakistani leadership to abandon its high-risk anti-India strategies that have relied on Islamization for national unity and allowed extremists to engage in dangerous terrorist provocations in India. He also warns the Pakistani leadership that their prior mix of policies was disastrous for the country and catastrophic for the region.

Surely, what Tripathi proposes is a series of sensible and desirable, if not indispensable, course adjustments, but these seem directly opposite to the policy initiatives that have been adopted so far by the Obama presidency. Consistent with his campaign pledge, President Obama has embraced the policy prescriptions advocated so persuasively by Gen. David Petraeus, whose strategic credentials rest on his influential reconceptualizing of counterinsurgency warfare (*Counterinsurgency Field Manual*, University of Chicago Press, 2007); on being given credit for successfully implementing "the surge" two years ago, which is widely believed to have avoided an American collapse in Iraq; on very effective briefings to Congress and the media; on his command responsibility for the entire Central Asia region (CENTCOM operations); and on retaining a seemingly unrivaled influence in the White House regardless of which party is in power. Next to Obama himself, Gen. Petraeus presently remains the most formidable political figure in the United States and a possible presidential candidate in 2012. This emphasis on counterinsurgency, together with reliance on an Afghan governmental partner tainted with corruption and electoral illegitimacy, may inevitably strengthen the comparison with the failed American effort in Vietnam, though the striking dissimilarities of the two situations should not be overlooked.

The result so far of this Petraeus phenomenon is to push the American approach in precisely the opposite direction from that urged by Tripathi. It is a policy that has emphasized bold and legally dubious cross-border military strikes by American aircraft, which have dangerously spread the war zone into the Pakistani heartland and pushed the Taliban eastward toward the Swat region. This policy also makes the Talibanization of Pakistan a genuine possibility. Such a misguided emphasis has been dramatized by General Petraeus's much publicized replacement of a more conventional American military commander in Afghanistan, Gen. Stanley McChrystal. McChrystal, an avowed counterinsurgency specialist, is notorious for his prior reliance on "special operations" across the Afghan border and for his particularly harsh prison detention policies in the country. In the second year of the Obama presidency this approach has come full circle. In an extraordinary exhibition of indiscretion, General McChrystal gave an intemperate interview to *Rolling Stone* magazine, insulting the Obama administration, which led to his dismissal as Afghan commander, and replacement by his sponsor and superior in the command structure, General Petraeus.

Unfortunately if this interpretation of the Obama approach is correct, it fully validates the major concerns expressed by Tripathi throughout this book. It also makes careful reading and widespread discussion of what Deepak Tripathi has to say an urgent priority for anyone concerned about correctly understanding, and hopefully challenging, the current dysfunctional drift of American policy in Afghanistan and Pakistan before it is too late. The haunting question that hovers over Afghan policy, and this book, arises: "Is it already too late?"

Richard Falk, Milbank Professor of International Law Emeritus,
Princeton University and Visiting Distinguished Professor since 2002,
Global Studies, University of California at Santa Barbara.
Santa Barbara, July 1, 2010

PREFACE

This book has been nearly thirty years in the making. In December 1979, I was in my early career as a journalist with the BBC World Service. My assignment was to write and produce an annual review of major world events, which was to be broadcast on the last day of the year. It had taken weeks of careful search through the sound archive and library material at the BBC offices at Bush House in London before I began to write the script in the middle of December. The hour-long program was recorded just before Christmas. My colleagues and I listened to the program again and again to make sure that the program was "perfect," so I could leave the tape with the duty officer for broadcast and go home for Christmas.

I was mistaken to assume that the job was finished and it would be all right on the day of broadcast. On Christmas Eve, reports of unusual military activity along the remote border between northern Afghanistan and Soviet Central Asia raised suspicions in Washington and London. Foreign diplomats had detected heavy air traffic between the Soviet Union and the Afghan capital, Kabul, for several days before, but it looked like a step up in the Soviet effort to support the struggling Communist regime in Afghanistan. The regime had been in place less than two years since the April 1978 coup, but was facing a growing insurgency in the countryside, mutinies within its own ranks, and food and fuel shortages in the midst of a harsh winter.

All of a sudden, my "perfect" review of the year belonged in the wastebasket and not on the air. Thousands of Soviet troops with tanks and heavy weapons had entered Afghanistan within a few days, assassinated the leader of the Afghan regime, Hafizullah Amin, and taken control of large parts of the country, including Kabul. Babrak Karmal had been installed as head of a new regime, and Amin was being denounced in the Soviet and Afghan media as a counterrevolutionary and an American agent. The Soviet Union had invaded Afghanistan, and whereas only a few minutes had been devoted to the Afghan situation in my original program, the Soviet invasion would now dominate the review of the year.

There was precious little information that could be used to rewrite and illustrate what had happened. Radio Moscow had made a brief announcement that Soviet forces had been invited by the friendly government of Afghanistan to help it deal with an insurgency fueled by certain foreign powers. In most world capitals, normal business had come to a halt in the Christmas holiday period and few senior figures were available to speak about the fast-moving situation. Those in Washington and London expressed shock and disbelief over the Soviet action in their statements, but were not very informative, and the wire services gave news of Soviet military advances into Afghanistan drip by drip. Every small piece of information, sound effect, reaction was priceless, and whatever we could muster had to be used in the most imaginative way possible. In the end, the program was completely rewritten and reproduced in two days, but it required working twenty hours a day.

The manner in which Afghanistan was closed to the outside world evoked memories of Churchill's Iron Curtain speech at Westminster College in Missouri way back in March 1946. The invading forces sealed the borders of Afghanistan overnight. Strict censorship prevented information from coming out, and under a blanket of secrecy, the Afghan population found itself subject to a high degree of control and oppression. Before the invasion, the Communist regime of Hafizullah Amin had appeared to be on the verge of collapse. Within hours of the invasion, Amin had been assassinated and Babrak Karmal, an Afghan exile living in Moscow, had been installed as Afghanistan's new leader. The invading Soviet forces had moved the Iron Curtain all the way to Pakistan's North-West Frontier, enveloping Afghanistan.

Over the next ten years, the story of occupation and the U.S.-led proxy war against the USSR in Afghanistan received ceaseless news coverage. Two things contributed to this media attention: the defeat of President Jimmy Carter in the November 1980 election and the return home of fifty-three American hostages from Iran two months later, which defused the immediate crisis for the U.S. administration and switched the attention to Afghanistan. Moreover, Ronald

•Reagan, the incoming Republican president, had promised a tough response to the Soviet invasion of Afghanistan and a revival of America's position in the world. True to his promise, Reagan presided over a relentless campaign against Soviet Communism during his eight-year presidency.

Reagan's decision to engage the Soviet occupation forces made Afghanistan a Cold War battleground in the 1980s and ensured that the country remained in the headlines for the rest of the decade. The American Central Intelligence Agency (CIA), Pakistani and Saudi secret services, China, Egypt, and a host of other countries took part in an elaborate military operation to recruit, train, and equip a large resistance force. America encouraged and financed the war against the Soviet Union. The CIA took the lead. Other members of the coalition were junior partners in the supply chain. The execution was the responsibility of Pakistan, which became the frontline state and journalists from all over the world descended on the Afghanistan-Pakistan frontier to cover the war against the Soviet Union.

With strict censorship imposed by the Soviet Union and its client regime in Kabul, little credible information came out of Afghanistan over the next few years. However, news was plentiful on Pakistan's frontier, where seven of the Afghan resistance groups had set up their offices and where refugees arrived daily. Stories of unspeakable brutality and human tragedy came to light with predictable regularity, but often there was little corroboration. Almost all Western embassies had closed down and diplomats returned to their home countries. News coverage was a mixture of facts, third-party accounts of events in the war zone, rumors, and speculation. The tactics of both sides were known, but the overwhelming sense that emerged was one of a conflict between good and evil. It was gripping stuff, but it was only part of the story.

Afghan society endured extraordinary violence over two decades. Both external powers and individual players—including Afghans themselves—contributed to the conflict. Only after three old-style Soviet leaders—Brezhnev, Andropov, and Chernenko—died within a two-and-a-half-year period and Gorbachev had risen to the leadership in May 1985 did the world have a better sense of events inside Afghanistan. Gorbachev soon decided to extract the Soviet Union from the conflict, but even he moved with caution. It took him two more years to reach the conclusion that the Soviet occupation forces could not achieve an outright victory and return home, and should therefore cut their losses and retreat. Since the history of the departure of Soviet forces from Afghanistan is well recorded, this is not the place to discuss it once more.

Prior to the late 1980s, Western journalists were rarely allowed to visit areas under Soviet or Afghan control. On significant occasions, such as the anniversary of the Communist coup in April 1978 or the arrival of Soviet troops in Afghanistan, a handful of correspondents were granted permission to visit Kabul or other selected places, but only under strict supervision and only for a few days. Many more clandestine visits by foreign journalists to the Afghan countryside occurred under Mujahideen escort. Only after 1987, when a Soviet withdrawal looked imminent and the Communist regime in Kabul had embarked on a policy of relaxation, did it become easier to visit the country. From the middle of 1988 until February 1989, the Soviet forces completed their withdrawal in the glare of foreign news media, and, at times, hundreds of foreign journalists were camped in the Inter Continental and Kabul hotels in the capital to cover the story.

In late 1989, the BBC decided to send a correspondent from London to be permanently based in Kabul. The corporation asked me if I were interested and I accepted the assignment. In January 1990, I left for Afghanistan via Moscow and Central Asia and spent the next fifteen months in the country with Kabul as my base. It took six months of negotiations with the Afghan authorities before the BBC was permitted to set up an office, but we succeeded. The last Communist leader, Najibullah, wanted to bring Afghanistan out of isolation, and the foreign minister, Abdul Wakil, was especially helpful in removing the bureaucratic obstacles. During my time as the BBC Kabul correspondent, I met regularly with Afghan leaders and ordinary citizens, and filed reports almost every day on the war and how it affected society. I returned to London in April 1991 and the Communist regime in Afghanistan collapsed exactly one year later amid the ruins of the Soviet state. Another decade of civil war followed the fall of Afghan communism. The end of the first phase of the Afghan conflict was a cause for some celebration in the West because of the defeat of the Soviet Union. The second phase led to the rise of the Taliban and turned the country into a haven for terrorism with all its implications for international security. This book is an attempt to determine how it happened.

A war correspondent lives in the midst of bombs, bullets, and human misery, and attempts to cope with the challenges of being in a conflict zone. One learns to take each day as it comes. Existence is basic and lonely and the days are unusually long. It is a life-changing experience, and between short bursts of activity aimed at meeting deadlines there is emptiness and time to reflect. The impact of witnessing violence by humans against other humans is profound and provides a broad scope for reflection.

Afghans are a deeply religious people known for their consideration and hospitality. They may be impoverished, but their acts of generosity are extraordinary and their two main languages, Pashto and Dari (Persian), and their literatures are rich. How then such people, with such qualities, can turn into monsters is a question with which I have often struggled. I decided to investigate the subject and what drove me was the attack on the United States on September 11, 2001. With my interest and accumulated experience, I felt I had something to give back. This book is also my attempt to contribute to the debate on terrorism.

The purpose of this book is to trace the origins of political violence during the Afghan conflict and to determine how that violence has contributed to the phenomenon of terrorism abroad. Research of this kind was difficult as long as official Soviet and U.S. documents remained classified. Even after the demise of the Soviet Union, publication of archive material on the Cold War was slow. The events of September 11, 2001, changed that. American policy entered a more aggressive phase, and many more secret documents on the Afghan conflict were declassified, thanks to the U.S. National Security Archive, which seeks to obtain classified papers under America's Freedom of Information Act.

American documents on Afghanistan between 1973 and 1990 had been available for a number of years. The period covers such major historical events as the overthrow of Zahir Shah, the last Afghan king; the country under Communism and Soviet occupation; and the U.S. proxy war against the Soviet Union. These documents tell some of the story of the early years of the Cold War and what is described as the "aid race" to Afghanistan. However, this collection would not have been enough.

In November 2001, just two months after the attack on the United States, the Woodrow Wilson Center of the Smithsonian Institute in Washington released a volume of Soviet documents from the same era, which had been translated into English. This collection gives the official Soviet version of history from the first Communist coup in Afghanistan in 1978 and the events leading to the Soviet invasion a year later, through the decade of occupation and war, until the Soviet retreat in 1989. These documents from the Russian and East German archives provide a fascinating account of decision-making in the

Kremlin during the last phase of the Cold War. Put together, the American and Soviet archives begin to tell a fuller story of the Afghan conflict and where it fits into the big picture of East-West rivalries.

In February 2002, the Woodrow Wilson Center published a manuscript, *The KGB in Afghanistan*, by Vasili Mitrokhin. Mitrokhin had spent almost his entire career as a KGB agent and worked as the main archivist at the KGB head-quarters outside Moscow from 1972 to 1984. During this period, Mitrokhin took meticulous hand-written notes from KGB files and then defected to Brit-ain with a large volume of secret service records just after the breakup of the Soviet Union.

The KGB in Afghanistan, edited by experts in Soviet history at the Wood-row Wilson Center, not only gives valuable insights into the role played by the KGB during the Afghan conflict, but also tells the story of infiltration by Soviet agents in years prior to the first Communist coup in Afghanistan in April 1978. He describes how the KGB recruited Afghans to work as informants, and what part the secret service played in the Soviet invasion of Afghanistan and subse-quent events.

The National Security Archive released another collection of official U.S. documents in 2003—this time from the Taliban period (1994–2001). These papers give insight into President Clinton's thinking and into America's busi-ness dealings with the Taliban when they were in control of much of Afghani-stan. There is evidence that the U.S. administration was concerned about the suppression of women and minority groups, as well as the Taliban's harboring of Osama bin Laden and his associates. President Clinton seemed indecisive about what to do with the Taliban until he ordered cruise missile attacks in retaliation for the bombing of the American embassies in Kenya and Tanzania on August 7, 1998. It looked like a brief diversion from Clinton's grand project of enlargement of free markets—a project on which America remained focused. Afghanistan was a low priority.

These sources provide the foundation on which this book is built. Other significant documents come from the *NATO–Russia Archive*, published by the Berlin Information-Center for Transatlantic Security. These documents shed light on the American preoccupation with the threat of proliferation of WMDs from the ex-Soviet arsenal and the need to help Russia recover from crisis while Afghanistan sank deeper into civil war and the Taliban emerged on the scene.

I have also used memoirs by a number of former American and Pakistani officials. Among them are Cyrus Vance, secretary of state, and Zbigniew Brzezinski, national security adviser, both during the Carter administration (1977–1981); Robert Gates, a career CIA official who served six American presidents from 1966 before becoming director of the CIA (1991–1993); and Brig. Mohammad Yousaf of Pakistan's Inter-Services Intelligence (ISI). Articles and books by specialists in terrorism and Afghan history have indeed been helpful, but this study would not have been possible without the new primary and secondary sources mentioned above.

This book is a result of a significant part of my professional life, as well as of archives that have become available since the end of the Cold War. If, as a young BBC journalist, I had not been given the task of producing the program that first ignited my interest in Afghanistan in December 1979, if the Soviet invasion had not led to a prolonged superpower conflict in that country, if I had not accepted the opportunity in the early 1990s to witness some of those events myself as the BBC Afghanistan correspondent, and if events of September 11, 2001, had not occurred, this book would not have been possible.

ACKNOWLEDGMENTS

I have to thank Hilary Claggett, my editor, and colleagues at Potomac Books, Inc., for making the publication of this study possible. My special thanks go to Richard Falk, Milbank Professor of International Law Emeritus, Princeton University, for writing the foreword to this book, and to Maharajkrishna Rasgotra, former foreign secretary of India and president of the Center for International Relations at the Observer Research Foundation. Both gave me their time, wisdom, encouragement, understanding, and support

I must also thank scholars like Walter LaFeber, Johan Galtung, and Shah Mahmoud Hanifi, for reading the manuscript with care and for endorsing the book. I would especially like to mention Howard Zinn, who died before he could see this book's publication. When I sent him the manuscript in 2009, Howard, at the age of 86, had just come out of the hospital and was recovering. He received my manuscript with the enthusiasm of a teenager. He read it, in bed, within seventy-two hours and sent one of the most generous reviews imaginable. He was looking forward to reading this book again, upon its publication. Along with millions of his admirers, I shall miss him. I think he would have liked it.

I am also grateful to the many people who read earlier drafts. The book is a study of archival material and, as such, is factual. The analysis goes where the archives take it. Where views are expressed, perceived or actual, they are mine. I cannot fail to mention here my beloved wife, Archana, who went through so much and helped me more than I can describe throughout my BBC career and when I was writing this book. In success and disappointment, she has always been with me.

NOTE ON STYLE AND SPELLINGS

The two main languages of Afghanistan are Pashto and Dari (Persian) and there can be a number of spelling variations of Afghan names when they are transcribed into English. For example, Mohammad can be Muhammad, Mohammed, or Muhamed. There are variations of Daud such as Daoud or Daod. Similarly, Russian names can be spelled in different ways. Vasiliy Mitrokhin can be Vasili Mitrokhin. Where possible, the author has used simplified spellings throughout this study, so Mohammed Daoud becomes Mohammad Daud and Vasiliy is Vasili. Elsewhere, it is Qandahar, not Kandahar, Jiddah instead of Jeddah, and Riyadh in preference to Reyadh.

GLOSSARY

Afghanistan. The word means "land of the Afghans." Afghanistan is a mountainous, landlocked country situated between Iran to the west, former Soviet Central Asian republics and China to the north, and Pakistan to the east and south. The Soviet invasion of Afghanistan in 1979 was followed by an East-West proxy war in the 1980s. Civil war among Afghan factions continued after the collapse of Soviet communism and disintegration of the Communist regime in Afghanistan.

Al-Jazeera. The term Jazeera means "island" or "peninsula" in Arabic and is the name of the satellite TV station, Al-Jazeera, based in the small Gulf state of Qatar. Through its broadcasts in Arabic, and in English since November 2006, Al-Jazeera has established itself as a prime source of news about the Middle East. It is a source that is quite distinct from Western media outlets and is known for carrying statements by al Qaeda leaders.

Al Qaeda. The term means the "base" or the "foundation," and speculations about what it references range from a protected region during the Communist era in Afghanistan to the title of Isaac Asimov's 1951 novel, *The Foundation* (translated into Arabic as *al Qaeda*), which describes the destruction of the mighty empire Trantor. Led by Osama bin Laden, the organization is believed to be responsible for a number of high-profile attacks on Western targets, including the World Trade Center and the Pentagon on September 11, 2001.

CIA. The Central Intelligence Agency, established under the National Security Act of 1947, is the biggest U.S. government organization involved in foreign intelligence gathering and covert operations to serve American interests. The CIA supplied weapons to Afghan resistance groups via the Inter-Services Intelligence Directorate of Pakistan during the Soviet occupation of Afghanistan in the 1980s. The agency is specifically prohibited from operating within the United States.

Culture of Violence. An overall condition, caused by traumatic events, which leads to a deterioration in the effectiveness of central political and societal institutions. This culture shapes the behavior of individuals, as well as state and non-state groups. Violence becomes part of the general lifestyle of people and determines their attitudes and mind-set.

HAMAS. *Harakat al-muqawama al-islamiyya*, which is translated as the Islamic Resistance Movement. HAMAS is a radical Palestinian Islamic group involved in armed conflict against Israel. The organization has also been involved in social and charitable work in Palestinian communities. HAMAS won a surprise victory in the January 2006 elections for the Palestinian Parliament.

ISI. The Inter-Services Intelligence Directorate is a highly secretive agency within the Pakistani armed forces. Founded in 1948 and trained by the Iranian secret service, SAVAK, and the American CIA, it has been described as a "state within the state" and is widely believed to have a key role in determining Pakistan's defense and foreign policies. ISI collaborated with the CIA in the war against the Soviet Union in Afghanistan. Otherwise, the ISI had its own interests in the region and developed close links with Islamic fundamentalist groups of Afghanistan.

Jihad. Arabic for "effort," whether of a political, military, or spiritual nature. The essence is to remove harm. Used by Islamic militants for "struggle." Translated by commentators and in the media as "holy war," which gives it a narrow meaning.

KGB. The Committee for State Security of the Soviet Union. First created in 1954, when the police apparatus was reorganized. Formally under the control of the Communist Party Politburo, but in reality enjoyed a large degree of independence. The organization had a highly centralized structure and its global rivalries with the CIA were legendary during the Cold War. The KGB penetrated Afghanistan at an early stage and was the prime mover behind the Soviet decision to invade the country in December 1979.

KHAD. *Khidmat-e Ittilat-e Dawlati*, which is the Afghan secret service created upon the Soviet KGB model in 1980. The name translates into the "State

Information Agency." Najibullah was the first chief of KHAD. In 1990, it was renamed *Wazarat-e Amaneyat-e Dawlati*, WAD. Dissolved at the fall of the Communist regime in April 1992.

Madrasah. An Islamic school where education is based on the Quran.

Mullah. A man of learning, equivalent to the clergy. Also known as *'alim*, plural *ulema*. Another term for a man of knowledge or piety is *Maulana*.

Pashtun. A community organized into tribes and consisting of just over 40 percent of the Afghan population and living in the neighboring North-West Frontier Province (now known as Khyber Pakhtunkhwa) of Pakistan. The *Durrani* Pashtuns, who ruled Afghanistan for three centuries until the April 1978 Communist coup, inhabit southern Afghanistan, while *Ghilzai* Pashtuns inhabit eastern Afghanistan and areas near the capital, Kabul.

PDPA. The People's Democratic (Communist) Party of Afghanistan. Founded in 1965, the party worked closely with the Soviet Communist Party and the KGB. The party rose to power in a coup in April 1978 and ruled until 1992. Leaders were Nur Mohammad Taraki (1978–1979), Hafizullah Amin (1979), Babrak Karmal (1979–1986), and Najibullah (1986–1992). The Najibullah regime fell to the Mujahideen in 1992, after which he lived in a United Nations compound in Kabul until September 1996, when the Taliban captured the city and tortured and executed Najibullah and his brother. The PDPA had two main factions: *Khalq* (the Masses) and *Parcham* (the Banner). Khalq members came mostly, though not always, from rural Pashtun areas; Parcham members were generally from Kabul and other cities and towns, and were part of Afghanistan's educated elite, some Pashtun, others non-Pashtun.

Shari'ah. The name originates from the Arabic root *shari'*, or "street." This is the legal system inspired by the Quran, the teachings and conduct of Prophet Mohammad (the *Hadith*), and the Islamic code of law, now invoked by fundamentalists. Only a small part of the Shari'ah is irrefutably based on the Quran. Fundamentalists assert that the Shari'ah cannot be proven wrong by human intelligence. It must be accepted, as it is "the will of God." The modernist movement in Islam opposes this view and insists that the Shari'ah should be applied to the actual situation and to new ideas, allowing for interpretations of the law.

Shi'a. The word means "faction." The Shi'a are the followers of Ali, the son-in-law of Prophet Mohammad, who formed a separate sect. A dominant sect of Islam in Iran, but a minority in Afghanistan.

Sunni. Originates from *sunnah*, or "tradition." This sect represents the majority in Islam and in Afghanistan. Puts emphasis on the adherence to text and revival of political authority. There are four Sunni schools of thought: *Hanafi*, *Maliki*, *Shafi*, and *Hanbali*. Of the four, Hanafi is considered to be the most liberal. It is based on customary practices and is the easiest to follow.

Taliban. In Persian, the term means "seekers of knowledge" (singular: *Talib*). The Taliban movement was formed in 1994, with recruits from religious schools (*madrasahs*) in Pakistan. Its members were mainly Pashtun, children of displaced Afghans, who were born or grew up in refugee camps in Pakistan.

Terrorism. The use of violence or the threat of violence by political actors, including opposition forces and states, to generate fear for the advancement of political ends. *Irhab* (intimidation) in Arabic, *terrorizm* in Persian. Terror is the effect of calculated and planned acts of violence on victims. Properties of terror include sudden and overwhelming acts of violence, which causes panic and uncertainty far beyond the immediate scene and which weakens public confidence in the ability of government and societal institutions to maintain security.

Wahhabism. The official ideology of Saudi Arabia since its formation in 1902. Most groups supported by Saudi Arabia or wealthy private citizens also champion Wahhabism. Its founder, Mohammad Ibn Abd al-Wahhab (1703–1787), branded all those who disagreed with him as infidels and declared jihad against them. Many Wahhabis still regard other Muslims, including members of the Shi'a community, as infidels.

1

THE CONCEPT OF TERROR

American Airlines Flight 11 from Boston crashed into the upper floors of the north tower of the World Trade Center. It hit the building between the 95th and 103rd floors. Thousands of people were already at their desks in both towers. About eighty chefs, waiters, and kitchen porters were also in the Windows on the World restaurant on the 106th floor. Many who worked for firms located in the crash zone were killed instantly. Those on the floors above were already doomed, their escape routes cut off by fire.[1]

The U.S. and its allies launched a massive aerial assault against Iraq on Friday. At 12:15 p.m. EST, antiaircraft fire could be seen rising in the skies above Baghdad. Within an hour, tremendous explosions began rocking the Iraqi capital, as the Pentagon announced "A-Day" was underway.[2]

The arrival of the twenty-first century brought with it a monster the likes of which had never been seen. The events surrounding the attacks on the World Trade Center in New York and the Defense Department in Washington on September 11, 2001, were unparalleled by anything previously seen in peace time. The hijackers came close to bringing America to its knees, as they had intended. The trail of these attacks took the Americans back to Afghanistan, where they had fought a proxy war against the Soviet Union before the Communist superpower disintegrated in 1991.

A decade later, President George W. Bush had been in the White House only a few months when the attacks were launched on the United States. The country had enjoyed eight years of prosperity during the Clinton presidency and was more confident of its world role. Bush had won the election in November 2000 on a conservative Republican agenda. The Bush vision for America reflected a more unilateral approach, with elements of isolationism.[3] He pointed out that the United States stood alone in terms of power and said that he wanted to project credibility by being strong and resolute. His message to America's adversaries, including Iraq and Iran, was "don't dare threaten our friends" or there would be consequences. The United States had to be guarded in its generosity, because it could not be all things to all people and put troops all around the world.

The atmosphere in the United States reflected aspects of both aggression and isolationism since Bush's ascent to the presidency, and the events on September 11 accelerated the change. On the one hand, Bush reminded the world of America's unmatched military and economic strength and warned adversaries not to threaten U.S. interests. On the other hand, he proclaimed that, under his administration, America's generosity toward others would have its limits; he was not prepared to help all people around the world without question. Reflecting the nation's shock and anger following the September 11 attacks, Bush declared a war on terror. He resolved to punish those responsible for the carnage and to remove future threats by a preemptive use of force.

The objective of this book is to determine how the U.S.-led invasion of Afghanistan came about. The book looks at the chain of events in Afghanistan during the Cold War and examines the impact of East-West rivalries on the internal politics of the country. The overthrow of the monarchy, the Communist seizure of power, and the Soviet invasion in the 1970s had a profoundly destabilizing effect in the region. These turbulent events led to a U.S. proxy war against the Soviet Union, which was eventually forced to withdraw from Afghanistan in 1989.

Soon afterward, the Soviet empire and Afghan communism collapsed, but the Afghan civil war continued and the country became identified with global terror in the 1990s. After the attacks on September 11, 2001, the United States and others felt that there was no recourse other than to invade Afghanistan and to remove the Taliban Islamic militia from power. In essence, the objective of this study is to determine how the conflict in Afghanistan created conditions that turned a generally peaceful kingdom into a haven for violent groups, and how the war contributed to the phenomenon of terrorism.

PROBLEMS WITH TERRORISM STUDIES

Both the effort to define terrorism and the international attempts to take mean-ingful measures to counter the phenomenon have faced obstacles since the early twentieth century. Initial attempts to establish an internationally acceptable definition of terrorism were made by the League of Nations, but a convention drafted in 1937 was never enforced.[4] More than seventy years later, member states of the United Nations are still struggling to reach a consensus on what constitutes terrorism.

The General Assembly continues to be split between members who see ter-rorist acts as nothing more than common crime and argue that terrorists should be brought to justice by strengthening the current international legal frame-work, and those who advocate that legitimate struggle for independence and self-determination must be distinguished from terrorism.[5]

There is general agreement among scholars that terrorism relates to the use of violence for political purposes. Beyond this, however, it has proved to be a complex subject to study because of the diversity of individuals and groups associated with it, the variability of their demands and motivations, and their different locations and areas of activity. Terrorism takes many forms: states or non-state groups may engage in terrorist acts; the organizations may be po-litical or religious; ideology may be left-wing or right-wing; or there may not appear to be a clear ideology; organizations may be little more than criminal gangs—indeed, there is evidence that many terrorist groups are involved in acts of kidnapping and extortion, robbery, and the smuggling of drug and weapons.

The difficulties do not end here. Perhaps the goal is independence from a foreign power or liberation from a brutal dictatorship. A state may use extreme and extra-legal force, including torture, to overcome an insurgency, and each side of the conflict may describe the other as "terrorist" while justifying its own, similar methods. Often, one side uses violence in the name of national security and stability, the other in the name of freedom. *Terrorist* then becomes a term of abuse to describe the opposing side in the propaganda war. A term loaded with political nuances such as these throws up many challenges.

Despite these difficulties, we need a clearly defined and widely applicable concept of terror. Our search for that concept begins with the questions: What do we mean by terrorism? What causes terrorism? A huge body of literature in which scholars have sought to answer these questions already exists.[6] The aim here is not to engage in a detailed review of the current literature—it is so vast and expanding that a review is neither practical nor realistic. Rather, the objective is to examine how different scholars have approached the concept of terrorism and how they have sought to go beyond the subjective character of the term to derive an ideal type with characteristics common to all acts of political violence. This chapter addresses the question of why there are problems with terrorism studies by examining the ways in which the subject is traditionally studied. In the next chapter, the goal is to develop a concept of terrorism that will allow us to understand Afghanistan's place in international affairs and how events there relate to terrorism.

There seems to be a common motive behind acts of terrorism. Terrorists aim to create a climate of fear that goes far beyond the immediate target group, and the intended victims are often civilians.[7] Frequently, terrorism is associated with private groups fighting against governments. The implication is that the effects of violence by private groups are somehow different from the effects of conventional war between states, in which a climate of fear is not created beyond the battlefield and civilians remain unharmed. This distinction is hard to maintain because it relies on an antiquated idea of what constitutes conventional warfare.

Warfare between states is no longer fought in trenches far from population centers. On the contrary, economic and industrial targets in civilian areas are often attacked to immobilize the national infrastructure, and as a result civilians are caught up in the cycle of violence. We have seen this in the Middle East and the Balkans in recent years. All acts of violence—whether they are considered conventional or unconventional warfare—produce terror and leave innocent civilians killed, injured, or displaced.[8] Fears over security and economic consequences are felt well beyond the immediate domain of violence, and there are always short- or long-term consequences. The effect of sudden, disproportionate violence on the morale and well-being of civilians and its further impact illustrate the common characteristics of terror regardless of whether the perpetrator is a state, a private individual, or a group.

What is the driving force behind terrorism and political violence?[9] It is sometimes tempting to describe terrorist behavior as crazy or mad, especially as part of the instant popular reaction to a major incident. Such a simplistic reaction, however, assumes that terrorists are unaware of their actions, that they have no goals or beliefs guiding their behavior, or that their actions are contrary to their objectives. Alternatively, one can recognize terrorist behavior as being driven either by deliberate, rational decisions or by certain psychological forces. These two approaches are opposite sides of the same coin: one explains terrorism as a product of strategic decision-making,[10] while the other attempts to show that psychological forces can compel people to commit violence.[11] The strategic choice approach emphasizes the logical processes that an organization pursues in considering alternative strategies before making a final choice. It describes the terrorist behavior as calculated.[12] The psychological approach emphasizes the emotional forces that drive terrorists to commit acts of violence and then rationalize them. These two approaches are not mutually exclusive and both can be employed in studying the subject.

RATIONAL CHOICE

The hijackers who attacked on September 11 were educated and intelligent people who had much to live for but who had chosen to die.[13] In his study of terrorist suicide attacks, Mark Harrison points out that both individuals and their organizations go through complex processes of planning, preparation, and deciding roles:

> Those who take part in suicide terrorism are self-evidently volunteers; they engage in it willingly, usually knowing what to expect and accepting the consequences. Most of them are not crazy and most are not being fooled. Moreover, although individuals do it, they do not do it alone. Suicide terrorism requires individuals to adopt coordinated roles: some recruit the volunteers and supply the means while others carry out the act.[14]

This does not only apply to suicide attacks but is true of all terrorist attacks. In another examination of the strategic choice theory, Martha Crenshaw defines the principal actor as a radical political organization with members who share common values and decide to adopt violence as their chosen strategy. It is a carefully considered option—a willful choice[15] made once the organization has concluded that violence will be the most effective of all available means to achieve its political goal.[16] Members of radical groups stand apart from others who consider violence morally wrong and often view such people as weak. Radicals consider themselves as prepared to make the ultimate sacrifice: to them, advocates of nonviolence are afraid of death or are hoping for future personal gains. By defining the organization as the central actor in the strategic choice approach, Crenshaw explains that her purpose is to avoid what is known as the "free rider" problem, in which individuals benefit from something without having to pay for it; when the organization is treated as the central actor, only active members can claim a share in the benefits of its operations.[17]

Individuals may join an organization because its size and solidarity are important to them, and when they become a member of the group, they contribute to both. On the inside, members are reasoned in their decision-making as a group. In the strategic choice approach, the emphasis lies in the collective rationality of the active members of an organization.

> As purposeful activity, terrorism is the result of an organization's decision that it is a politically useful means to oppose the government. The argument that terrorist behavior should be analyzed as rational is based on the assumption that terrorist organizations possess internally consistent sets of values, beliefs and images of the environment.[18]
>
> If the costs of rebellion are great, or if peaceful strategies of political action are available that may be as effective or more effective than rebellion, rational actors will not rebel.[19]

The term *collective rationality* in the world of the terrorist raises some questions. Does it refer to the accumulated rational choice of each member of a group? Are there forces that compel certain members to remain in the organization? By the time someone has joined an underground group, the basic choice for political violence has already been made. Once a member, the possibility of being expelled, tortured, or killed by fellow members is usually a strong enough reason not to advocate anything other than the continuation of violence. Opportunities of returning to normal life are remote. Avoiding capture is usually of greatest importance and rationality under the circumstances may mean simply carrying on with the campaign of violence. Pressures such as these indicate that group rationality is not a result of the free rational choice of individuals.

Since the organization is the central actor in the strategic choice approach, this perspective relies heavily on the assumption of organizational cohesion. There may be compelling reasons for unity, but it cannot always be taken for granted. From the IRA in Northern Ireland to the PLO and other radical factions in the Middle East, from the Tamil guerrilla movement in Sri Lanka to Sikh and Kashmiri groups in India, organizations have often been divided. Such divisions may create many more, yet much less cohesive, groups, or even provide the opportunity for some individual terrorists to go their own way and "freelance." What happens then? How do we deal with situations in which there is a war of all against all, like those seen during the conflicts in Afghanistan, Chechnya, and Lebanon? Conditions in these places are so chaotic and fluid, and individual loyalties change so frequently, that studying organizations in any consistent manner may be impossible.

Crenshaw suggests that past experience and observation of other terrorist campaigns are among factors that organizations consider before making decisions. Beginning in the early 1980s, the use of suicide bombers by the Tamil Tiger group in Sri Lanka and the pro-Iranian Hizbollah based in Lebanon proved devastating.[20] Militant Palestinian groups such as HAMAS and Islamic Jihad in the occupied territories later adopted this method to attack Israeli targets. Al Qaeda's campaign of violence since the early 1990s has also relied on suicide attacks—the most spectacular of which were seen on September 11, 2001. However, whether the increased use of suicide bombings is the result of past experience and rational decision-making or a tendency to copycat the tactics of other groups is difficult to say.

Organizations may sometimes decide to launch violent campaigns even when the costs are too high. This can happen for a number of reasons. It is possible that they have miscalculated the consequences;[21] perhaps the attackers are unconcerned that the consequences are inflicted on large numbers of innocent victims;[22] or it could be that the attackers wish to provoke a disproportionate response by the government they oppose.[23] As David Lake points out, reprisal attacks by governments can lead to consequences that are helpful to such groups:

> Extremists seek to provoke a response from the target that, through its disproportionate and indiscriminate nature, punishes the broad population of which the terrorists are part.[24]

There is indeed evidence that terrorist activities are calculated to alter the behavior of their adversary, for instance provoking the state to use force against the civilian constituency.[25] This has been witnessed in the occupied territories, in Arab countries facing internal uprisings, and in Indian-controlled Kashmir.

Insurgents hope that the more repression a government uses against civilians, the more alienated the population will become and support the insurgents against the government. Conversely, if an organization is fighting for a cause with popular support and the government is already weak, then the possibility of the government giving in to the group's demands, or even collapsing, is greater.

PSYCHOLOGICAL FORCES

The other side of the coin is the proposition that the causes of terrorist behavior are related to psychological forces, which compel certain people to commit acts of violence.[26] Advocates of *psycho-logic* do not dismiss the thesis that such individuals think strategically. Jerrold Post, a leading proponent of this approach, accepts that there is a special logic that characterizes terrorists' reasoning. But he says he takes significant issue with the proposition that terrorists willingly resort to violence and that terrorism as a course of action is an intentional choice selected from a range of perceived alternatives.[27]

The central argument in this approach is that terrorist behavior is rooted in the psychological system of the individual. Ted Gurr describes it as the "frustration-aggression mechanism."[28] In developing his thesis, Gurr begins by arguing that mass deprivation tends to turn people toward large-scale violence of low intensity while frustration among privileged and aspiring individuals causes organized civil violence of high intensity. There is something of a contradiction in this, because Gurr relies on external causes—deprivation or affluence—and argues that these alter the psychological state of mind of certain individuals. As a result, terrorists see the world around them as sharply divided and this view is reflected in their rhetoric.

With such a polarized view of the world goes the unshakeable belief that their cause is always just and moral. While others are the "source of all evil," terrorists see themselves as freedom fighters. The enemy, representing the privileged, the powerful, or the infidel, must be destroyed. Post describes this type of reasoning as *psycho-logic*, but he also argues that it does not mean that terrorists are "psychologically well balanced" or that their behavior is the "product of a rationally derived strategic choice." He asserts that many display "borderline personality disturbances," but acknowledges that insufficient data makes this line of inquiry difficult to pursue. In describing Mohammad Atta, the ringleader behind the September 11 attacks, Post makes these observations:

He was dedicated to his studies, was polite, engaged, bright . . . until he made a trip to Afghanistan and it was when he came back . . . he seemed to be in his own world marching to a different drummer at that point. . . . There was almost a psychological transformation and he became then totally absorbed in the cause, the cause as articulated by Osama bin Laden.[29]

A deranged individual is usually a loner, not likely to plan and execute attacks with others in a group. What Jerrold Post suggests is that the visit to Afghanistan triggered certain processes in Atta, and when he returned, he began to live in a different world—the world of a loner. However, psycho-logic is a more subtle approach than this, and experts, including Post, accept that the link between political violence and psychological disorders is unproven. While Post does not believe that terrorists are crazy, deranged people, suffering from psychological disorders, he does imply that their view of the world contrasts sharply with that of others in society.

There seems to be an inconsistency in the way terrorism is explained here as a product of psychological forces. On the one hand, it is acknowledged that terrorists are not mentally disturbed individuals; on the other hand, it is implied that they are somewhat imbalanced, because their view of the world is very different from that of the majority of society. Does it translate into a comment on human nature in general? Does conformity always suggest balance in people? Are all nonconformists imbalanced? Applying this logic more widely would result in many more people being condemned as imbalanced.

In the literature explaining the psychological causes of terrorist behavior, individuals and their characteristics are often treated pejoratively. Post sees a surprising degree of uniformity in the rhetoric of terrorists. He describes it as "polarizing" and "absolutist," and says that the logic of this rhetoric is what justifies their acts of violence. He claims that people with certain personality traits are drawn toward terrorism in disproportionate numbers. They often include "aggressive, action-oriented," and thrill-seeking individuals; their tendency to rely on "splitting" and "externalizing" is high.[30] *Splitting* and *externalizing* refer to traits that prevent a person from being able to "fully integrate the good and bad parts" of their personality. They accept what they find good and like as part of their self and project what they hate outwardly. The outside world, which they blame for perceived wrongs and consider the source of evil, reflects their own inadequacies. This type of logic is sometimes used by law enforcement agencies in search of solutions to the problem of terrorism. Writing in the FBI Law Enforcement Bulletin, Randy Borum puts forward the following model:

> (It) begins by framing some unsatisfying event or action as being unjust, blaming injustice on a target policy, person or nation, and then vilifying, often demonizing, the responsible party to facilitate justification for aggression.[31]

Borum goes on to recommend to the law enforcement community:

> Investigators and analysts who must attempt to understand and anticipate how a person will act in a given situation should seek to understand that individual's "map," or perception, of the situation. Ideology may be a part of that, but other important dynamics and behavioral factors may contribute as well.[32]

How do psychological factors affect terrorist groups and their behavior? The psycho-logic response is that such organizations would not be formed in the first place if people with the personality traits discussed above did not join them.[33] For many individuals who become terrorists, it is the first time they have truly belonged to any organization and they believe that their new identity is entirely dependent on their association with the group. Through this association and interaction with fellow members, this singular platform enables them to identify with a certain ideology, establish goals, and exercise power.[34]

Psychological forces play a fundamental role in ensuring group cohesion and advancement. Cohesion requires forces that make members subscribe to certain ground rules and tactics. Other psychological forces promote internal conflict, which is a continuous battle for power and ideas. Groups that are able to operate within this state of conflict survive and the interaction of their members creates new, more powerful forces. These forces influence the conduct of all members and give organizations the power they exercise, power enforced by these terrorist groups in their campaigns of violence. In a terrorist organization, the need to belong and affiliate with each other often prompts members to surrender their personal identities and assume the collective identity of the group.[35]

The tendency to sink one's personal identity into the organization is particularly strong in militant religious groups. The reason may lie in the demand made by these groups for complete surrender to the authority of God, in whose name all activities are carried out. Leaders of religious groups that preach violence project their own hatred on to the enemy and may interpret their holy texts in ways that sanctify their own prejudices. Their call to the faithful is often to make the ultimate sacrifice in the name of God, securing a supreme place in heaven for those who die.

It has already been said that the psychological approach to study terrorism contradicts the strategic choice proposition that violence is a willful strategy. The implication of the rationalist argument is that since terrorism is the weapon of the weak, a group will renounce violence once its goals have been achieved. Advocates of psycho-logic, however, regard violence not as a means but "the end itself."[36] It is because the terrorist rhetoric is absolutist and seeks to achieve total victory. This would explain why radical leaders often find it difficult to stop even after seemingly achieving their goals.

Evidence exists to support this crucial difference between the strategic choice and psychological models. Certain groups cease their violent campaigns once their objectives have been achieved: for example, the African National Congress after the end of apartheid in South Africa, pro-independence groups in India after British withdrawal, Sukarno following Indonesian independence, the Communists after gaining control of South Vietnam, and the Sandinista movement after the 1979 revolution in Nicaragua. It seems perfectly rational to stop fighting once the objective has been met. However, for some actors, when violence is no longer a means but becomes the end itself, as advocates of psycho-logic suggest, then such actors find it difficult to stop. Organizations like al Qaeda, Islamic Jihad, the Chinese Communist Party under Mao, and the revolutionary leader Che Guevara demonstrate this.[37]

The psychological approach is about exploring the inner state of mind of terrorists, rather than examining the external political factors that influence their behavior. Those who advocate it are, in general, psychologists and forensic experts associated with law enforcement and crime prevention. Their logic often leads to the determination that the problem could be solved if only law enforcement agencies had enough resources to remove the tiny minority of terrorists from the general civilian population.

This view neither takes sufficient account of the external factors—poverty, unemployment, injustice, weak institutions—nor of the wider support such individuals are able to attract in society. Instead, it is used to argue that those who take up arms do so because of certain abnormal processes taking place in their minds; a thesis that is difficult to prove. Even if proved, there are problems with the explanatory status of the proposition itself: a person with a mental abnormality is likely to be a drifter and therefore unsuited to working effectively within an organization. Further evidence that people convicted of terrorist offenses are mentally unstable is hard to come by.

STRUCTURAL FACTORS

The third approach to studying terrorism is described as "structural analysis." In this approach, external causes in the environment—including political, cultural, social, and economic factors—are investigated. It is argued that the interaction of such factors with each other and with certain individuals results in terrorist behavior.[38] Again, advocates of the structural approach do not dismiss the possibility that decisions by individuals or groups to resort to violence can be explained by either strategic choice or psychological analysis or even by both. Rather, they promote the ease and practicality of the structural approach as a research strategy.[39]

Jeffrey Ian Ross begins the construction of his structural model by dividing the causes of terrorism into two categories. The causes are separated by *permissive* (indirect) causes and *precipitant* (direct) factors. For Ross, general features of a society—specific "geographical location," "type of political system," and the "level of modernization"—are some of the indirect factors that are present in one form or another in all countries. Geographical location cannot be altered, but the political and economic systems in societies normally evolve over time.

Ross makes the assertion that these permissive or indirect factors do not foster terrorism on their own. Rather, he says that their nature contributes to the emergence of direct causes in a given environment. It may be so where a slow corrosive process in an organized society creates conditions that promote political violence. But Ross's model does not explain the consequences of unexpected events, like a military coup or an invasion, bringing about abrupt change in the system. Sudden, traumatic events in a coup or invasion damage or destroy a country's existing system of organization and its replacement may be painful and slow in coming. People in authority in the government are removed, the armed forces and internal law enforcement agencies often disintegrate or are depleted; new leaders are forcefully imposed, creating resistance, and attempts at suppressing the opposition only triggers more of it. The new rulers may belong to a different ethnic group or nationality, or may represent a different ideology that is not readily acceptable to the population. There may be attempts to reorganize society by force, triggering even further resistance. All these are relevant points in our study of the Afghan conflict.

But Ross's structural model is overly focused on urban settings. He says that, unlike rural settings, cities offer certain advantages to terrorists, like prominent targets and media presence for instant publicity. His logic applies to acts of urban terrorism.[40] Therefore, while ethnic and ideological conflicts and military coups mentioned in Ross's model can help our study of terrorism in Afghanistan, his emphasis on urban settings begins to pose difficulties. Others, though, including Timo Kivimaki and Liisa Laakso, have looked at the relationship between poor, underdeveloped societies and oppositional political violence.

> Fundamentalist terrorism develops in a context of economic and political grievances of a perceived terrorist constituency. This includes a lack of public goods like education and health services. Such conditions are needed for the perceived legitimacy of terrorism and for the emergence of a culture of tolerance towards terrorism.[41]

While it is possible to study political violence by structural analysis in some situations, it does not provide satisfactory answers in others. For example, reasons behind state terrorism are difficult to explain by structural analysis.[42] How external forces influence the environment in which a state exists, and what motivates that state to adopt a culture of terror, can best be studied by examining the broader environment. The Afghan conflict began in the 1970s at the peak of the Cold War between the Soviet Union and the United States; Afghanistan was caught up in the rivalries triggered by the Cold War. Two decades later, the demise of the USSR and the withdrawal of U.S. interest gave rise to a new set of conditions in which radical Islamic forces became dominant. The Taliban rose to power in that setting.

Strategic choice may be a more useful method to study state terrorism in these conditions rather than the psychological or structural approach, because the leaders of a state may have concluded that terror is the most effective way of controlling their subjects and influencing the policies of adversaries. To perceive regimes that use terror as irrational would not serve a valuable purpose in this study.

We will now summarize the main points of our discussion and develop a concept of terrorism that will be useful in our study. We recognize that terrorism means different things to different people and is contingent on beliefs. Two conflicting views of terrorism are found today. The first sees terrorist incidents as acts of violence by private individuals or groups, determined to create an atmosphere of fear and panic in the general population. The aim of the terrorist is to undermine public confidence, weaken or overthrow the existing order, or force a change in government policy. This line of observation normally suits the establishment, meaning governments and others in authority. We will call it the *conventional view* of terrorism. The second view, often adopted by guerrilla organizations, liberation movements, and their supporters, is that political violence is the weapon of the weak against an enemy of overwhelming strength. An insurgent organization would therefore accuse the government it opposes of using state terrorism to suppress a minority.

Our aim now is to arrive at a single definition that assimilates these two opposing views of terrorism. To achieve this, we will remove the subjective nuances associated with the term and adopt a guiding principle that is common in all cases of political violence. That principle will be a definition that takes into account the impact of terrorism on its victims, not the way in which it is described by those who use violent force. The essence of such a definition must be that violence in all forms involves a degree of terror, whether justified as legal or claimed as illegal. This is not a pacifist argument, for violence may be necessary in certain situations, notably in self-defense. Rather, our definition has to be based on a statement of fact as violence affects its target and sends a wider message. We define terrorism in the following terms:

> Terrorism is the premeditated use of violence by an individual, group, or state to achieve political goals; it is intended to generate shock and panic in the short term and long-term uncertainty beyond the actual scene of violence, to compel the existing political order to change policy, or to surrender in the face of sudden and disproportionate force. Once the consequences of violence are established, a threat of repeating similar acts can be sufficient to terrorize the target.

We have considered the strategic choice, psychological, and structural approaches, which researchers use to explain the causes of terrorism. These approaches are not mutually exclusive, and it is accepted that one or more of them can be employed to investigate the subject. It may be possible to apply any one of the three approaches to our study of terrorism in the context of Afghanistan, but to do so would not take the other important factors into account.

The strategic choice approach would seem appropriate to explain the involvement of outside powers like the Soviet Union and the United States in Afghanistan during the Cold War. Afghanistan was in the midst of intense rivalries in West Asia and the Indian Ocean, and there was no way for a weak state to avoid the consequences. It is also possible to apply the strategic choice theory to study the presence of regional powers like Pakistan, Iran, and Saudi Arabia, and the conduct of significant internal players—the royal family, the armed forces, and the pro-Soviet communist factions. Each was driven by its own interests.

However, the strategic choice approach to study the Afghan conflict would not take into account psychological forces that influence human behavior and structural factors like poverty and abundance of weapons. Similarly, the psychological route would exclude the strategic choice and structural approaches. The psychological approach appears to be the weakest of the three, because there is not sufficient evidence, including data, to support it. We need a new, more appropriate concept to examine how Afghanistan became a terrorist sanctuary by the end of the Cold War.

2

CULTURE OF VIOLENCE

The Afghan conflict and events that triggered it span over thirty years, a fact that gives us an opportunity to develop a new, more appropriate concept for understanding the phenomenon of terrorism. That concept is one of culture of violence. The main benefit of pursuing this route lies in the broad understanding of the concept of culture, which encompasses all that members of a society think, have, or do. *Culture* is the sum total of a society at a given point and explains how it reached such a pass, as we will now learn.

Culture, as defined by E. B. Tylor, is "that complex whole which includes knowledge, belief, art, morals, law, customs and many other capabilities and habits acquired by . . . [members] of society." Culture is the way of life that people adopt in society without ever consciously considering how it came into being. It incorporates the impact of events, cultivated behavior, experience accumulated over time, and social learning, and is transmitted from generation to generation over years, decades, even centuries.

The fundamental building blocks of a culture are traits. Traits assume many forms such as tools, houses, and lifestyles. Culture represents patterns of behavior—family relationships, attitudes, and acts toward neighbors and foreigners. The way government encourages citizens to conform, or imposes sanctions on them, indicates a certain culture. It is a collective mentality involving shared ways of seeing, understanding, and experiencing the world, and it distinguishes the members of one group from another.

The obvious trigger for the Afghan conflict between 1978 and 2001 appears to be the communist coup by a group of pro-Soviet military officers in

April 1978. The cold-blooded nature of the murders of the overthrown Afghan leader, Mohammad Daud Khan, his family, and close associates installed a culture of violence, which was replicated by subsequent events over more than two decades. We will take a systematic look at the stages of evolution of this culture.

Internal conflict. Afghanistan was ruled under a monarchy in which the king, Zahir Shah, took a benign role, while loyalists, including family members and technocrats, ran the day-to-day affairs of the country. Internal conflict in the 1960s upset that careful arrangement. While communist and Islamic groups agitated, a directly elected parliament loosened the royalists' grip on power and a split occurred between the king and his cousin, the Prime Minister Daud Khan. Daud was forced to resign, and in 1973 he overthrew the king in a coup. Five years later, Daud was assassinated by pro-Soviet military officers in the coup that began Afghanistan's long descent into war.

Great power involvement. The country was in a region at the center of superpower rivalries since the beginning of the Cold War. By the 1970s, the United States had become focused on Iran and the Middle East, and had been left behind in the race for influence in Afghanistan. The Soviet Union had firmly established itself in the country, and the KGB had infiltrated almost every level of Afghan society—infiltration that only grew after the 1978 communist coup and the Soviet invasion a year later. These events convinced the United States to confront the Soviet Union. The consequences of the U.S.-Soviet proxy war in the 1980s contributed to further divisions within Afghan society. Numerous factions and warlords came to the fore, and vast quantities of money and weapons supplied by external forces accelerated the conflict.

State disintegration. The communist takeover in 1978 was a political earthquake that shook the foundations of the Afghan state. The structure created under the monarchy and the five-year rule of Daud (1973–1978) suddenly disintegrated and was replaced by a Soviet-type system. Widespread purges by the communist regime removed large numbers of people from the armed forces, the judiciary, and other state agencies. The state system was also under attack by outside forces and, in the end, was no longer able to defend itself or its citizens.

Foreign indifference and the rise of extremism. With the demise of the Soviet Union in December 1991, the West became indifferent to Afghanistan, leaving the country to regional players like Saudi Arabia, Pakistan, and Iran. The collapse of Afghanistan's communist regime in April 1992 led to a more turbulent phase in the conflict. With no single opposition group or alliance able to take control, Afghanistan rapidly descended into full-scale civil war. From the growing turmoil rose the Taliban, an extremist Islamic militia supported by powerful elements within the Saudi and Pakistani ruling classes. The Taliban represented a particularly fanatical brand of Islam, founded on an intolerant, anti-Western, Sunni theocratic ideology. As more and more Afghan territory fell under Taliban control, the country developed into a sanctuary for extremists, attracted to Afghanistan for ideological and military training before returning to fight wars elsewhere.

Violence replicated itself throughout these stages, often running simultaneously. Internal conflict was a feature of both Afghan regimes and opposition groups throughout the war; the involvement of great powers continued to varying degrees during much of the conflict; and disintegration of the Afghan state was a gradual process, resulting in a complete breakdown of institutions after the collapse of the communist regime. By the early 1990s, terror had become a way of life in Afghan society.

In defining the term *culture of violence* we have drawn out the following: a condition in which violence permeates all levels of society and becomes part of human thinking, behavior, and way of life.

Essential characteristics of a culture of violence are as follows:

Dialectical: a pattern of replicating once established. Coercion leads to resistance, which necessitates even greater coercion to suppress, thereby generating a cycle of violence.

Prompted and shaped by external forces: intervention by outside powers upsets the local balance of forces, resulting in disorder and conflict. As hostilities escalate, they attract more external forces in defense or opposition of local players, and increasingly, these external forces determine the scale and course of events.

Develops along with institutional breakdown: the culture of terror grows as the capacity of local institutions such as security forces, judiciary, and legislature to maintain order deteriorates.

Law superseded by violence: institutional collapse makes the system of law enforcement increasingly irrelevant and results in an environment in which violence replaces law as the primary means of maintaining order.

Expectations altered and adapted to force as a way of life: actors acquire a habit of using
  force. Citizens expect solutions to be found through violence.
Culture distorted: the cycle of violence thus created distorts the culture and creates
  a climate of fear that drives human behavior and lifestyle.

Having defined the concept of terrorism and culture of violence, we will
proceed to determine how the conflict in Afghanistan has contributed to the
global phenomenon of terrorism. We will learn how the involvement of external forces in the early years of the Cold War upset the delicate equilibrium in
Afghan society and how the ensuing turbulence led to the country's occupation
by the Soviet Union in the late 1970s; how the Soviet invasion of a deeply religious country in December 1979 provoked local resistance and deeper external
involvement, leading to one of the most brutal regional conflicts of the Cold
War; and how events over the following two decades shaped a culture of terror
in Afghanistan, the consequences of which had not been foreseen.

3

AFGHANISTAN IN THE COLD WAR

The communist coup in April 1978, which overthrew the Afghan president, Daud Khan, came during a particularly turbulent period in East-West relations. The structure of détente so carefully built during the Nixon presidency in the early 1970s was collapsing. The consequences of America's military withdrawal from Vietnam were there to see. With the collapse of the pro-U.S. regimes in South Vietnam and Cambodia, Indochina had fallen under communist rule, and a vast region on the southern fringes of the Soviet Union had become the central theater of the Cold War in Asia. This region included countries around the Gulf in the Middle East. In this chapter, we will examine what forces were at work in the region in 1978 and establish why Afghanistan attracted little attention from America.

Iran

Afghanistan, a landlocked, mountainous country surrounded by the USSR, Iran, Pakistan, and China, was in the middle of the Cold War theater. Iran shares a long border with western Afghanistan, consisting of Herat province and its surrounding areas and Iranian influence is prominent throughout western and northern Afghanistan. Dari, the Afghan version of Persian, is widely spoken in all but the Pashtun areas of the south.

A water dispute had caused tensions between the two countries in the 1950s, but relations improved after settlement in the mid-1960s.[1] With Iran's oil wealth grew Shah Reza Pahlavi's ambition to extend Iranian influence in the region. In 1974 an agreement committing Iran to an investment of $2 billion in

Afghanistan was announced.[2] The Iranian secret service, SAVAK, also began to help in setting up a similar organization in Afghanistan.

By 1978, though, Iran was in crisis. Popular opposition to the pro-U.S. regime of the Shah was growing under the leadership of the Islamic clergy, throwing America's strategy to safeguard oil supplies into disarray. Memories of the 1973 Middle East war and the Arab embargo were still fresh,[3] and the prospect of another threat to energy supplies was of great concern to the United States. In January 1978, there were antigovernment demonstrations in the holy city of Qum, but these were suppressed by Iranian security forces with heavy loss of life. The violence in Qum sparked widespread protests in other parts of Iran, and Ayatollah Khomeini became the central figure in the revolutionary movement. His portraits could be seen everywhere; his name was constantly chanted in slogans.

Iranians representing three powerful sectors of society—the mosque, the bazaar, and the intelligentsia—had gathered around Ayatollah Khomeini's name in opposition to the Shah. Radical Islam was on the rise, but it was Shi'a Islam and it was fervently anti-American. It could be a threat to America's close ally in the region, Saudi Arabia, the world's largest oil exporter and the leader of the majority Sunni sect of Islam.

The sense of alienation in Iranian society was reinforced by high inflation and corruption. Massive oil price rises had meant a big increase in Iran's oil revenues, which were being used to finance industrial and military projects. Cooperation between the Shah and Israel in security and energy matters had angered many conservatives. His secret service, the SAVAK, was hated for its coercive tactics at home.[4] The American administration continued to believe, until it was too late, that the Shah was going to survive the crisis. It was not to be.[5]

The crisis in Iran was something of a mixed blessing for the Soviet Union. There were potential advantages because of the problems the Iranian upheaval would create for Western security in the Indian Ocean.[6] However, an Islamic clerical regime in Iran might raise the morale of long-suppressed Muslim minorities in large parts of the Soviet Union, from Tajikistan to Azerbaijan, bordering on Iran. Religious fundamentalism could also spread to other countries, including Afghanistan, where the Soviet Union had influence.

PAKISTAN

Among Afghanistan's immediate neighbors, Pakistan had particularly close links with Afghan society. The Pashtun community in Pakistan's North-West Frontier Province had strong ties with Afghan Pashtuns, the country's dominant race. Their trading links, official and unofficial, played an important role in both economies. Pakistan also had a keen strategic interest in Afghanistan. Vast areas along the open Afghan-Pakistan frontier were vital for maintaining strategic depth—an essential element of Pakistan's defense doctrine.[7] In the event of an all-out attack from India to the east, Pakistan could evacuate its key military and civilian personnel to relative safety along the Afghan-Pakistan frontier to the west.[8] However, it required a friendly government in Kabul, and therefore successive Pakistani administrations had shown a keen interest in the affairs of Afghanistan.

From the Pakistani perspective, the "Pashtunistan" issue had dominated relations with Afghanistan since 1947, the year in which Britain granted independence to Pakistan and India. The issue centered on demands for a separate Pashtun homeland across the Afghan-Pakistan frontier and caused strong resentment and fear among the mainly Punjabi rulers of Pakistan.[9] Had these demands been successful, Pakistan would have become a reduced entity. Moreover, integration with Pakistan's Pashtun tribes would have turned Afghanistan into a Pashtun-majority state. For these and other reasons, the military-intelligence establishment of Pakistan became deeply involved in Afghan society soon after 1947, with profound consequences during the conflict in Afghanistan.

In 1978 Pakistan was ruled by a military regime led by Gen. Zia-ul Haq, who had overthrown the elected prime minister, Zulfiqar Ali Bhutto, and seized power in a coup a year before.[10] Initially, General Zia had promised to hold free and fair elections within ninety days, but cancelled them in early 1978.[11] All political activity was outlawed, large numbers of opponents and journalists were arrested, and a number of newspapers shut down. Instead, General Zia began making overtures to small religious parties and installing prominent members of these parties in the corridors of power.[12] This turn of events alienated many Pakistanis and isolated the military regime on the international scene. With increasing popular disaffection and a deteriorating economy, Pakistan's military regime was in desperate need of support at home and help from abroad.

Problems for Pakistan were compounded because its strategic relationship with the United States had cooled off. In the early years of the Cold War, their alliance was based on two factors: America needed Pakistan to contain the spread of Soviet communism and Pakistan wanted U.S. support against the threat from India, which was close to the Soviet Union. Pakistan received large amounts of military and economic assistance in return for joining the Western alliance and allowing American reconnaissance flights over Soviet territory.[13]

The picture was different in early 1978. There was criticism of the military takeover by General Zia in the West. Pakistan was a much reduced country following the loss of its eastern wing back in 1971. There was concern in Washington over Pakistan's secret nuclear program.[14] The unrest over allegations of rigged elections, which incited the military takeover, had caused instability in Pakistan. The overthrow of Prime Minister Zulfiqar Ali Bhutto was an unwelcome development for both the United States and China; Bhutto had played a key role in bringing the two countries close to each other, including facilitating Henry Kissinger's 1973 visit to China. The visit marked the beginning of a strategic alliance of the United States and China against the Soviet Union.

Despite all this, the foreign policy of Pakistan in 1978 was still governed by the twin necessities of defense against India to the east and a friendly government in Afghanistan to the west. After a period of chaotic civilian rule, the military in Pakistan had reasserted itself, but the challenge it now faced was how to revive Western interest and attract much needed political and economic assistance to turn the nation's fortunes.

CHINA

Afghanistan has a narrow border with China through the Wakhan corridor linking Afghanistan's northeastern Badakhshan province with Chinese mainland.[15] It is one of the world's highest borders, with some mountain passes through the Hindu Kush rising to an altitude of almost 16,000 feet (5,000 meters). On the other side of the border is the Chinese autonomous region of Xinjiang. It is a sparsely populated area inhabited by several Muslim groups, including the Uygurs, the Kazakhs, the Tajiks, the Kirghiz, and the Uzbeks.

The split from the Soviet Union that began in the 1960s made it necessary for the Chinese leadership to attempt to counter Soviet influence in the region. This resulted in China attaching greater importance to developing relations with Kabul. Though China's long years of isolation imposed limits on how rapidly ties with other countries could be cultivated, Afghanistan received Chinese aid, mainly in the form of credits for irrigation and rural development projects and a textile factory outside Kabul.[16] By 1978, the Sino-Soviet split was complete and Chinese relations with the United States were improving.[17] In the developing strategic alliance with the United States, China appeared likely to follow Washington's lead.

THE UNITED STATES

Besides the crisis in Iran, the United States had other worries in 1978, both in the region and at home. The Southeast Asia Treaty Organization (SEATO) had been disbanded.[18] The Central Treaty Organization (CENTO) had been ineffective in preventing Soviet expansion to other countries in the region and the Iranian crisis was to spell the end of the organization.[19] All this after the American withdrawal from Indochina contributed to the impression that the United States was retreating in the face of Soviet expansion.

At home, the United States was going through a period of deep introspection after Vietnam and the Watergate affair, which forced President Nixon out of office and contributed to the defeat of his successor, Gerald Ford.[20] Many Americans did not trust their national leaders, whose actions were often questioned. U.S. president Jimmy Carter, a southern Baptist Christian, was determined to establish America's moral leadership in the world.[21] His dedication to human rights had given American foreign policy an aggressive tone, especially in relations with the Soviet Union. It also had the stamp of Carter's national security adviser, Zbigniew Brzezinski, a strong advocate of America establishing its ideological ascendancy.[22] Brzezinski's assertion was that America's image and ideological influence abroad had deteriorated and a new offensive emphasizing freedom, democracy, and human rights was one way for America to reassert itself.

Serious disagreements between Brzezinski and U.S. secretary of state Cyrus Vance were pulling American foreign policy in different directions.[23] Vance, who had to negotiate with the USSR on a range of issues, including arms limitation, regional crises, and economic matters, was in favor of a cautious approach. America's aim, according to Vance, should be to establish a relationship with a Soviet Union that did not "seek to dominate other countries" and that accepted a "responsible role in the world."[24] Before the communist coup in April 1978, Afghanistan was not on the agenda for either Brzezinski or Vance. With the crisis in neighboring Iran deepening, it was not a significant issue for the U.S. administration.

AFGHANISTAN

President Daud had been in power for almost five years when he was deposed by pro-Soviet military officers on April 27, 1978. Daud, eighteen members of his family, and a number of his ministers were assassinated in the coup.[25] It ended nearly four decades of rule by King Zahir Shah and Daud, his cousin, who had seized power in a palace coup in July 1973, abolished the monarchy, and declared Afghanistan a republic.

Society

The shape of Afghan society has largely been determined by its geographic location at the crossroads of Central, West, and South Asia. Wave after wave of migrating people have passed through the region, leaving behind a variety of ethnic and linguistic groups. In 1978, the population of Afghanistan was estimated at a just over 15 million; the Pashtuns, politically the most powerful group, amounted to just under half of this number.[26] Significant among other groups were Tajiks, Hazaras, Uzbeks, Turkmen, Baluch, and Nuristanis. Pashtuns were largely concentrated in the southeast of Afghanistan and spread across the open frontier with Pakistan;[27] Tajiks, Uzbeks, and Turkmen lived along the Afghan-Soviet border. Communities often overlapped in much of Afghanistan, creating conditions in which distrust and discrimination existed along with extraordinary acts of tolerance and generosity.

Pashto and Persian (Dari for Afghans) evolved as the most important languages of Afghans, although each language has an array of dialects. Both belong to the Iranian branch of the Indo-European language family. Persian was the primary language in the capital, Kabul, and areas farther north. In some cases, Pashtuns could well be Persian-speakers while some Tajiks and Uzbeks spoke Pashto.[28]

About 85 percent of Afghans belonged to the Sunni sect of Islam, the rest were Shi'a. Most Sunnis were from the Hanafi school, which is dominant in the Arab Middle East, Afghanistan, and Pakistan.[29] Founded by one of the earliest Muslim scholars, Abu Hanifa, the Hanafi school is based on the most liberal interpretation of Islam and is extremely tolerant of differences between communities.[30] It makes considerable use of reason and practical legal opinion in case law. This liberalism was reflected in the way different Afghan communities generally lived in harmony.

Foreign relations

Great powers had been interested in Afghanistan for hundreds of years. The British and Tsarist Russian empires had vied for influence there in the nineteenth and early-twentieth centuries. So did the United States, the Soviet Union, and the neighboring powers of Iran and China, after the Second World War. Driving this competition was the belief that whoever gained control of Afghanistan would then be tempted to move into Pakistan to secure access to the Indian Ocean's warm-water ports. Close proximity to the Gulf's oil reserves gave Afghanistan strategic importance as a buffer state, which each power was determined to prevent its rivals from crossing.[31]

Since the 1950s, the United States and the Soviet Union had used aid to gain influence in Afghanistan. Between 1950 and 1977, the total U.S. assistance in the form of loans, grants, and agricultural commodities amounted to some $450 million.[32] America's stated purpose was to develop transportation facilities, increase agricultural production, expand the educational system, stimulate industry, and improve government administration. In the 1950s, U.S. money was used to build roads, dams, and hydro-electric power plants. In later years, the focus of American aid switched to technical education and training.

The main objective of the United States was to foster an independent Afghanistan, "willing and able to impose limitations on the Soviet Union."[33] This was the basis on which America had decided to enter the "aid race" with the USSR. However, American diplomats acknowledged in 1977 that U.S. assistance had fallen "short of balancing the Soviet Union" and had lost the race.[34]

Daud was partly responsible for this outcome. From 1953 to 1963, he had served as Afghanistan's prime minister and his brother, Mohammad Naim, as the country's foreign minister. In effect, the two ruled the country and the king kept away from the day-to-day administration. Daud's personality was forceful. His ambition was to see rapid economic development, but he did not want the country to become too dependent on Western help.[35] There had been tensions between Daud and the United States as far back as the 1950s, in particular over American aid for the ambitious Hilmand Valley Project. The plan was to build an irrigation network around Afghanistan's longest river, which would run across western Afghanistan and Iran, and turn vast, barren areas into green fields. However, repeated delays in completing the project led to acrimonious exchanges between American and Afghan officials.

Daud had also decided to avoid the Western-sponsored Baghdad Pact, later known as CENTO. He had already committed Afghanistan to the Non-Aligned Movement at its founding conference in the Indonesian city of Bandung in 1955. The decision formalized Daud's desire to follow a policy of neutrality—a policy designed to attract aid and investment from all possible sources. It seemed to pay off when, in the same year, the Soviet leader, Nikita Khrushchev, visited Kabul and announced a loan worth $100 million. Soon afterward came Afghanistan's first five-year development plan, marking the beginning of Soviet-style state planning.

However, the main factor shaping Afghanistan's foreign policy was its relations with Pakistan. The Durand Line dividing the two countries had not been recognized by successive Afghan governments. Demands were growing in Pakistan's North-West Frontier Province for a separate state for ethnic Pashtuns, to be called Pashtunistan. It would incorporate Pashtun tribal areas on the border with Afghanistan, where Pashtuns were the dominant ethnic group. Daud was a strong advocate of these demands, but the Pakistani authorities were determined to resist because they saw the Pashtuns as a serious threat to their country's integrity.

Tensions with Pakistan had underscored Afghanistan's vulnerability as far back as the 1950s. Afghans' dependence on transit facilities through Pakistan for trade with the outside world was undeniable, as was the annual migrations of hundreds of thousands of nomads between northern Afghanistan and Pakistan's border areas. Occasional Pakistani moves to close the frontier created serious problems for the Afghans in the 1950s. It was, however, the Pakistani blockade between September 1961 and June 1963 that caused the biggest crisis for the Daud government and ultimately forced his resignation.[36] A proud man, Daud felt humiliated by the king's decision to accept his resignation. The manner of his departure caused a permanent breach in their relationship, and in July 1973, when the king was on a European visit, Daud staged a coup and overthrew him. The monarchy was abolished and Daud assumed the presidency of Afghanistan.

The coup, which brought Daud back to power, was made possible by a group of young Soviet-trained army officers.[37] American diplomats in Kabul informed the U.S. secretary of state, Henry Kissinger, that, in the capital at least, residents appeared to be expressing support for the new regime and relief that the ineffective, corrupt leadership of the king was at an end.[38] The diplomats alerted the State Department that the new government headed by President

Daud was likely to be "authoritarian and highly nationalistic," similar to his previous regime between 1953 and 1963.

They informed Washington that, in foreign affairs, Daud would seek to maintain close and friendly relations with the USSR. However, they said that the new regime did not necessarily pose a threat to any major U.S. interests and the main foreign policy issue in the region would be the Pashtunistan question. The U.S. administration feared that the Pashtunistan issue could inflame secessionist demands in Pakistan, America's close ally. For the United States, the defense alliance with Pakistan was too important to risk.

4

AFGHANISTAN UNDER COMMUNISM

The role played by Soviet-trained officers in the 1973 coup highlighted the foothold the USSR had secured in Afghanistan since 1956—the year in which the country started to receive significant military aid from Moscow. The Afghan Military Academy had become heavily dependent on Soviet help, and by the end of the 1970s, more than 3,700 Afghan officers had been trained in Soviet military establishments.[1] Soviet military assistance to Afghanistan amounted to some $1.25 billion during this period. Afghan requests for U.S. military aid, however, were rejected.[2]

SOVIET INTELLIGENCE IN AFGHANISTAN

Much more has come to light in recent years about the extent of infiltration by Soviet intelligence in Afghanistan during this period.[3] For almost twenty years, the KGB was involved in building up an elaborate spy network in the country. It included officers working under diplomatic cover in the Soviet embassy in Kabul (known as the Residency), advisers assigned to Afghan ministries and offices (Representatives), and hundreds of Afghans who were mostly paid KGB agents.

One of the oldest, Nur Mohammad Taraki, had been a Soviet agent since 1951 and maintained close contacts with intelligence officers in the Soviet embassy in the Afghan capital.[4] Taraki acted alone in the beginning, but later met another Marxist activist, Hafizullah Amin. Together, they established a group called *Khalq* (the Masses). Another agent, Babrak Karmal, formed a separate faction with Communist leanings known as *Parcham* (the Banner) in 1957. The two factions united in 1965 to form the People's Democratic Party of Afghanistan (PDPA). Taraki was elected first secretary of the Central Committee and Karmal became his deputy.

Soon afterward, Taraki was invited to Moscow by the Soviet Communist Party, where he met with party officials, including the head of the International Department, Boris Ponomarev. Manifesto, rules, strategy, and financing of the PDPA were discussed, but the Soviets advised Taraki to be extremely cautious.[5] The party suggested that he publish a newspaper, but only through a "figurehead, a man of means," so that suspicions were not raised over the source of the paper's financing. In fact, the PDPA and its newspaper, the *Khalq*, received finances from the Central Committee of the Soviet Communist Party. Taraki was given a monthly allowance and food supplies. The Soviet Communist Party and the KGB both preferred Taraki as leader, but accepted that Karmal, as head of the Parcham faction, was also politically important because he had contacts within the Afghan intelligentsia and had won a seat in parliament in Kabul in the 1965 elections.

KGB officers working under diplomatic cover in the Afghan capital asked Taraki to carry out operations for them, and he regularly passed on intelligence about the Afghan army and government to them. Taraki assisted in recruiting more agents, and he was instrumental in organizing anti-Chinese demonstrations in the Afghan capital.[6] The KGB had advance knowledge of the 1973 coup and that Daud was planning to overthrow the monarchy. After the coup, Taraki was given instructions "to move loyal supporters into leading posts in the new state apparatus;" in turn, he received more secret funds from the KGB in 1974.

DAUD'S REPUBLIC: A ONE-PARTY STATE

The 1973 coup, in which the Communists had helped Daud overthrow the king, radicalized Afghan politics. The king was humiliated, the monarchy abolished, and the democratic experiment ongoing since the mid-1960s came to an abrupt end. The rise of pro-Soviet communists caused great anger among the right-wing religious groups. Islamist leaders Gulbuddin Hikmatyar, Abdul Rasul Sayyaf, and Burhanuddin Rabbani had been concerned with the growing communist influence since the 1950s, and now their worst fears were realized. Soon after the 1973 coup, the Daud regime, in collaboration with the PDPA, launched a campaign against the Islamic Alliance, which had just won a big victory in elections for the Kabul University Students Union. A number of prominent Islamist activists, including Hikmatyar and Rabbani, escaped to Pakistan. The movement went underground in Afghanistan.

Daud calculated that he had overcome the challenge from the Islamic Alliance, and his next political move was to the right. A proud man with a secular, independent mind and a strong determination not to become a client of any big power, Daud reduced the number of Soviet military advisers in his ministries and signed an ambitious agreement with Iran in 1974.[7] The deal promised an investment of $2 billion in Afghanistan—more than the combined total Soviet aid over the previous two decades. Officials in Tehran began to talk of growing Iranian influence on the Afghan government, and Daud's visits to Iran, Saudi Arabia, Kuwait, and Pakistan seemed to confirm a fundamental shift in Afghanistan's foreign policy.

Daud then turned against communists at home. Pro-Soviet figures were removed from their ministerial posts, and military officers known to be Soviet sympathizers were marginalized. In 1977, a new constitution was approved at a traditional grand assembly. It elected Daud as president for a term of seven years and Afghanistan became a one-party state. His National Revolutionary Party was the only one allowed to operate. These were unwelcome developments for the Soviet leadership.

The People's Democratic Party had split in 1967—just two years after the Khalq and Parcham factions came together to form the single party. Ten years later, as Daud moved to neutralize the communists, the KGB initiated efforts to reunite the two factions. The presence of United Nations and NATO experts coupled with multinational projects in northern Afghanistan, near its border with the USSR, alarmed the Soviet leader, Leonid Brezhnev. While Daud was visiting Moscow in April 1977, Brezhnev angrily demanded that the Afghan government send these experts back as they were foreign spies promoting imperialism. In a blunt exchange, Daud told Brezhnev that he would not allow the USSR to dictate the governing of Afghanistan, and stated that how and where foreign experts were employed in the country was the sole prerogative of the Afghan authorities.[8]

The security situation in Kabul became compromised in the wake of Daud's campaign against his opponents. The minister of planning, Ahmad Ali Khorram, was assassinated at the end of 1977. In February 1978 came a treason trial, which implicated some twenty-five Islamists. During this time rumors of a left-wing plot to overthrow President Daud persisted. In the midst of all this came the murder of a prominent member of the PDPA, Mir Akbar Khyber, on April 17, 1978.[9] His death triggered a chain of events that would lead to the communist coup within a matter of days.

At Khyber's funeral, thousands of Kabul residents came out to protest the Daud regime. The leaders of both PDPA factions gave fiery speeches, accusing the imperialist forces of the murder. Calls to overthrow the government were reportedly made.[10] Daud retaliated and ordered the arrest of senior PDPA leaders. Taraki and Karmal were detained in the early hours of April 26, 1978. Inexplicably, Hafizullah Amin was not detained, and news of the arrests was communicated to the rest of the party network. Between April 27 and 28, a small group of military officers—almost all Khalq members—carried out the coup.[11] Daud and most of the members of his family were assassinated.

CONFLICT WITHIN AFGHAN COMMUNISM

The decision of the rebel leaders to give the KGB advance notice of the coup demonstrated the importance they placed on the need for Soviet support. First, Taraki asked the Soviet embassy for help in case Afghanistan was attacked by neighboring Iran or Pakistan.[12] The Politburo of the Soviet Communist Party met on April 30 to consider the situation in Afghanistan.[13] Soviet instructions were conveyed to the PDPA through KGB officials. Hafizullah Amin was told that the Soviet leadership wanted Taraki to be proclaimed president but not general secretary for the time being. That announcement should be left for a later date.

Disputes between the Khalq and Parcham factions came to the fore soon after the communist coup, the allocation of senior posts being the main bone of contention. Military officers, many of whom belonged to Khalq, were opposed to the inclusion of Parcham members. Conversely, the Parcham leader, Babrak Karmal, resisted the expansion of the Revolutionary Council to give greater representation to the armed forces. The situation became so serious that the Soviet ambassador and advisers had to intervene.[14]

This new power struggle was a serious setback to Soviet hopes that the communist regime would expand its popular base.[15] Babrak Karmal bitterly complained to the Soviet ambassador that a number of leading members of his Parcham faction were about to be sent abroad as "ambassadors" or "under the pretext of medical treatment."[16] Karmal protested that he was being isolated from the affairs of the country even though he held the number two position and warned that the PDPA was headed for another split. Barely a month later, the split did occur and the alliance between Khalq and Parcham collapsed.

The conflict between the PDPA factions was rooted in a mix of ethnic, class, and ideological tensions.[17] With some exceptions, Khalq members were mainly Pashtun nationalists from rural Afghanistan, where tribal loyalties and feuds prevailed.[18] Khalq officers had a higher representation in the military and security services than those from the Parcham faction.[19] Although Khalq was by no means a monolithic group, given the tribal rivalries and personal ambitions of its members, it was nonetheless closer to the levers of power.

Members of Parcham were generally from the capital, Kabul, and other urban centers of Afghanistan. They were by and large more educated and articulate than their Khalq counterparts. Ideologically, Parchamis were less conservative and more internationalist in outlook. Many of them belonged to non-Pashtun ethnic groups and resented the historical dominance of Pashtuns. Since the April coup, the PDPA had been engaged in a campaign of reprisals against Western-educated Afghan technocrats, who were seen as supporters of Daud or of the deposed king. They were replaced by mainly Khalq members in senior government positions. Mass arrests, torture, and executions of suspected opponents had begun. In May about nine hundred people were thrown into prison in the northern province of Balkh alone, and many were shot to death in subsequent weeks.[20] A new prison, still under construction outside Kabul, was being used to lock up thousands of political prisoners. Interrogations under torture and executions were routinely carried out by the Afghan secret service, which was being restructured on the Soviet model.

In July the Khalq leadership launched a drive against Parcham with the aim of removing all potential rivals of Taraki and Amin. In the first phase, a number of senior Parcham figures were removed from power and sent abroad as "ambassadors," only to be dismissed later. Karmal himself was sent into exile in Czechoslovakia.[21] His half-brother, Mahmood Baryalai, was sent to Pakistan and Najibullah to Iran. Both were eventually stripped of their Afghan citizenship. The most prominent woman in the PDPA leadership and Karmal's close companion, Anahita Ratebzad, was exiled to Belgrade.

"Conspiracies" against the ruling party were uncovered, and suspected enemies of the state still in the country, including senior civil servants and military officers, were targeted. After the discovery of an "anti-revolutionary network" in August 1978, the defense minister, Abdul Qadir, and the chief of the general staff, Maj. Gen. Shapur Ahmadzai, were taken into custody.[22] Confessions were extracted from both officers under torture, which led to further arrests and purges. Major General Rafi, one of the leaders of the communist coup, and Sultan Ali Kishtmand were removed from the cabinet and imprisoned. These events made the Soviet leadership increasingly uneasy, and Taraki and Amin were told to halt "unjustified repression."

By late 1978, Amin was in firm control of the organs of state security. The KGB made several direct appeals to him to end the prosecution of so-called conspirators and to release a number of dissident army officers, including Rafi and Qadir.[23] Amin was told that these people had done "useful work for Soviet intelligence" and made a significant contribution to the "Afghan revolution." Amin replied that he was willing to release individuals close to Soviet officials, but accused some of them of being out of touch with the latest situation, comments that caused irritation and annoyance in the Soviet leadership.

The Afghan crisis had worsened within months of the April coup. The PDPA organization was hemorrhaging because of internal purges. With most of their rivals exiled or jailed, power was concentrated in the hands of Taraki and Amin. State security forces were under the effective command of Amin, who became defense minister in July 1979. Meanwhile, the regime became increasingly isolated. It was all very different from the promises made by the PDPA to build an "antifeudal" alliance consisting of "the working class, the peasantry, the intelligentsia, and the artisans."[24]

Marxist cadres believed that all landlords were "feudal" and saw no distinction between tribal chiefs and landowners. The way officials treated chiefs and village elders sparked widespread anger in Afghan society, uniting large sections of the population and contributing to uprisings against the communist regime. The decision to adopt a red national flag in October 1978 was extremely provocative and was followed by the announcement of a land-reform program.[25] The drive to redistribute land and set up Soviet-style cooperatives was launched with little preparation. This led to the collapse of a well-established system under which relatively prosperous landowners had traditionally provided peasants with seeds, access to water for irrigation, animals, and machinery.[26]

Challenges to the Afghan regime were mounting, but so was the Soviet commitment to support it. Brezhnev and Taraki signed a friendship treaty in Moscow in December 1978, and a commission for economic cooperation was set up to provide the basis for massive Soviet economic and military aid to the

PDPA regime. Armed resistance began to spread in early 1979, causing a sharp deterioration in the security situation. In February the American ambassador, Adolph Dubs, was abducted by gunmen and taken to the Kabul Hotel, where he was kept hostage for several hours. He was killed in a failed rescue operation. Afghan security forces launched the assault despite several appeals by American diplomats at the scene in the presence of Soviet advisers.[27] The United States reacted with outrage, which was compounded when Taraki suggested that all four abductors of Dubs had been killed, so there was nobody left to interrogate.[28]

At this stage, the U.S. administration was consumed by the crisis in Iran after the fall of the Shah and the subsequent disruption to oil supplies to the West. Nevertheless, President Carter imposed sanctions against the Afghan regime immediately after the ambassador's death. Economic aid was cut and plans to resume the military training of Afghan officers were dropped.[29] On August 14, 1979, Carter signed a directive prohibiting further assistance to Afghanistan. Other noncommunist countries and international organizations, including the World Bank, began to cut back their aid programs.[30] These measures further isolated the PDPA in the international community and increased its dependence on the Soviet Union.

Violent Transformation of Society

Inside Afghanistan, a series of uprisings in 1979 proved catastrophic for the communist regime. The most serious rebellion occured in March in the western city of Herat, near the Iranian border. Units of the local military garrison joined angry crowds that had earlier attacked the office of the provincial governor.[31] Military installations were ransacked and vehicles set on fire. Pitched battles were fought between rebels and retreating government forces. The rebels stormed the prison and freed opponents of the regime. Dozens of Soviet military officers, technical advisers, and their families were captured, publicly tortured, and killed. These gruesome acts caused a profound sense of shock in the Soviet Union. Government forces were only able to crush the uprising after reinforcements arrived from Kabul and other eastern garrisons, and planes—probably flown by Soviet pilots—bombed the city, killing or wounding thousands of people.

The revolt in Herat made Taraki very nervous. There had been desertions from military units elsewhere, but this uprising signaled a much deeper crisis in the Afghan armed forces. During urgent consultations with the Soviet leadership, Taraki admitted that his government had no support in the population and that the situation was only deteriorating.[32] In a desperate move, he proposed that the USSR send its own Tajik, Uzbek, and Turkmen soldiers disguised as Afghans to control the situation. He suggested that they would be indistinguishable from Afghans of the same ethnic groups.

Taraki traveled to Moscow in an attempt to persuade the Soviet leadership personally, but was told by Brezhnev that Moscow had decided against the idea because it "would only play into the hands of the enemies—yours and ours." Instead, Brezhnev lectured Taraki on the need to adopt tactics to split the Afghan clergy, to exercise caution in using "repressive measures" against army officers, to unite the party, and widen the support base of the regime.[33]

April 1979 brought another mutiny at an army base in the eastern city of Jalalabad, followed by an uprising by ethnic Hazaras in June and a mutiny by government troops in Kabul in August. All three revolts were suppressed by brute force, using artillery and aerial bombardment.[34] But the Afghan armed forces were disintegrating, popular resentment was rising, and the country was only weeks away from yet another coup.

A rapid and violent transformation of Afghan society was under way, driven by the creation of new forces in opposition to the existing order. Internal conflicts made the communist regime weak and unstable. The more brutal tactics the regime imposed, the more determined the opposition became, prompting the subsequent use of even greater coercion.

With this pattern taking hold in Afghan society, the United States and its allies remained preoccupied by the mounting crisis in Iran and the Gulf while the military rulers of Pakistan struggled with their own isolation. For most of the Cold War years, the Americans had viewed a strong friendly government in Iran as vital to Western interests, and friendship with Pakistan as more important than Afghanistan. As the 1980s approached, the Americans had lost the race for domination in the Gulf region by turning Iran into a proxy. However, with the rise of communism and growing Soviet involvement, Afghanistan was about to become a key battleground in the East-West conflict. Pakistan was to be America's base in its war against the Soviets.

5

TOWARD DISINTEGRATION

The Communist takeover in Afghanistan in April 1978 was the beginning of an increasingly unstable and violent period, which was to lead to a Soviet invasion in December 1979. The murders of President Daud, his family members, and his close associates in the 1978 coup were gruesome and demonstrated the degree to which pro-Soviet army officers and communist activists hated Daud. The desire to seek revenge after Daud's decision to purge communists and distance himself from the USSR was overwhelming. These were the officers who had helped Daud overthrow his cousin, King Zahir Shah, five years before, but he had turned against them. The leaders of the 1978 coup were determined not to leave any vestiges of the old regime, nor did they want to share power with anyone else. It was all very different from the coup in 1973, which transpired with hardly any bloodshed and restored normality the following day.

This and the following chapters explore the increasingly fractured nature of 1970s Afghan society along ethnic, sectarian, and ideological lines and how these structural factors began to create a culture of violence and to attract external powers to the Afghan theater. Conflict within Afghanistan's first communist regime and the external opposition that contributed to its failure are examined. It becomes clear how this failure led to the Soviet military invasion of Afghanistan in December 1979—an invasion that prompted a proxy war between the USSR and the United States and its allies as Afghanistan spent a decade under Soviet occupation.

STRUCTURAL FAULT-LINES IN AFGHAN SOCIETY

The four key military officers behind the communist coup in 1978 were ethnic Pashtun and three of them belonged to the Khalq faction.[1] Other individuals from non-Pashtun ethnic groups and from the Parcham faction were brought into the regime when the coup leaders handed over power to the People's Democratic Party. This sequence of events pointed to broader social and political divisions between Pashtun and non-Pashtun, and between Khalq and Parcham.[2] Besides these twin factors, there was another source of conflict in Afghan society—tribal and personal hostilities and the ambition for power. Often, some or all of these factors fueled conflict simultaneously, and it was often difficult to identify exactly the root cause.

Above all, the most significant source of conflict related to the historical development of the Afghan nation. It was a diverse and complex society with competing internal forces and external influences. Afghans were a deeply religious people and the clergy had a special place in society. The Pashtuns dominated the south, but were not a unified community, with numerous tribes and rivalries among them. However, there were close social and economic links between the Pashtuns and their southern neighbors in Pakistan's autonomous tribal agencies. In northern Afghanistan, however, there lived a number of non-Pashtun ethnic groups.[3] These communities had links with their counterparts in Iran to the west and with Soviet Central Asian republics to the north. Communities in the northeastern Afghan province of Badakhshan were close to ethnic groups across the border in China's Xinjiang region.

These sociological forces and religious influences often pulled communities in opposite directions and produced tensions within Afghan society: Shi'a, who looked to Iran, versus Sunni, who looked to Pakistan and Saudi Arabia; Pashtun versus non-Pashtun, as well as tribal rivalries within Pashtun communities. Likewise, the Tajik, Turkmen, Uzbek, and other minorities, which competed with each other in the north, sometimes found common ground in uniting against the Pashtuns.

Despite all these divisions, the traditional conservative nature of Afghans and their deep religious beliefs meant that there was an inherent resistance to communism and a system of state control over every sphere of life. It was no surprise that the imposition of a communist regime provoked widespread alienation among Afghans, and many prominent opposition figures either went underground or into exile to fight it.

Before the overthrow of the monarchy in 1973, distant communities of Afghans throughout the country had lived under considerable local autonomy and looked to the king for guidance and help in times of crisis. Without the monarchy, the institution that held the country together no longer existed. Other forces of ethnic, tribal, and external nature began to exert greater influence, pulling the communities away from the center.

The Soviet Union had advance knowledge of the 1978 coup and was actively involved in the formation of the communist regime afterward. It would stand to reason then that the attempt to accommodate the Pashtun and non-Pashtun, Khalq and Parcham, was made at the behest of the Soviet leadership. But the appearance of unity was artificial and short-lived: first came a purge of Parcham members from the regime followed by rebellions of civilians and troops, which began to spread across the country. The cycle of violence rapidly gathered momentum, and by April 1979 the regime seemed to be losing control.

VIOLENT AND OPPORTUNISTIC PASHTUN NATIONALISM

Another factor affecting events in Afghanistan was violent, opportunistic Pashtun nationalism, personified at the highest level by Hafizullah Amin. For more than a year after the communist coup, Amin had taken advantage of Taraki's personality cult and presented himself as his disciple, when in reality the two men were very different and represented rival Pashtun constituencies in the Khalq faction of the PDPA. Taraki, a self-educated writer of modest means from the southern province of Ghazni, liked to think of himself as someone who would lead the peasants and the landless to a Marxist revolution in Afghanistan. In Kabul, Taraki's relations with the Soviet embassy and KGB officers were close; in Moscow, he was the preferred leader of the People's Democratic Party of Afghanistan.

Hafizullah Amin, a Pashtun from a village near Kabul, was educated at Columbia University in New York. Upon returning home, Amin worked as a teacher for several years and became active in the PDPA and focused his considerable organizational skills on recruiting Pashtun students to the party. These new recruits were mainly rural Pashtuns, who became part of the Khalq faction, never forsaking their nationalist roots. Many of them later joined the Afghan armed forces. At the same time, Amin cultivated close relationships with pro-Soviet officers serving in the security forces. Despite his Soviet connections, prominent Afghans viewed Amin not so much as a communist but rather as an ambitious and ruthless Pashtun nationalist who would not hesitate to use any means to eliminate his rivals. This became obvious as a power struggle broke out in the communist regime after the coup.

By July 1979 the relationship between Taraki and Amin had suffered a sharp deterioration and Amin had begun to wrest control. At a Politburo meeting that same month, Amin launched a personal attack on Taraki, accusing him of dictatorial behavior and holding him responsible for the government's failures. Amin then introduced a resolution that called for a "collective leadership" to rule the country. The resolution was approved, and the Politburo agreed to expedite the establishment of this new leadership. Amin's motive appeared to be to win control of the defense ministry, and Taraki was eventually forced to accept Amin's appointment as de facto defense minister, which gave him a tighter grip over the military establishment. Other prominent figures were given less important posts in the reshuffle. Aslam Watanjar, a key figure in the 1978 coup, was moved to the interior ministry, which controlled the police. Meanwhile, Amin's brother Abdullah was appointed as supervisory governor for the four northern provinces, and his nephew, Asadullah, became the deputy minister for foreign affairs—appointments that brought accusations of nepotism against Amin, but represented a fundamental shift in power, leaving Taraki as a figurehead.

Within days of gaining control of the defense ministry, Amin's authority faced a serious challenge and his response to the crisis strengthened his reputation for ruthlessness. Rebel troops, under the command of officers recently recalled from eastern Afghanistan, staged a mutiny at an army brigade in Kabul.[4] As the rebellion broke out, the command center inside the Bala Hisar fort was seized and tanks appeared on the road to the presidential palace. On Amin's orders, the rebels were intercepted and the fort was surrounded by government tanks and attacked by helicopter gunships. After several hours of heavy fighting,[5] the revolt was brutally put down and Amin emerged as the strongman in Kabul.

The scale of popular uprisings in the countryside was different, however. The Afghan regime made a number of requests to the Soviet Union for troops to help crush growing revolts in the provinces, but the Kremlin turned them down.[6] One such appeal was for the deployment of two Soviet brigades; another asked for a Soviet parachute division to be sent to deal with emergencies. The Soviet leadership continued to deny Afghanistan's requests.[7]

Many in the Kremlin were aware that such a move would provoke the Americans into increasing their aid to the Afghan resistance. Soon after the Kabul mutiny was crushed, the Soviet deputy defense minister, Gen. Ivan Pavlovsky, secretly visited Afghanistan to assess the situation.[8] He told the Kabul regime that the introduction of Soviet fighting units would further complicate the military and political situation,[9] and would be seen as a direct intervention in an independent, non-aligned country. The USSR would face severe international criticism, which would aggravate the crisis in East-West relations. It was not in the Soviet interest to draw too much American attention to Afghanistan.

THE ROLE OF THE SOVIET UNION

It is now known that hundreds of troops serving with the Soviet special forces were quietly airlifted into Afghanistan in the summer of 1979—but not to help the Kabul regime in putting down rebellions. A small number of KGB troops were also flown to the capital with the stated aim of supporting the communist regime.[10] Two more airborne battalions were secretly stationed at the vast air base at Bagram, north of the capital.[11] Meanwhile, the Soviet Politburo told Amin and Taraki to build up security throughout the country—a move that would further stretch the depleted and demoralized Afghan forces. Anti-Amin leaflets, from an unknown source, began to circulate in Kabul in mid-July.

The Soviet Union had several possible motives for these actions. Although Amin's control of the Afghan defense and security apparatus was stronger than ever, it was being drained of its effectiveness due to growing desertions, mutinies, and incompetence. Taraki's position in the regime was weakening, and the need for the Kremlin to bolster its favored player was urgent. With thousands of officials and advisers operating from the Soviet embassy complex and from various Afghan ministries, security was a constant concern.

The arrival of the KGB and special forces in Kabul gave the Soviet Union a platform to launch a military operation independent of the Afghan forces, if necessary. The deployment of Soviet airborne troops at Bagram was particularly significant for two reasons: it gave the USSR control over a vast, modern base, from which aircraft of any size could operate; and the base could also serve as a bridge between military facilities in the Soviet Union and the Afghan capital, where facilities were limited.[12]

American diplomats in Kabul had begun to detect signs of a rift between Amin and the Soviet embassy, particularly with the Soviet ambassador, Alexander Puzanov. A number of Soviet advisers had been withdrawn from the Afghan foreign ministry, and meetings between Amin and Puzanov had become less frequent.[13] The Soviets were unhappy with Amin's maneuverings at the Afghan Politburo meeting in late July and with his takeover of military affairs.[14]

At a meeting with Taraki the Soviet ambassador demanded an explanation for the decisions taken in the July meeting of the PDPA Politburo.[15] The Soviets seemed largely unaware that the tide had turned against Taraki, who no longer commanded a majority in the Politburo. The Soviets were troubled by the unforeseen reshuffle resulting from the July meeting, and Amin was well aware of that fact.[16]

As the frequency of independent Afghan decision-making increased, Soviet advisers and specialists in Kabul were instructed to keep a closer watch on the internal workings of the regime. KGB and Soviet counterintelligence services escalated their activity and Soviet advisers in Afghan ministries became more involved, some even demanding that all decisions be made jointly. It amounted to a Soviet veto in the running of the regime, which only served to provoke senior figures in the PDPA.

In August 1979, some members of the anti-Amin faction in the Politburo tried to turn others, especially neutral parties, against Amin.[17] Tempers exploded when Taraki accused Amin of nepotism, citing the appointments of his brother and nephew in senior positions.[18] Amin's supporters responded by claiming that their leader—whom they described as a true Marxist-Leninist—was merely following the example set by Cuban leader, Fidel Castro, who had appointed his brother as defense minister.

In early September, the KGB submitted its recommendations on handling the situation to its top leadership.[19] The report acknowledged that the Afghan regime was losing authority and that the population was turning against the Soviet Union. The KGB complained that repeated advice to Taraki and Amin to expand their support base had been ignored and charged the Afghan regime with relying too much on military force to solve internal problems. It concluded that many of the coercive measures being taken to suppress the opposition were "unjustified" and laid blame on Amin.

Their recommendation was to somehow "remove Amin from the leadership" and press Taraki to form a "coalition government," in which the PDPA would play the leading role while still including "suitable" members of the clergy, tribes, and minorities. They advised release and rehabilitation for illegally arrested political prisoners, in particular Parcham faction members—and suggested the preparation of an alternative leadership in the event the crisis intensified. For all of its objectivity, the KGB analysis of the situation and some of its recommendations were explosive. Amin had been identified as the main cause of instability in the Afghan communist party, but it was doubtful whether the Soviet leadership would be able to control him.

The question then was how to remove Amin. He had almost complete control over the security apparatus and persuading him to give up was not a likely option. If the KGB recommended the use of force, then who but the USSR would execute this? The consequences of a Soviet military intervention would be far-reaching, as history would later demonstrate. Perhaps at the time these considerations contributed to the reluctance of certain Soviet leaders to support full-scale invasion of Afghanistan.

6

THE SECOND COMMUNIST COUP

Taraki left Kabul in early September 1979 to attend a summit of the Non-Aligned Movement in Havana. It was there that he was asked to stop over in Moscow for a meeting with the Soviet leader, Leonid Brezhnev, on his way back home.[1] The meeting took place on September 10, when Brezhnev spoke to Taraki from notes approved by just three of the Politburo members: KGB Chairman Yuri Andropov, Defense Minister Dmitri Ustinov, and Foreign Minister Andrei Gromyko. Brezhnev expressed to Taraki his grave concern over the deteriorating situation in Afghanistan and the ruling PDPA. Implying Amin, Brezhnev suggested that it was not sound for a single individual to simultaneously hold all powerful positions in the party, the armed forces, and the state security apparatus; he described it as a formula for dictatorship. The Soviet leader almost hinted to Taraki to "get rid of" Amin.

On September 13, two days after Taraki's return to Afghanistan, the Soviet embassy in Kabul informed the Soviet Politburo of a sharp deterioration in the relationship between Amin and Taraki.[2] Amin told Taraki that the "gang of four" had orchestrated an attempt on his life while Taraki was abroad.[3] This was the beginning of Amin's drive to overthrow Taraki. Amin ordered the commanders of the armed forces and the National Guard to ignore Taraki. Amin gave up the post of prime minister and assumed total control over the defense ministry. All of his supporters were instructed to remain in their posts and to report to him.

Realizing that the crisis was grave, the Soviet Politburo instructed the ambassador, Alexander Puzanov, to meet with Taraki and Amin—together or separately—and tell them that their rift would prove fatal should they fail to "demonstrate a sense of responsibility."[4] Puzanov was also directed to inform Taraki that Soviet troops stationed in Kabul could not be used to arrest Amin, because that would be seen as a direct interference in the internal affairs of Afghanistan and would have far-reaching consequences for the USSR.

Over the next twenty-four hours the Soviet embassy made frantic efforts to defuse the crisis, but failed to dissuade Amin from moving forward with a coup. By the evening of September 14, Taraki had been overthrown and imprisoned in solitary confinement. The Soviet leadership was enraged. The visiting deputy defense minister, General Pavlovsky, bitterly protested against Taraki's removal, but Amin's mind remained unchanged. That same day, Amin carried out an extensive reshuffle: three prominent members of the anti-Amin faction—Watanjar, Mazdooryar, and Gulabzoi—were dismissed from the Politburo,[5] and took sanctuary inside the Soviet embassy complex.[6] A fourth member, Asadullah Sarwari, was removed from his post as head of state security. Puzanov's decision to grant refuge to three of his rivals greatly angered Amin, but the Soviet ambassador would soon leave his post and return to the Soviet Union.

The Central Committee of the PDPA met on September 16 in the defense ministry, which had become Amin's fortress. Taraki was accused of being involved in terrorist activities and of conspiring in the attempted murder of Amin. The Central Committee then removed Taraki from all his posts—as general secretary and as a member of both the Politburo and the Central Committee. Amin replaced him as general secretary of the PDPA.[7] The Soviet Union was informed that both resolutions were approved "unanimously," with 26 of 31 members of the Central Committee present.

Taraki's fall deepened the sense of crisis in the Kremlin. The Soviet Politburo noted that Amin had "used Taraki's absence" (from Afghanistan) to seize control of "all the levers of power."[8] The urgent question before the leadership was how to deal with Amin after the coup. In the end, it was decided that the Soviet Union should continue to deal with him, but that Amin should be asked to clarify his intentions and that Moscow should make every effort possible to "restrain him from carrying out repression against Taraki's supporters."[9] The Politburo also agreed that Soviet advisers assigned to various departments in the Afghan government should remain in their posts, but do nothing to assist Amin in any repressive measures against his opponents in the party. The Soviet leadership also decided to curtail the supply of weapons and military equipment to the Afghan regime, while continuing the supply of spare parts and ammunition for combat operations against insurgents. Amin was to be warned against harming Taraki or putting him on trial. Amin's September 1979 coup went contrary to everything the Soviet leadership had wanted in Afghanistan. Taraki had been overthrown and his life was in danger. The man that Moscow regarded as highly unpredictable had seized power. The formidable military machine and repressive secret service that the Soviet bloc had helped Afghanistan build was now being used by Amin against his opponents in the party. As a result, his repressive policies were doing great harm to the image of the USSR.

The Kremlin was alarmed at the prospect of the Soviet Union losing control of Afghanistan. The leadership had conveyed its grave concern in private meetings and messages from Moscow.[10] It had repeatedly appealed to Taraki and Amin to settle their disputes. The Soviet Union feared that Amin's coup was unlikely to reduce the tensions in the ruling PDPA.[11] The USSR informed its close allies of the gravity of the situation and stated that it would be difficult to predict the course of future events. Brezhnev himself acknowledged what little power the Soviet leadership had in preventing Amin's coup.[12] Despite Moscow's repeated pleas, Taraki was murdered three weeks later.

SOVIET DILEMMA

What immediate options were available to the Soviets? Confrontation with Amin was very risky. Soviet commandos were stationed in the Afghan capital and at Bagram in the north, but only in relatively small numbers. The "alternative leadership" of which the KGB had spoken did not really exist. The pro-Taraki group in the Khalq faction of the PDPA had suffered a crushing defeat and was left leaderless. Almost all prominent figures of the Parcham faction were in exile. Amin was firmly in control of the armed forces and the secret service. A Soviet-led military operation to remove him was bound to be bloody, and there was no guarantee of success.

The Soviet leadership decided that it had to preserve its influence in Afghanistan.[13] The assumption in the Kremlin was that there would be no major change in the policy of the Amin regime, because it would continue to "face difficulties for a long time" and remain dependent on Soviet assistance—possibly become even more dependent than before. The Soviet leadership, therefore, calculated that Amin would be obliged to maintain the status quo. However, he was unpredictable and the task of keeping Afghanistan in the Soviet domain was going to be "difficult and delicate."

Nevertheless, Amin's coup wounded the KGB's and the Kremlin leadership's pride, and they soon began to notice unwelcome changes in Amin's behavior. He instructed the Afghan media to soften their criticisms of imperialism and Pakistan.[14] The October 1979 purchase of an American DC-10 aircraft by Ariana, the Afghan national airline, was given wide and enthusiastic coverage in the media. During meetings with Soviet officials, Amin looked willing to listen to suggestions, but the Soviets suspected that his seemingly cooperative attitude was merely a ploy to buy more time to strengthen his position while continuing to purge his opponents. Amin was aware that the Soviet leadership favored Taraki and his supporters, and his goal was to "get rid of them as quickly as possible."

Relations between Amin and Puzanov had broken down, and Amin launched a campaign to discredit the Soviet ambassador. Describing Puzanov as a tactless individual and a liar, Amin claimed that the ambassador misrepresented the events of the September coup.[15] At a gathering of ambassadors from Communist countries in the Afghan capital, one of Amin's close allies suggested that Puzanov had guaranteed Amin's safety during his visit to Taraki's office on September 14.[16] On that day a shooting incident came to light, resulting in the death of two security men. Amin managed to escape, but the statement implied that the Soviet ambassador had been involved in a conspiracy to kill Amin. It was clear that Puzanov's days in Kabul were numbered; he was recalled to Moscow in November 1979.[17]

Amin's relationship with the KGB had also broken down. In their messages to Moscow, Kabul-based Soviet agents accused Amin of misrepresenting the Soviet position in the PDPA Central Committee and the Revolutionary Council meetings on September 16.[18] It was said that Amin gave the impression that the Soviet Union "would not object to the dismissal of Taraki" because of his ill health. Since Amin's coup, KGB officers in Kabul also reported an increase in the anti-Soviet sentiment—including an increase in incidents of harassment of Soviet citizens—and a rise in American influence.[19] The Soviet leadership reacted with dismay over the prospect that the regime in Kabul might be prepared to move toward the United States, and the mood in the Kremlin began to change. In late October, a group of senior political figures reported to the Central Committee of the Soviet Communist Party that it had become necessary to do "everything possible" to prevent a "political reorientation of Amin toward the West."[20] However, secrecy was of utmost importance and Amin must be given no reason to believe that the Soviets did not trust him or want to deal with him. To ensure this, a two-pronged approach was suggested: "assert appropriate influence" over his regime and "further expose his true intentions."

One of Puzanov's final acts before leaving his post as Soviet ambassador was to hold a meeting with Amin. Puzanov assured Amin that the Soviet Union was ready to welcome him in the country.[21] The Afghan crisis was worsening, Amin's support base was rapidly disintegrating, and he was running a brutal campaign to eliminate his opponents. Still, Puzanov told Amin of Moscow's satisfaction at steps being taken by the Afghan leadership for "party and state building."

Amin, too, was reticent. He described the turn of events as achievements and told the Soviet ambassador of a revolt by troops at the Rishkor army base near Kabul that had been crushed by his forces.[22] Tribal guerrillas were active in eastern Afghanistan, but as long as Amin's troops were present in the region, they would be able to keep control of the roads and towns outside the capital. Nevertheless, Amin suggested that the regime could do more with Soviet help. In response, Puzanov told him that the Soviet Union would send a drilling specialist to work in the northwestern province of Herat, rather than promising any military support. The strategy was aimed at keeping Amin under the impression that he was trusted, while doing nothing that might help him stay in power.

American diplomats on the ground had alerted the U.S. administration about a very significant political crisis developing in Afghanistan.[23] The intelligence reports that reached Washington indicated that the loyalties of military units in the southern Afghan provinces of Qandahar and Ghazni, both bordering on Pakistan, and Qunduz near Soviet Central Asia in the north, were "not clear." In Kabul, tensions were high; major streets around ministries were blocked and Soviet-built tanks were deployed at strategic points, including the U.S. embassy. Diplomatic messages described the self-destructive behavior of the ruling PDPA. Sinking morale, fear, and uncertainty were widespread. The U.S. embassy described the effect of cabinet reshuffles and purges from the party as "paralyzing."[24] One message quoted an Afghan official as saying that the communist leaders were like "a bunch of scorpions biting each other to death." Brutal repression had become the sole instrument of survival for the regime, and it was impossible to know exactly how many political prisoners had been killed or detained. American assessments indicated that the number of people killed had reached six thousand, and as many as four times more had been imprisoned.[25]

After the assassination of Taraki in early October, it was easier for Amin to blame him for the atrocities since the 1978 Communist coup.[26] For a brief period, Amin portrayed himself as a benevolent leader. Releases of some prisoners were announced on Kabul radio, and in mid-November, the interior ministry began to publish lists of people who, according to the regime, had died in detention in the previous eighteen months. The announcements came to an abrupt halt, however, when crowds of grief-stricken relatives became too hysterical to handle.

Some leading figures also received leniency. Death sentences reportedly imposed upon Abdul Qadir and Sultan Ali Kishtmand were commuted to fifteen years in prison, and the twenty-year sentence passed on to Mohammad Rafi was reduced to twelve years. It has been suggested that Amin's real motive in taking these actions could well have been to win some favor in the military units that resented his treatment of PDPA officers.[27] If it were indeed the intention, his efforts did not work: the mutiny in the Rishkor barracks near Kabul occurred only one week later. Yet, the campaign to eliminate prominent figures who could replace Amin was still under way. Nur Ahmad Etemadi, a former prime minister under the king, was executed to warn the Soviet Union "not to think of alternative leaders."[28] Similarly, Tahir Badakhshi, a founding leader of the PDPA who had since left the party, was also killed.

Many opponents of the communist regime had fled to Pakistan and Iran, and a number of Islamic groups had established offices in Pakistan's North-West Frontier Province. The Kabul regime and the Soviet Union had been accusing Pakistan of supporting the efforts of the Afghan guerrillas by allowing training camps and supply routes. In order to neutralize them, Amin appealed for talks with Pakistan and Iran, but to no avail. Pakistan was unwilling to negotiate. Pakistan's military ruler, Gen. Zia-ul Haq, was pursuing an Islamic agenda to consolidate his own position in the country. Soviet support for the communist regime in neighboring Afghanistan had huge potential advantages for Zia, in terms of aid from wealthy Islamic countries and from the West. Zia could silence his critics at home if he became an important player in the fight to defend

Islam against communism. Similarly, the chances of talks between the Kabul
regime and Iran's ruling clergy were bleak.

During the brief three months when Amin was in power, armed resistance
to the regime spread rapidly, spawning both organized and spontaneous rebellions, in which virtually all social groups participated.[29] Afghans fled the
country at a rate of sixty thousand every month. Many young people joined
Mujahideen groups based in Pakistan and Iran, and some took up arms and
headed for the mountains to fight the regime. By December 1979 as many as
twenty-three of Afghanistan's twenty-eight provinces were believed to have
come under rebel control.[30]

The opposition stranglehold on Kabul was tightening. The highway linking the capital with the eastern city of Jalalabad was cut off at the end of November. A power station that supplied much of the electricity needed for Kabul was
under constant threat. The road from Kabul to Gardez, an important garrison
town, was cut off, and heavy fighting continued in the area until after Amin
was deposed. Amin's brother was seriously injured in an assassination attempt,
reportedly planned by Taraki's supporters.

It was clear by early December that Amin's overtures toward Pakistan's
military rulers to dismantle rebel bases inside their territory had failed. With
few options left, he made desperate appeals to the Soviet Union to send troops
to rescue his regime.[31] At that point, Amin calculated that the deployment of
Soviet forces to defend Kabul would release Afghan army units to fight the rebels in other places. Amin was uncertain of the loyalty of many of his troops, and
redeployment outside of the capital would minimize the possibility of a coup
against him.

The Invasion

The entire Soviet strategy in Afghanistan was close to collapse toward the end of
1979. Personal and factional rivalries in the PDPA had caused many headaches
for the Soviet leadership. Attempts to unite the party had been frustrated; the
man the Kremlin wanted to lead Afghanistan's communist regime had been assassinated; and Hafizullah Amin, viewed as a "power-driven" man with a habit
of using "disproportionate harshness" to control others, had seized power.[32]
The Soviet Union provided significant military and economic assistance to the
Kabul regime and was not pleased with Amin's methods and actions.

Under the Soviet system, religious minorities in the Central Asian republics had been suppressed for more than fifty years. It was the Kremlin's hope that the communist regime in Afghanistan would restructure the country on the Soviet model and keep Islamic groups under strict control. Afghanistan would serve as a permanent buffer between Soviet Central Asia and Pakistan. At a time when Islamic movements were on the ascendancy in Iran and Pakistan, the imagined order would help to contain the threat of Islamic resurgence within the Soviet borders. With Afghanistan in turmoil, these plans were in disarray.

The Soviet leadership was particularly incensed following a KGB tip-off that Amin's regime had met with the Islamic opposition inside Afghanistan.[33] Intelligence reports said that Mujahideen representatives had traveled from Pakistan, and the two sides had discussed the possibility of Amin sending back Soviet advisers and specialists should the resistance groups end their armed struggle. The Kabul regime was willing to release suspected rebels from its prisons and even change the national flag. Reportedly, Amin's emissary gave the Mujahideen representatives this assurance: "Everything is acceptable, but it will take time."

The possibility of close relations between Afghanistan and Iran was equally alarming for the Soviet Union. The Islamic revolution had brought the clergy to power in Iran, and the likelihood of Afghanistan falling under its influence was contrary to Soviet interest. Even more worrisome was the prospect of an Islamic regime in Kabul. While the Soviet leadership was pleased at the overthrow of the Shah and the loss of American influence in Iran, it was very concerned at the mass executions and imprisonment of members of the pro-Soviet Tudeh party. The establishment of an Islamic regime in Kabul, while the political left in Iran was simultaneously being crushed, would have been a double blow to the Soviet strategy in the region.[34]

At the end of October 1979, KGB Chairman Yuri Andropov, Defense Minister Dmitri Ustinov, Foreign Minister Andrei Gromyko, and Head of the International Department Boris Ponomarev had advised the Central Committee of the Soviet Communist Party that Amin should not be given any impression that he was not trusted in the Kremlin, but that his true intentions should be exposed.[35] Now Amin had been exposed and the Kremlin resolved to take "decisive action."[36] Officers of the KGB's First Chief Directorate, responsible for foreign intelligence, were told that the situation in Afghanistan had become quite unacceptable and needed to be addressed.[37]

A KGB envoy was sent to Prague to work with Babrak Karmal, who was said to be very eager for a direct and immediate Soviet intervention.[38] In November, several Afghan exiles, who could potentially form an alternative leadership, were brought to the Soviet Union from Bulgaria, Czechoslovakia, and Yugoslavia.[39] They remained in Moscow for extensive briefings until December 12, when they were moved to Soviet Central Asia, near the Afghan border.

The KGB chief, Yuri Andropov, made a final case for intervention in a secret memorandum to Brezhnev in early December.[40] In the document, Andropov accused Amin of destroying the army and government by mass repression, which, he said, had created an acute situation in Afghanistan. He reminded Brezhnev of Amin's secret activities, indicating a "possible shift to the West." The KGB chief repeated that Amin had opened up secret contacts with the Americans, made promises to Afghan tribal leaders to distance the regime from the USSR, and attacked Soviet policy in meetings of his inner circle. Andropov told Brezhnev that diplomats in Kabul were openly talking about "Amin's differences with Moscow." There was a growing danger that the gains made by the 1978 communist takeover were about to be lost and Soviet interests in Afghanistan compromised.

The KGB proposed that the Soviet Union launch a "limited" military operation aimed at helping Afghan exiles such as Karmal to create a new party and state structure in Afghanistan. Andropov suggested mobilizing Soviet forces close to the Afghan border in order to deal with "unforeseen complications." Other matters, such as the "liquidation" of opponents, could be decided later. A plan had already been worked out in November during long discussions with a number of Afghan exiles:[41] Amin was to be removed from power and Karmal was to be installed as leader of the ruling People's Democratic Party of Afghanistan.

The Soviet operation was launched with a massive airlift of troops and military equipment to Kabul in the early hours of December 25.[42] Within twenty-four hours, some two hundred transport planes landed and Kabul Airport was secured. Special frontline units of the Soviet army encircled the capital to prevent any liberation attempt by forces loyal to Amin. Soldiers of the 103rd airborne division, supported by paratroopers, seized key installations. The task of other Soviet regiments was to disarm Afghan units trying to break into the city. With lightning speed, tens of thousands of Soviet ground troops—with tanks and armored carriers—crossed the Amu (Oxus) river and occupied large parts of northern and western Afghanistan.

The next phase of the Soviet operation, to eliminate Amin, began in the evening of December 27. A bomb, which paralyzed Kabul's entire telephone network, also served as a signal to attack Amin's residence. He had escaped from the presidential palace near the city center and taken shelter in a building just outside Kabul. More than seven hundred KGB troops in Afghan military uniform had been flown in from Moscow with orders to assassinate Amin.[43] His base came under heavy air bombardment while commandos of the Alpha squad of the KGB led the ground attack that included as many as five thousand Soviet troops.

The assault force met fierce resistance from about three hundred soldiers of Amin's Presidential Guard and two thousand infantrymen. There was heavy fighting overnight, but the last pockets of resistance had been overcome by the early hours of December 28. Amin and two of his sons were killed and a number of close relatives captured. Babrak Karmal was installed in power, and Watanjar, Sarwari, and Gulabzoi had all returned with the Soviet invasion forces.

It was the third time in less than two years that Afghanistan had undergone violent change in leadership. In every coup, the deposed leader was assassinated.[44] Associates were murdered, tortured, or purged, leaving the subsequent regime more isolated and reinforcing the climate of fear in the society. The consequences of this upheaval were profound. Members of the royal family still left in Afghanistan were wiped out in the first communist coup in April 1978.[45] The coup destroyed the very institution meant to uphold the social accord among the divergent ethnic groups in Afghan society.

Within weeks of the 1978 coup, conflict had broken out in the PDPA regime, resulting in extensive purges of Parcham members by the Pashtun-dominated Khalq faction. The Khalq leadership then turned on itself. In the ensuing feud, President Taraki was murdered by his own deputy, Hafizullah Amin, who seized power and began to target people he perceived as Taraki's supporters. This internal conflict left the Amin regime with a narrower base, but its determination to maintain power was stronger than before. The consequence was the rise of a more extreme form of Pashtun nationalism, determined to use even more ruthless tactics against the resistance that grew daily.

The murder of Taraki, together with escalating military and civilian rebellions, finally convinced the Soviet Union to invade Afghanistan and replace

Amin with a compliant leadership in Kabul. The aim of the Soviet invasion might have been to restore order in Afghanistan, but the actual result was very different. The invasion unleashed internal resistance on a much greater scale and attracted other outside powers, marking the beginning of a new and more violent era in the history of the Afghan conflict.

7

LET BATTLE COMMENCE

The Soviet invasion of Afghanistan in December 1979 marked the onset of a decade-long proxy war in which the United States and its allies supported the anticommunist Mujahideen forces. Billions of dollars worth of weapons were poured into Afghanistan, the number of dead and wounded ran into hundreds of thousands, and millions of Afghans were forced out of their country as refugees. It was one of the longest and most expensive conflicts in the history of the Cold War. In the end, the Soviet occupation forces withdrew and the USSR crumbled, while violence penetrated every level of Afghan society. This chapter will examine the initial phase of the American proxy war against the Soviet Union and how the actions of both superpowers fueled the culture of violence in Afghanistan.

For almost two decades following the Soviet invasion in 1979, the U.S.-inspired version of history was that the Central Intelligence Agency had begun to provide aid to the Mujahideen in 1980, after Afghanistan had fallen under Soviet occupation. This became the official version of America's role in Afghanistan, a result of the impression left by President Carter immediately after the Soviet invasion, and others in later years. More historians picked up and reinforced this version.

> The region which is now threatened by Soviet troops in Afghanistan is of great strategic importance. It contains more than two-thirds of the world's exportable oil. . . . An attempt by any outside force to gain control of the Persian Gulf region will be regarded as an assault on the vital interests of the

United States of America and . . . will be repelled by any means necessary, including military force.

—President Carter, State of the Union address, January 1980 [1]

The Soviet invasion changed the nature of the Mujahideen resistance. . . . The United States, People's Republic of China, Britain, France, Italy, Saudi Arabia, Egypt, and the United Arab Emirates began funneling military, humanitarian, and financial aid to the Mujahideen through Pakistan.

—Lt. Col. Lester Grau, U.S. Foreign Military Studies Office [2]

Initially for a few months [after the Soviet invasion], the Americans disappointed Zia . . . and adopted a wait-and-see attitude. . . . President Carter was locked into the intractable Tehran hostage crisis . . . while advice from the Pentagon and the CIA was that, with or without Pakistan's backing, Afghanistan was a lost cause. Why throw good money after bad and needlessly antagonize the Soviets by aiding the Afghan resistance?

—Brig. Mohammad Yousaf, Pakistani Army [3]

Soviet intervention and the arrival of foreign aid transformed the structure of the resistance and its relation to Afghan society.

—Barnet Rubin, American academic [4]

It was generally accepted that the United States had been caught unprepared by the invasion, which came at the end of a very difficult year for President Carter. The Islamic revolution in Iran had established a ruling order deeply hostile to American interests in the Gulf region. Even more serious was the crisis at the American embassy in Tehran, where Iranian militants had seized approximately seventy U.S. citizens.[5] America was looking powerless and Carter's inability to deter the Soviet Union from occupying Afghanistan reinforced that image.

Concerns in the United States about Soviet intentions were aggravated by the discovery of a brigade of Soviet combat troops in Cuba in September 1979.[6] Articulating these concerns, Francis Fukuyama wrote that the danger to American security existed on two levels. On one level there existed a "straightforward military threat," meaning that the Soviets could gain control over the energy resources through "direct invasion and occupation of one or more oil-producing countries." On the other, it consisted of "active interference in a country's internal politics" in the region, with the aim of "weakening it and ultimately making it susceptible to Soviet influence."[7] To many Americans, the events in Afghanistan illustrated the true nature of the Soviet threat.

In the Senate, the Second Strategic Arms Limitation Treaty with the Soviet Union came under persistent attack from an alliance of Republicans and conservative Democrats. The president's authority was undermined by rivalries within his own administration, most notably between Secretary of State Cyrus Vance and National Security Adviser Zbigniew Brzezinski. These differences deepened in the administration's growing atmosphere of crisis. By the time Carter stood before the U.S. Congress to deliver his State of the Union speech in January 1980, it looked as though Brzezinski's strong anticommunist views had gained a decisive influence over the president. In an illuminating passage about Brzezinski's increasingly dominant role in the Carter administration, the United Nations special envoy for Afghanistan, Diego Cordovez, wrote:

> In the immediate aftermath of the [Soviet] invasion, Secretary of State, Cyrus Vance, proposed to President Jimmy Carter that the United States offer to neutralize Iran and Pakistan in exchange for a Soviet withdrawal [from Afghanistan]. . . . Brzezinski was able to kill the idea in one of the least-noticed but most important of his many clashes with Vance. . . . Brzezinski wanted the Soviet Union to be cast in the role of defendant before the court of world public opinion.[11]

Carter's reaction was intense and extreme, but his exact motives were unclear. He said that the Soviet invasion was "perhaps the most serious threat to peace since the Second World War" and that the Soviets must be made to realize that they "cannot take such action with impunity."[9] The United States had to respond strongly "to impress upon the Soviet Union the cost of its behavior." We know now that the State Department wanted to continue the policy of détente, but was frustrated by Brzezinski's confrontational approach.

Carter's statements following the Soviet invasion of Afghanistan have been described by some as signaling a return to America's policy of containment with regard to the Soviet Union and effectively ending constructive dialogue between the two nations.[10] In this instance, the term *containment* is taken literally, meaning an aggressive policy of building military alliances in order to check a hostile power or ideology. However, a broader view of containment is helpful in understanding the nature of U.S.-Soviet relations after the Second World War. The need for the United States to check Soviet communism never ceased, but the methods to achieve this aim varied.

Sometimes, America's methods to contain Soviet expansion involved aggressive militarism; at other times, U.S. methods were conciliatory, involving what is described as constructive dialogue, including seeking opportunities for cooperation in areas of common interest rather than permanent confrontation. Carter's response after the Soviet invasion of Afghanistan was a swing of the pendulum toward an aggressive posture, not a radical departure from the policy of his predecessors. When the U.S. leader stated that the invasion of Afghanistan had brought a "dramatic change" in his view of the Soviets' ultimate goal, it was an attempt to increase the pressure on the Soviet leadership.[11] Thereafter, Carter's actions changed the balance of rewards and penalties for the Soviet Union.

Events in Iran and Afghanistan before the Soviet invasion had already turned Carter into an enthusiast for higher military spending, and plans had been announced for a Rapid Deployment Force, enabling U.S. forces to intervene quickly to protect its interests around the globe.[12] After the Soviet move into Afghanistan, attempts to secure ratification of the Strategic Arms Limitation Treaty in the Senate were abandoned and the administration announced its intention to introduce compulsory military service. A policy of economic retaliation against the USSR was adopted: exports of high-technology equipment were restricted, sales of grains and meat were suspended at a time when the Soviet Union was experiencing acute food shortages, Soviet boats were no longer permitted to fish in American waters, scientific and cultural exchanges were halted, and President Carter announced a boycott of the 1980 Moscow Olympics.[13]

THE SOVIET INVASION: A CIA TRAP?

An authoritative rejection of the official version of events surrounding the Soviet invasion and the U.S. response came from ex-CIA director Robert Gates in 1996.[14] According to Gates, the Carter administration began considering the possibility of providing secret aid to the Afghan insurgents in early 1979— long before the Soviet military invaded Afghanistan. As part of this policy, the CIA had provided a number of options to the National Security Council.[15] The agency argued that the Afghan insurgents had achieved what they considered to be surprising successes against the pro Soviet government in Kabul, citing rebellions in the countryside and the army. The military government of Pakistan had indicated that it might be more forthcoming in terms of helping the insurgents than previously expected and that Pakistani assistance might include small arms and ammunition. However, the Pakistanis made it clear that they would not risk Soviet wrath without a firm commitment from the United States. American intelligence officials had also learned that Saudi Arabia was about to appeal to the Carter administration to help the Afghan rebels. The Saudis could provide money and encourage Pakistan, and possibly other countries, to offer at least tacit support to the Afghan resistance.[16]

These developments came to light almost twenty years later, but at the time they influenced the Carter administration to increase the combat ability of the anticommunist forces in Afghanistan. On July 3, 1979, Carter signed a presidential order that authorized secret aid to the Afghan Mujahideen.[17] The aim of the order was to support "insurgent propaganda and other psychological operations" in Afghanistan and to provide funding or non-military assistance, either unilaterally or through third-party countries. Although U.S. aid was non-military, the path was open for spending those dollars to obtain military equipment from other sources.

Brzezinski spoke in public about the matter for the first time in 1998.[18] He confirmed that President Carter did indeed sign the first directive for secret aid to the Mujahideen in July 1979. He revealed that he told Carter on the same day that the American action was, in his opinion, "going to induce a Soviet military intervention" in Afghanistan. Brzezinski denied that the United States had pushed the Soviets in any way to intervene, but maintained that the Carter administration "knowingly increased the probability that they would." Brzezinski described it as "an excellent idea," because it had the effect of drawing the Soviet Union into "the Afghan trap." He said that on the day the Soviets crossed into Afghanistan he wrote President Carter that the United States had "the opportunity to give the USSR its Vietnam War."

The justification the Kremlin offered for the Soviet military intervention at the end of 1979 was that America and its allies were secretly trying to destabilize the Communist regime in Kabul. The admission by Brzezinski adds substance to the Soviet claim. Twenty years after the Soviet invasion, Brzezinski was unapologetic. Did the Western support, weapons, and military training for the fundamentalist groups not create future terrorists? Did America's failure to bring stability to Afghanistan after the defeat of communism not contribute to the rise of the Taliban? Was the outcome a military success or a political blunder? Brzezinski sounded as certain in 1998 as he was twenty years before:

> What is most important to the history of the world? The Taliban or the collapse of the Soviet empire? Some stirred-up Muslims or the liberation of Central Europe and the end of the Cold War?[19]

The account by Brzezinski is informative, but must be treated with caution. First, it reflects his flamboyant style and seems to be aimed at drawing attention to Brzezinski's own role during the Carter presidency. Second, his explanation is simplistic in that it does not consider the pressures inflicted upon the Soviet leadership because of the chronic failure of the Communist regime in Afghanistan, before the Soviets decided to invade. It may also be part of a wider tendency among senior public figures in America and among its allies to claim credit for dismantling the Soviet empire.

Brzezinski's brief interjection nearly two decades later may be a one-sided and personal view of events toward the end of the Cold War, but it does help us to understand his role in convincing President Carter to take a hard line with the Soviet Union. While the crisis in Iran and the Gulf dominated most people's minds, Carter had secretly embarked on a policy that would make the United States a major player in Afghanistan and would bring America in direct confrontation with the Soviets after the invasion in December 1979. This policy was part of a much bigger strategy against the Soviet Union. Its consequences were profound and went beyond the Cold War.

CARTER'S LEGACY

The first Carter directive authorizing secret aid for the anticommunist Afghan guerrillas in July 1979 consisted of only about half a million dollars.[20] It soon acquired momentum, and by late August, Pakistan's military ruler, Gen. Zia-ul Haq, was encouraging the United States to supply weapons to the Afghan opposition. Quite separately, Inter-Services Intelligence Directorate of the Pakistani army was also pressing for the insurgency to be expanded.[21] As a result, the CIA Director, Stansfield Turner, gave his approval for a number of "enhancements." These included the provision of communications equipment for the guerrillas via Pakistan and Saudi Arabia, funds for Pakistan's military regime to purchase weapons for the insurgents, and a similar amount of arms and equipment provided to Pakistan directly from the United States, which were to be distributed among the insurgent groups.

The guiding principle of the new relationship between the United States and Pakistan was settled upon during a meeting between Brzezinski and General Zia in Islamabad.[22] Zia demanded that all arms supplies, money, and training for the insurgents "be provided through Pakistan and not directly by the CIA." Brzezinski readily agreed, saying the decision had approval from "the top echelons of the Carter administration." A senior ISI officer who was once directly responsible for the operation later confirmed: "As soon as the arms arrived in Pakistan, the CIA's responsibility ended. From then on, it was our pipeline, our organization that moved, allocated and distributed every bullet that the CIA procured."[23]

Pakistan was vital for the American scheme because of its common border with Afghanistan and the presence of millions of ethnic Pashtuns on both sides of the open frontier. After the invasion of Afghanistan, active collaboration with the Pakistani military became even more important as large numbers of Afghan refugees began to arrive in Pakistan. They would be housed in refugee camps just inside Pakistan, and the vast camp cities would be an ideal ground to launch guerrilla operations into Afghanistan.

Brzezinski's next destination was Saudi Arabia. The United States had calculated that support from the custodians of two of the holiest places in Islam was essential.[24] The influence of the Saudi royal family in the Muslim world could also be a great advantage. With its enormous wealth of oil, Saudi Arabia was in a position to make a significant contribution to the war effort in Afghanistan. In Riyadh, Brzezinski secured agreement from the Saudi rulers to "match the U.S. contribution to the Mujahideen."[25] This also suited General Zia, because it would end the international isolation of his regime.

So the foundations of an elaborate plan to confront the Soviet military power were drawn by bringing Pakistan, Saudi Arabia, China, and Egypt into a pact under just the right conditions. America's alliances with Saudi Arabia and Pakistan went hand in hand as both of them followed the same Islamic ideology, which was hostile to Soviet communism. The Saudi royal family had been a close American ally in the region and Pakistan was eager to reenter into the U.S.

fold because of its newfound importance as a frontline state confronting Soviet occupation forces in Afghanistan.

China's strategic alliance with the West had already been developing, and the Soviet move into Afghanistan gave it a new urgency. President Anwar El Sadat of Egypt had broken ties with the USSR in 1976 and made peace with Israel a year later.[26] His decision to realign himself with the United States had begun to attract large-scale American aid and there was every prospect of increasing such aid if Egypt joined the CIA-led war against the Soviets in Afghanistan.

Both China and Egypt had extensive knowledge of Soviet-style weaponry and manufactured hardware of old Soviet designs. This would make them important suppliers of weapons to the Mujahideen resistance. Afghanistan thus became part of the wider American strategy to confront the Soviet Union. At about the same time, Carter ordered other "covert operations to counter Soviet advances in the Third World," in countries including Yemen, Grenada, Jamaica, Nicaragua, and El Salvador.[27] All these operations would undergo a vast expansion under President Ronald Reagan's administration.

8

THE REAGAN OFFENSIVE

Ronald Reagan's inauguration in January 1981 ushered in a more aggressive American administration. During the presidential campaign, Reagan had consistently attacked Carter's record on foreign policy and his weakness in dealing with the Soviet Union. Once he was in office, Reagan's approach to foreign and defense policies was to vigorously challenge the Soviet Union in the third world. While Carter used largely covert actions to counter Soviet activities, Reagan was far more confident and belligerent. He denounced the brutal invasion of Afghanistan and warned the Soviet Union against intervening in Poland, where the Solidarity trade union movement was challenging the communist system.[1]

Reagan called for measures to ensure that aggression was never again attempted by a false perception of American weakness. He said that the free world must do everything necessary to maintain its security "so long as our adversaries continue to arm themselves at a pace far beyond the needs of defense." To this end, his administration would use all possible means—secret operations, financial aid, diplomacy, even military intervention—and on a much bigger scale "to reverse both the reality and the perception of which country was stronger," America or the Soviet Union.[2]

Afghanistan thus became a strategic battleground for Reagan's fight against Soviet communism, and Pakistan was turned into a frontline base for the United States. Negotiations on a big aid package to Pakistan began soon after Reagan assumed office in 1981, and that June its details were announced: worth $3 billion, it would consist of economic and military assistance over six years.[3] The deal included the sale of advanced F–16 aircraft to Pakistan to strengthen its air defense capabilities as well as offering development assistance, support funds, and loans to help purchase other military hardware from America.

The resumption of American aid to Pakistan raised sensitivities in India, which complained that the sale of F-16 fighters was the start of a new arms race in the region. Meanwhile, Congress asked whether it was wise to supply expensive, high-technology military hardware to third-world countries. What would the U.S. administration achieve by equipping the armed forces of Pakistan with sophisticated weapons? Would Pakistan ever be expected to respond militarily to Soviet forces? The Reagan administration was uncompromising in its justification. It insisted that Pakistan required immediate air superiority over the Soviet Mig-23 and Mig-25 aircraft based in Afghanistan.[4] The F-16s would give Pakistan a credible air defense capability to "deter or repel limited air attacks or incursions out of Afghanistan."

Getting Pakistan firmly on its side was just one part of the Reagan administration's plan. It also pursued a top-secret program, code-named SOVMAT, to help prosecute the war against the Soviet Union and its client regime in Afghanistan. Developed in the CIA headquarters in Langley, Virginia,[5] the program bought Soviet-style weapons and equipment from a number of countries. China and Egypt had the expertise to manufacture the required hardware as well as Israel, which had captured vast quantities of Soviet-supplied weapons from Egypt, Syria, and Jordan in the 1967 and 1973 Middle East wars. East European organizations also made deals, lured by large offers of money from CIA-sponsored corporations.

William Casey, Reagan's CIA director, had a central role in the war against the Soviet Union.[6] He had served in the Office of Strategic Services (OSS), a forerunner of the CIA, during the Second World War, but afterward he opted to practice law instead of making a career in the intelligence services. His nomination to head the CIA in 1981 caught Congress and the press by surprise, although, in the end, an overwhelming majority in the Republican-controlled Senate approved it.[7]

THE INITIAL PHASE

The CIA's effort to help the Mujahideen fight the Soviet forces got off to a slow start in the Reagan administration's first year. Before leaving the presidency, Carter had proposed military assistance worth about $60 million a year between

1981 and 1983.[8] The Reagan administration initially stuck to these levels, which were matched by Saudi Arabia. In the meantime, Casey instigated a fundamental change in the way the CIA conducted its operations. From his early OSS experience, he had learned to value the basic data military planners used. As head of the CIA, Casey spent a great deal of time reading intelligence analyses, questioning their conclusions, and pushing his staff to find new, remote sources. He had little time for career analysts who did not question their own assumptions and look "beyond the walls" for new information and insight.[9]

To stretch the Soviet military power in as many flash points as possible, the CIA began gathering much more information about the Soviet economy, its military-industrial complex, social and ethnic problems, and military developments.[10] In the first year of the Reagan presidency, CIA analysts predicted extremely serious consequences if Soviet defense spending continued to rise at a faster rate to support its intensified military competition. The study concluded that the Soviet state's ability to increase its investment for long-term economic growth would be reduced substantially, per capita consumption might decline "in real terms," and key sectors of the Soviet economy would be disrupted by the late 1980s.

The Reagan administration's offensive against Soviet communism had begun to take shape and the tables had begun to turn as the political crisis in the Kremlin worsened toward the end of 1982.[11] Soviet gains of the 1970s in Indochina, Afghanistan, Angola, Ethiopia, and Nicaragua no longer seemed as solid as they had a few years before.[12] The Soviet occupation forces appeared to have become stranded in Afghanistan, the Marxist regime in Angola was struggling against a U.S. backed insurgency, the Marxist government in Nicaragua faced a growing challenge from the right-wing rebels, and the Kremlin's efforts to support the Communist regime of Cuba were draining the Soviet economy. Meanwhile, U.S. public opinion had become disillusioned with détente, and people were ready to support Reagan's defense buildup. The Reagan administration's next move was to intensify military and economic pressure on the Soviet Union in all these areas, as well as to launch new weapons programs.[13]

Egyptian president Anwar Sadat, in September 1981, lifted the blanket of secrecy from the CIA's Afghan operation. In an interview with the American television network NBC, Sadat revealed that the United States was purchasing Soviet-designed equipment from Egypt and shipping it to Afghan freedom fighters.[14] These weapons, "either originals or duplicates," included shoulder-fired anti-tank and antiaircraft missiles, guns, and ammunition. He said that the American administration originally contacted him; thereafter, "the transport of arms started from Cairo on U.S. planes." The NBC report also revealed that the operation had been going on for twenty-one months. If true, it clearly started in January 1980, a year before Carter left the White House.[15] Carter himself did not comment on the report.

The Soviets' reaction was swift and hostile. The Communist Party daily, *Pravda*, described Sadat's remarks as the "first official confirmation" that the United States had been arming Afghan terrorist groups from the beginning.[16] "Washington was silent for a long time," *Pravda* said, but Sadat had removed "the mask of hypocrisy from the American administration." The Soviets accused the United States of doing everything possible to stir up trouble in Afghanistan. The administration responded that the bulk of the resistance fighters' arms had been obtained from indigenous sources and included weapons "captured from the Soviets, from defecting or cooperating Afghan army personnel," and "existing supplies in local hands."[17]

The United States, meanwhile, was working hard at strengthening its alliance with the People's Republic of China. Defense Secretary Harold Brown had made a low-key visit to China within days of the Soviet invasion of Afghanistan.[18] Within two weeks of Brown's visit, Congress approved a trade agreement and put China on the most-favored-nations list. In May, the Chinese vice premier for security and head of the Communist Party's Military Affairs Committee, Geng Biao, toured the United States. Brown announced that the administration had authorized American companies to sell nonlethal military equipment to China, including transport planes, helicopters, and air defense radar systems, and the Chinese were reportedly pleased with the formal establishment of military relations with America.[19] It emerged many years later that Brown's negotiations had also led to two American electronic intelligence-gathering posts being constructed in the northwestern Chinese province of Xinjiang, close to the Soviet Union and Afghanistan.[20]

The Chinese strongly condemned the Soviet invasion of Afghanistan, reflecting their fears that the Soviets were extending their influence in Asia to encircle China.[21] Soon after the invasion, China began providing military aid to the anti-Soviet guerrillas. The Chinese leadership favored using firm military force and urged America and Western Europe to provide coordinated support to the Afghan resistance. It was totally opposed to any diplomatic compromise that allowed the Soviet troops to withdraw and still keep the Babrak Karmal regime in Kabul.

While the exact Chinese military assistance is not known, U.S. intelligence thought it consisted of small arms, mortars, antitank mines, rocket-propelled grenade launchers, and ammunition. Intelligence reports show that Chinese shipments arrived by air or by sea in Pakistan, where the ISI assumed the responsibility for "delivering the weapons and selecting the recipients." American intelligence predicted that Chinese aid to the Afghan resistance would increase, but it would "remain dependent on Pakistani cooperation."[22]

INVADERS, FREEDOM FIGHTERS, AND A SUPERPOWER BATTLEFIELD

We have seen how the U.S. strategy of confronting the Soviet invasion of Afghanistan evolved and what its objective was. The Americans had decided to draw out the Soviet military machine by supplying and training the anticommunist forces in the Afghan theater and by steadily increasing the pressure until the occupation of Afghanistan became unsustainable. To this end, the United States had built up a formidable coalition of European allies, Pakistan and other Islamic states, and China. We will now see how this strategy worked in practice and how, as a result, both sides poured massive military resources into the Afghan conflict.

Within six months of the invasion, more than eighty thousand Soviet troops occupied Afghanistan.[23] Further reinforcements arrived to suppress revolts across the country. A number of Soviet civilians and troops were "hacked to pieces" in Qandahar in early January, and troops brutally quelled riots in Kabul and the western city of Shindand a month later.[24] The Soviets launched repeated offensives in several areas in 1980.[25] Despite heavy reinforcements, however, the occupation army had spread out too quickly. Soviet troops that were to have been garrisoned and given time to settle down were brought out early owing to the resistance fighters' harassment tactics. The Soviets began to take significant casualties.[26]

At first, anticommunist guerrillas had only light assault weapons and some remote units were short of arms and ammunition.[27] The major groups still lacked "the heavier weaponry needed to turn the situation" to their advantage. The Americans also identified other major deficiencies: more and better surface-to-air missiles and antiaircraft guns, heavy machine guns, antitank missiles, land mines, and radio equipment. American intelligence services were convinced that the Soviet army could not permanently seal off Afghanistan from the outside world. The rugged terrain, the limited manpower of the Soviet-Afghan army, the hostile local population, and the resourceful resistance fighters all conspired against any attempt to close the Afghan border. The United States and its regional allies could always supply the guerrillas fighting deep inside Afghanistan.

What if they did give the Mujahideen all this equipment? American intelligence expected the Soviets to resort to high-altitude bombing to protect their aircraft and crew members. They would escort their helicopter gunships with other gunships or high-performance aircraft and use heat flares and so on to avoid enemy missiles. While the superiority of the Soviet forces was overwhelming, morale among the Mujahideen was high. They enjoyed widespread support in the countryside, where the populace gave them food, shelter, and safe passage. They could move around at will.

An occupation army that fails to win the hearts and minds of local inhabitants is likely to resort to brute force. The Soviets used extreme coercion against the population in the countryside, not only to break the opposition's spirit, but also to convince Afghans that the price of supporting the resistance was high. The number of people fleeing the intense bombardment of their villages and towns rose steadily. By the end of February 1980, just two months after the Soviet invasion, more than half a million Afghans had arrived in Pakistan, and by that summer, officials expected a million refugees or perhaps more if the Soviet and Afghan forces launched an all-out assault against the inhabitants.[28]

It began to look as if the Soviets were deliberately driving the Afghans from their homes. Pakistani officials and resistance leaders reported that Paktia Province in eastern Afghanistan had been virtually depopulated. In mid-1981, Soviet attempts to drive the Mujahideen guerrillas out of the Paghman Mountains northwest of Kabul failed. Both sides suffered heavy casualties, but hundreds of innocent villagers also died.[29] Other offensives around Kabul encountered fierce resistance, most notably in the Panjshir Valley, where Soviet troops were locked in a prolonged, unsuccessful campaign to dislodge the Tajik guerrilla commander, Ahmad Shah Masood.[30]

The consequences of Soviet bombing were disastrous. Guerrillas and civilians alike suffered casualties, and agricultural land and infrastructure were devastated, often displacing entire communities. Despite all this havoc, the resistance took over towns from time to time and "could be repelled only when air support and tank reinforcements arrived. Even in the capital, nightly gun battles, assassinations and attacks on government and Soviet installations" occurred.[31] No amount of brutality could stop anti-Soviet demonstrations in Kabul.[32]

At the end of 1982, the Reagan administration claimed to have convincing evidence of the Soviets' "selective use" of toxic chemical agents since at least 1980.[33] Victims and medical staff treating them reported blistering and burned skin, nausea, and vomiting. Mujahideen commanders' graphic accounts revealed that "bodies decomposed rapidly and flesh peeled away" when victims were moved. After examining victims in several refugee camps in Pakistan, foreign relief workers also confirmed reports that poisonous gases had been used.

DEATH BY A THOUSAND CUTS

The Afghans' strategy of defeating the vastly superior Soviet army has been described as "death by a thousand cuts."[34] Operating in small guerrilla bands, the anti-Soviet forces were relentless in their attacks, which included staging ambushes; conducting assassinations; sabotaging bridges, roads, and power plants; and intercepting supply convoys. These tactics and heavy rocket attacks on civilian areas caused fear and panic in Soviet-held parts of Afghanistan and gradually starved them of essential supplies. Kabul and other urban population centers became more and more dependent on Soviet handouts.

Pakistan's army and the military intelligence service, ISI, were both heavily involved in directing the guerrilla war on behalf of the United States. Early on, regular soldiers attached to the Afghan Bureau of the ISI were sent inside Afghanistan to accompany Mujahideen fighters on special operations. They acted as advisers and helped in various operations such as blowing up an oil pipeline, mounting a rocket attack, or laying an ambush.[35] These offensives were "at their peak in 1984, when no less than eleven teams operated" around the most important targets: Kabul, Bagram airfield to the north, and Jalalabad in eastern Afghanistan. Guerrilla raids on Soviet and Afghan posts along security rings around these targets benefited the opposition in three respects: they kept large numbers of troops tied to their posts, created opportunities for the Mujahideen to capture weapons and ammunition, and damaged morale on the Soviet-Afghan side.[36]

A more intensive phase began toward the end of 1983. CIA director William Casey had been in his post for nearly three years and overseen a great deal of planning in the meantime. In the first half of 1984, the number of Mujahideen guerrillas trained in Pakistan increased from four hundred to about a thousand men a month. By 1987, the total number of ISI training camps around the Pakistani border towns of Peshawar and Quetta had gone from two to seven.[37] Between 1983 and 1987, "at least eighty thousand Mujahideen received training in Pakistan" and thousands more inside Afghan territory.[38] To improve communication, the CIA provided the training camps in Pakistan and guerrilla bases throughout Afghanistan with secure radio sets.

The amount of arms and ammunition going through the CIA pipeline to the Afghan resistance also increased dramatically—from 10,000 tons in 1983 to 65,000 tons in 1987.[39] The sixfold rise of materials arriving in Pakistan made the ISI's task much more difficult. They had to move supplies and, at the same time, maintain strict secrecy. Soviet and Afghan intelligence agencies were bound to pick up any leaks, which would allow the enemy greater time to prepare. In any event, the commander of the ISI's Afghan operations claimed that his troops miraculously protected the delivery and distribution system for the increased weapon supplies. It was never exposed.[40]

As it turns out, this increased CIA military aid to the Mujahideen was the result of President Reagan's conscious decision two years before. From late 1984 to early 1985, the administration had debated what direction America's war against the Soviet Union should take. On March 27, 1985, Reagan signed a presidential directive that proved decisive. In the war's first five years, America's purpose had been to increase the Soviets's costs for invading Afghanistan; however, Reagan's directive changed the purpose *to win* the war.[41]

Thereafter, General Zia of Pakistan became bolder and opened the way for far greater incoming military aid. The risk of Soviet retaliation still existed, but Zia took his chances. The ISI distributed the bulk of weapons supplies and financial aid among fundamentalist Mujahideen groups whose religious zeal was great and determination to defeat the Communists unshakable.[42] These fundamentalist fighters were willing to endure extreme hardships and make the ultimate sacrifice—martyrdom.

Another big question before the Reagan administration in 1985 was whether to provide Stinger antiaircraft missiles to the Mujahideen.[43] The CIA had long opposed the idea for fear the technology would reach the Soviet armed forces if they captured a missile from the Afghan resistance.[44] After months of deliberation, the objections were dropped. The administration decided to supply four hundred Stingers to the resistance, who first used them in combat in the autumn of 1986, hitting three out of four targets. It was not long before the resistance mounted a devastating campaign against Soviet and Afghan government aircraft.

Undoubtedly the introduction of Stinger missiles proved a turning point in the war against the Soviet Union in Afghanistan. They altered the balance of power by providing the Mujahideen with "sheltered enclaves."[45] For instance, out of fear of losing too many aircraft, Soviet and Afghan government forces were compelled to limit their activities to defending large cities and communication links. The Soviets no longer attacked except to disentangle themselves, and their priority changed to avoiding major losses. As Soviet troops retreated to well-defended positions within Afghanistan, the opposition forces extended their control over vast areas of the country.[46]

General secretary of the Soviet Communist Party Mikhail Gorbachev's description of Afghanistan as a bleeding wound in February 1986 had signaled a desire to bring Soviet troops home.[47] Further, the Soviet Union preferred to extricate itself with its reputation intact. To achieve that goal, Gorbachev decided to replace the widely hated Afghan leader Babrak Karmal with Najibullah in 1986 and encouraged a policy of national reconciliation in Afghanistan. In the end, the pressures on the Soviet Union became so great that Gorbachev had to withdraw his troops probably sooner than he would have liked.

At a Politburo meeting in November 1986, Gorbachev gave a gloomy assessment of the Soviets' military involvement in Afghanistan.[48] "We have already been fighting in Afghanistan for six years," he said, and unless they changed their approach, they would "continue to fight for another 20-30 years." He recalled that in October 1985, the Politburo had discussed the possibility of withdrawal "through a combination of military and political measures." Now, a year later, the Soviet leader admitted the Afghan government's military position was still weak, the policy of national reconciliation had not worked, and the Soviet plan "had been badly realized." Gorbachev proposed withdrawing half of the Soviet troops from Afghanistan in 1987 and the rest in the following year.[49]

By Moscow's own admission, its costs in the Afghan conflict were devastating. Officially, the war resulted in an estimated fifty-five thousand Soviet casualties, including dead, wounded, and mentally ill, without realizing "the desired victory."[50] The Russian General Staff conceded that the Soviets' goals in Afghanistan were extremely vague and their time for military planning was limited. The Soviet army's style of warfare—that is, fighting a conventional war with heavy ground weapons and airpower—was not suited for the mountainous Afghan terrain. Further, the Soviet armed forces struggled to understand the resistance fighters' tactics.

From January 1987 to February 1989, as the Soviet Union completed its military withdrawal under the Geneva Accords,[51] its forces conducted virtually no offensive action in Afghanistan.[52] They fought only when attacked or when supporting Afghan forces in their operations. Although the Soviet Union took two years to complete its retreat, the Kremlin leadership had already accepted defeat.

For almost the first three decades of the Cold War, the United States had regarded Afghanistan as a low priority even as it fell under Soviet domination. Jimmy Carter's election as president in November 1976, however, brought a significant change. Détente, which Republican administrations had nurtured since 1968, ended. As U.S. foreign policy acquired an aggressive tone, the Soviet leadership felt under attack by Carter's ideological offensive based on human rights and democracy. Attitudes in the Kremlin hardened, causing a deterioration in East-West relations.

Events after the Communist coup in Afghanistan in April 1978 changed America's Afghan policy. President Carter initiated a policy of active confrontation with communism in Afghanistan, authorizing secret aid to Mujahideen groups fighting the pro-Soviet regime in Kabul. The Communist takeover was a seismic event that set off a process of radicalization in Afghan society. The ensuing Soviet invasion not only accelerated the process but also transformed Afghanistan into a theater for East-West conflict. Over the next eight years, Carter's successor, Ronald Reagan, prosecuted America's proxy war against the USSR.[53] Carter, a Democrat, and Reagan, a Republican, represented different ends of the American political spectrum; however, their strong religious beliefs heavily influenced both men's politics. Thus, both chose to align themselves with radical Islamic groups close to Saudi Arabia and Pakistan to fight Soviet communism.

The superpowers and their allies introduced vast quantities of weapons to fight the war. They also recruited and trained hundreds of thousands of troops to outdo each other. Ideological incitement and mutual hatred exacerbated the conflict, dividing communities, tribes, and even families. State and social institutions under sustained attack and coercion became the primary instruments in society. In this toxic environment, the culture of terror grew in Afghanistan.

9

CONSEQUENCES OF THE U.S.-SOVIET WAR

The Soviet military's retreat from Afghanistan in February 1989 ended a complex and costly phase in the Cold War. The Soviets' initial plan had been to commit a limited number of troops to the Afghan Communists' cause for a short period.[1] In reality, the invading forces found themselves trapped in a vicious conflict with the Americans and their allies for nearly a decade. The Soviet planners' original intent was to occupy the major Afghan cities and air and logistic bases; "to protect the main roads to ensure the safe movement of troops, equipment and supplies"; and to keep the Afghan military supplied with equipment, ammunition, and fuel. Success in these operations would have released Afghan government forces to attack the resistance in the countryside and would have kept the Soviets' contact with local Afghans at a minimum and Soviet casualties low. Once the Afghan forces had overcome the resistance and the Communist regime was strong enough to deal with further unrest, the Soviets had planned to withdraw. Instead, the retreat of the occupation forces took place in very different circumstances ten years later.

For these reasons, the invasion of Afghanistan was a historic failure. This chapter looks at some of its consequences. It examines the role each of the principle actors played after the Soviet occupation of Afghanistan ended and how subsequent events on the war front destroyed what order remained in the ruins of the decade-long U.S.-Soviet proxy conflict. The Afghan state system suffered a complete collapse, as war of all against all led to terror everywhere.

Military commanders of the bygone Soviet era maintain that they believed the plan for Afghanistan was based on their experience in the East European countries—in particular, East Germany, Hungary, and Czechoslovakia—after 1945.[2] The explanation of this view is simple. The Soviet Union intervened in these countries with overwhelming force. Tanks rolled in to impose the Kremlin's will. The Soviets removed counterrevolutionaries from the regime and replaced them with compliant officials. The situation was then stabilized before Soviet troops withdrew from the streets. Thereafter, the country's client regime was left to rule according to Soviet guidance. This strategy worked for nearly fifty years. Its armed forces did not suffer the sort of casualties they did in Afghanistan. Moreover, the Kremlin was able to keep control over the client regimes until just before the Soviet state itself collapsed in 1991.

Afghanistan was not a developed society like East Germany, Hungary, or Czechoslovakia; rather, it is a country of vast mountain ranges and wilderness. It was ideal territory for guerrilla warfare, and the Soviets did not apply the lessons drawn from their postrevolutionary counterinsurgency operations in Uzbekistan and Tajikistan through the early 1930s. This proved to be a fatal mistake. The Soviet Union also failed to learn from Britain's unsuccessful attempts to subdue the Afghans during the nineteenth and twentieth centuries.[3] It took almost a decade after the Soviet Union's disintegration for a more realistic appraisal of its losses in Afghanistan to emerge.[4]

Soviet military tactics against the Afghan population were brutal and overwhelming. Heavy, sustained bombardment forced men, women, and children out of their communities. Damage to the rural infrastructure in much of Afghanistan was severe and widespread. The Soviet military's coercive tactics were not only directed at the active Mujahideen resistance. The Soviets' aim was also to spread fear, to break the will of the Afghan population, and to demonstrate that any sympathy for anti-Soviet activities would be costly for entire communities. Supply routes were cut in areas where opposition was strong, leaving countless inhabitants destitute. Families were split, often never reunited, and hunger and disease became prevalent. Terror was fundamental in the Soviet occupation of Afghanistan.

The war left many scars on Soviet society, too. The problems of drug addiction, low morale, smuggling, and corruption reached alarming proportions, and tensions between Soviet soldiers of different ethnic backgrounds rose markedly.[5] To avoid service in Afghanistan, significant incidents of draft evasion occurred. The antimilitary sentiment among Soviet troops was noticeable, and leaders feared it could impair the discipline and effectiveness of Soviet forces worldwide. Soviet troops who had served in Afghanistan shared their experiences and shaped the views of millions of their relatives and friends, and discontent with the Afghan war effort was rife in Soviet society.

The human cost to Afghanistan, however, was far greater. By the time the Soviet occupation forces withdrew, more than 1.3 million Afghans had been killed and over a third of the entire population had become refugees.[6] Many internally displaced Afghans, unable to leave the country, had fled from rural areas to Kabul and other government-held towns searching for relative safety, work, and handouts from aid agencies. Permanently disabled Afghans of all ages could be seen begging for food and clothing, and the newly wounded arrived in hospitals run by humanitarian organizations such as the Red Cross and Médecins Sans Frontières (Doctors without Borders).

TOWARD THE FINAL BREAKUP OF THE AFGHAN STATE

Following the Soviet retreat in February 1989, Afghanistan's significance as a theater of superpower conflict began to recede, and war fatigue settled among players who had fought for more than a decade. The Najibullah regime remained in Kabul, however, looking very exposed. Other regional and global events quickly eclipsed the alliance of two key players in the Afghan conflict—the American CIA and the Pakistani ISI. The United States had shown exceptional determination to triumph over the Soviet Union during the Reagan presidency, but in January 1989 Vice President George H. W. Bush succeeded him in the White House. Euphoric after the Soviets' retreat from Afghanistan, Washington believed the client regime in Kabul would soon collapse.

The Soviet Union, too, was beginning to look vulnerable. So, continuing the anti-Soviet policy of the Reagan administration, Bush turned his attention to other flash points, including the USSR itself and its East European satellites, which were in turmoil.[7] The CIA's new target was the Soviet Union, not Afghanistan. For the ISI, its target remained Afghanistan, where it had invested a great deal in supporting fundamentalist Islamic groups and where Pakistan wanted to see a compliant government. As soon as the close link between the Soviet Union and Afghanistan loosened and the two intelligence agencies' paths diverged, the turmoil in Afghanistan grew, with several highs and lows before the state finally collapsed.

The ISI's Afghan mission was not yet over, and a number of large urban centers, most notably Kabul, were there to be taken. Seizing a big Afghan city would be seen as a dramatic opposition victory in the region and beyond. The sponsors of the war against the Communists in Afghanistan—the United States, Saudi Arabia, and China, in particular—would be delighted, and Pakistan's military intelligence, together with its Mujahideen soldiers, would be rewarded. Further, losing an important city would have demoralizing consequences for Afghanistan's Communist regime while raising the opposition forces' morale.

Although these pressures had existed since 1988, months before the Soviets' withdrawal, numerous setbacks to the Afghan resistance and its ISI sponsors made the need for a spectacular success in the battlefield even more urgent. Only a month before the Soviet withdrawal was to begin, one of the ISI's vast weapons stores had blown up, destroying ten thousand tons of arms and ammunition.[8] More than a hundred people, including Pakistani intelligence officers, were killed and as many as a thousand injured. The ISI depot was said to have contained at least four months' supply of weapons for the Mujahideen. All of it went up in smoke at once.

Conspiracy theories about the explosion abounded. If it had been an act of sabotage, then the Soviets had the "most obvious motive."[9] Senior Pakistani officers who had past associations with the ISI blamed the Americans, pointing to their changing foreign policy and claiming that they wanted a stalemate in Afghanistan to "prevent [the] fundamentalists winning the war." Their suspicion, right or wrong, was reinforced after the U.S. administration decided to cut back on supplies after the destruction of the weapons depot. The Pakistanis bitterly complained that the next CIA consignment took eight months to arrive; meanwhile, the offensive against the Communist regime in Kabul lost precious time.

For years, the ISI had controlled the system of distribution of military and financial aid to Afghan resistance groups based in Pakistan.[10] Thus, the ISI gained a high degree of influence over Mujahideen leaders such as Gulbuddin Hikmatyar,[11] Yunis Khalis,[12] and Abdul Rasul Sayyaf.[13] The Pakistanis justified the amount given to each group based on the performance of its fighters in battle. In fact, the main beneficiaries of the weapons pipeline were Pashtun nationalist groups that espoused fundamentalist Islamic ideology. They vehemently opposed Western liberal values, but they hated communism even more. Their ISI-facilitated alliance with the United States was only a matter of convenience.

While America's attention moved on to other areas of East-West rivalry following the Soviet military's retreat from Afghanistan, the Pakistanis' interests, and those of the ISI, were strictly regional. The ISI's long-term strategy was to prop up Islamist Pashtun groups to retain its influence in Afghanistan. ISI officers sought to justify this plan by claiming that the military aid given to each Mujahideen party was dependent on its performance in the war, but this assertion does not stand up to scrutiny. If that had indeed been the case, then Ahmad Shah Masood and Ismail Khan, two of the most effective guerrilla commanders, should have received much more than they did. In fact, in their battles they often had to rely on weapons seized from Soviet forces. Relations between the ISI and Masood were particularly bad, and he rarely visited Pakistan during the conflict.[14] Meanwhile, Hikmatyar, who had bases in Pakistan, received generous help from his hosts.[15] The Americans had little say in this distribution system, and their influence declined further once the U.S.-Soviet proxy war ended.

A major tragedy in Pakistan increased the ISI's isolation from America. On August 17, 1988, the military ruler of Pakistan, General Zia, and several other senior officers and American diplomats were killed in a plane crash en route to a military display.[16] It was a disaster for the ISI and its client groups in the Mujahideen resistance. Zia had played a pivotal role in persuading the Americans that his plan to fight the Soviets was sound and likely to succeed. He had raised the banner of Islam at a difficult time and succeeded in creating a patchwork of religious parties, social groups, and donors to support the war. His sudden death would complicate the flow of aid to Pakistan.

CRISIS IN THE ISI AND THE JALALABAD OFFENSIVE

The ISI had faced severe criticism since the disaster at the weapons depot. The controversy over its role in the Afghan conflict and in Pakistan's national defense grew after Zia's plane crash. The agency felt particularly vulnerable because its new chief, Lt. Gen. Hamid Gul, was a controversial figure with powerful enemies. A staunch Muslim, he was daring and always ready to play for high stakes.[17]

Following Zia's death, the first democratic elections in more than a decade were held in Pakistan in November 1988. The elections were won by Benazir Bhutto, whose father, Zulfiqar Ali Bhutto, had been overthrown by Zia and executed. Benazir became prime minister, but the ISI maintained its grip over the conduct of the war in Afghanistan. The ISI and the new civilian government viewed each other with deep suspicion, and the agency was still eager to prove itself to the Americans. The ISI saw a big Mujahideen victory under its command in the Afghan theater as essential. Jalalabad, a major city not far from Pakistan, was supposed to be the answer.[18]

The CIA delivered a new shipment in December 1988. ISI officers felt that the weapons would not reach the Mujahideen for another three months, making any offensive on a major Afghan target unlikely before March 1989; but the Soviet forces would be withdrawn by then. Under the Geneva Accords, the United States and the USSR had promised to refrain from any interference and intervention in the affairs of Afghanistan and Pakistan.[19] The superpowers had also urged all states to do likewise, but these promises were not kept.

Military hardware through the CIA pipeline still arrived in Pakistan, albeit belatedly and on a smaller scale. The Soviet Union also continued to supply large quantities of weapons and ammunition for the Communist regime in Kabul, and hundreds of Soviet military officers remained in Afghanistan as "advisers."[20] Among them were Soviet military experts deployed to service and fire Scud missiles at enemy targets. Senior Pakistani officers bitterly accused both America and the Soviet Union of pursuing the same agenda—that is, to ensure that fundamentalist Mujahideen groups did not win power in Kabul, but that Afghanistan had a broad-based coalition government.[21] Was their assertion the case? Or did America want to see an unimpeded Soviet withdrawal? (That was certainly the intention of the Geneva Accords, although in the great spirit of revenge among fundamentalist Mujahideen groups, they might have wanted to inflict more damage on the retreating Soviets.) Or had the United States decided to slowly disengage itself from the conflict? There were no clear answers.

There was little doubt, however, that the ISI would continue to be a major player in Afghanistan. The other significant player was Iran, which shared a border and trade routes with Afghanistan and newly independent countries of Central Asia. With the Shi'a minority in Afghanistan under pressure from Pakistani and Saudi-backed fundamentalist Sunni groups, Iran's interest was obvious.[22] In Afghanistan, Iran did not have the ability to overcome the influence of Pakistan, and Saudi Arabia, while backed by the United States. Instead, Iran's interests could best be served by supporting mainly non–Pashtun and Shi'a ethnic groups in northern and central Afghanistan and by staying passive in the Pashtun south, where the influence of Pakistan was strongest, as we shall see.

After weeks of propaganda that a big Mujahideen offensive was imminent in an area vacated by Soviet troops, several thousand anticommunist fighters assembled in the hills around Jalalabad in March 1989. The propaganda campaign might have been instigated by the ISI chief, General Gul himself, or it could also have been a ploy to generate fear and panic in the Afghan armed forces. Its biggest drawback, however, was that the element of surprise was lost. The Kabul regime sent heavy reinforcements to its garrison in Jalalabad that strengthened the outer defenses with new bunkers, barbed wire, and extensive minefields.

The Mujahideen offensive on the city began with a direct, frontal attack from the east, and the initial momentum led them to capture a strategic village and the nearby airport.[23] It was not a guerrilla attack but a conventional assault, launched under cover of intense artillery and rocket bombardment. They captured a number of Soviet-built tanks from government forces and used them to advance toward the city. The initial Mujahideen success was short lived as they, along with their ISI advisers, were driven back.

It was the beginning of a stalemate that would continue for four months. The ISI deployed eight senior commanders and their groups, but no overall leader emerged who "could command obedience" of all the men. Some groups suspected that Pakistan was planning to install its favorite, Hikmatyar, in Kabul. Few Pashtuns outside Hikmatyar's own party, or in the Tajik and other Afghan minorities, wanted to die for that cause. Coordination among the Mujahideen was lacking, and, strangely, the guerrillas fought by day and returned to neighboring villages to sleep by night. They could be seen walking or cycling toward the frontlines each morning and were exposed to attacks from the Afghan government forces. Meanwhile, the Afghan government troops fought for their own survival. Soldiers who had surrendered to the Mujahideen in the early phase were brutally killed; laying down their weapons was not an option.[24]

The siege of Jalalabad brought untold misery to the local population. The Kabul regime was able to supply its armed forces, but the residents were left to endure acute shortages of food and other essential goods. Tens of thousands of refugees—old men, women, and children—had left for Pakistan by June.[25] Jalalabad was heavily damaged, and hundreds of civilians died or were wounded. Estimates are that up to a thousand government soldiers were killed in the campaign and the number of deaths on the resistance side was thought to be four times more.[26]

The siege of Jalalabad was a military blunder, and the attempt to capture the city ultimately failed. For a while, it served to raise the government forces' morale and turned the local population against the resistance. To abandon guerrilla tactics in favor of full-scale conventional warfare was a fundamental mistake that reflected the daredevil approach of ISI director-general Hamid Gul. After that humiliation, tensions grew between Prime Minister Benazir Bhutto and General Gul. He was removed from his post in June 1989.[27]

U.S. STRATEGY AFTER THE SOVIET WITHDRAWAL

The decade-long occupation of Afghanistan had been a costly and painful experience for the Soviet Union, and its military withdrawal without leaving a strong, friendly government in Kabul did great harm to its image. The United States had succeeded in giving the USSR its "Vietnam." The next step was to bring down Najibullah's regime in Kabul. By then, the Americans were pressuring the resistance to bring all the groups together. But a U.S.-inspired attempt to form a broad-based coalition government collapsed when the parties meeting in the Pakistani capital, Islamabad, in February 1989 could not agree on the inclusion of Shi'a groups based in Iran.[28] Hikmatyar, Sayyaf, and Khalis—all Sunni Pashtuns who were close to the ISI—resisted attempts to grant the Shi'a parties an acceptable share of power, and the move failed.

Influential American figures complained that the Afghan interim government did not have the support of many key commanders who controlled significant territory inside Afghanistan.[29] These commanders, in turn, wanted the political leaders to take their views into account. Concerns over human rights began to be expressed. The interim government was also accused of having "alienated many Afghans because of its stand on important political and social issues." The views of Hikmatyar and other fundamentalist leaders on the status of women and minority groups heightened fears in many communities across the country, especially in the cities, where people enjoyed a relatively liberal lifestyle. The assault on Jalalabad was described as a major error as was the Mujahideen's mistreatment of defectors and prisoners, many of whom were tortured or killed.

These developments signaled an important shift in American tactics. In the war against the Soviet Union, the U.S. administration had started from a position of unreserved support for the Mujahideen. Under President Reagan, the United States gave the resistance vast amounts of military and financial aid, much of which was channeled to fundamentalist religious groups via the CIA-ISI pipeline. As the Soviet military withdrawal was completed and the 1990s approached, however, the same parties found themselves out of favor in Washington. The Bush administration's preference had switched to the idea of a moderate Mujahideen government that would limit the influence of Islamic fundamentalists in the new Afghanistan.

10

THE FINAL DAYS OF COMMUNISM

The Najibullah regime may have survived the siege of Jalalabad, but the fighting left the government garrison exhausted and its military hardware depleted. It also demonstrated how much the regime's survival depended on massive Soviet aid, including all essentials ranging from food and oil to military hardware and money. Before the withdrawal of Soviet troops, concern over Najibullah's fate had been growing in the Kremlin, and much anger was directed at Pakistan's open and flagrant violations of the Geneva Accords.[1] Discussions in the Politburo focused on instances of Pakistani soldiers directly participating in military operations. In addition, Kremlin reports expressed alarm over the frequent bombardment of border areas and the continuous flow of weapons and armed groups crossing into Afghanistan.

The Soviet leadership was also worried about the state of the ruling People's Democratic Party of Afghanistan (PDPA). Leading figures in the Kremlin complained about the "factional, tribal and other disagreements" that continued to harm the PDPA. They spoke of Afghan leaders' impulsiveness and how they let memories of years of internal conflict dominate their thinking. Personal rivalries often came out into the open in the Afghan Politburo and the cabinet.[2] Ensuring the survival of Najibullah in power became the Soviet leadership's main concern. It needed unity in the Kabul regime and control over large cities, especially the capital, where the situation was critical.

In the Soviet view, Afghanistan's main problem involved the economy. The Kremlin feared that the Afghan opposition was going to launch an economic blockade of Kabul, choking the supply of food and fuel to the city and provoking discontent in the population. The Soviets also knew the Mujahideen continued to rob and intimidate drivers of vehicles transporting goods to the capital. All of these strong-arm tactics created acute shortages and disruptions from time to time. If a full-scale Mujahideen blockade of Kabul were successful, it would bring down the Communist regime.

There was an air of desperation in the Afghan capital. Najibullah had pleaded with the Kremlin to somehow keep open the route between Kabul and the Soviet Central Asian republic of Uzbekistan until at least May 1989.[3] He thought it would ensure the immediate survival of his government. There was no guarantee of the route staying open, however, which became clear soon after the Soviets' withdrawal. Mujahideen guerrillas often blocked the Salang tunnel, which ran through the Hindu Kush Mountains three thousand meters (about ten thousand feet) above sea level, and frequent avalanches created obstructions in winter months. Supply convoys traveling to Kabul were long and slow, and lives were often lost in moving them. These difficulties meant that the air corridor once used to supply the Soviet occupation forces remained busy even after their withdrawal.

The amount of Soviet aid to Kabul increased in the short run, and attempts to intimidate the Afghan opposition continued from inside Soviet territory. Military aircraft regularly deployed near the border with Afghanistan.[4] Some were even ordered to fly without any camouflage so that the Pakistanis and the opposition could see them. Soviet reconnaissance planes also flew missions over Afghanistan to take aerial photographs of "military concentrations of the enemy."

The Soviet leadership considered Najibullah's suggestion about using foreign volunteers in Afghanistan to help his government repulse enemy attacks. Who would they be? If Najibullah was thinking of inviting volunteers from Muslim countries, there was little prospect of it happening. His government was widely seen in the Islamic world as a puppet regime that foreign and Afghan Mujahideen were fighting to overthrow. If Najibullah's idea was to get fighting men from Soviet bloc countries, or India, again it was a nonstarter. Communism was collapsing in the Soviet bloc, and Gorbachev was unlikely to agree to the scheme, having just withdrawn his own troops from Afghanistan. Further, there was a serious risk that introducing new foreign forces would refuel the conflict.

Was Najibullah probing whether the Kremlin would give a tacit approval to Muslim volunteers coming from Soviet Central Asia to defend his regime? The Soviet leaders did not seem enthusiastic. They responded that the plan was unobjectionable if it involved a number of countries, "particularly Muslim ones." However, they knew the international climate was so hostile and the will to fight for the Kabul regime so weak that Najibullah's idea stood little chance to succeed. Instead, the Soviet leaders repeated their intention to continue the diplomatic campaign to influence public opinion in the United States, Pakistan, Iran, and Saudi Arabia, and, if possible, to use India's influence in the Non-Aligned Movement.

Najibullah made the most of the Mujahideen's failure to capture Jalalabad and widened the rift between exiled resistance groups and their field commanders inside Afghanistan. In the name of national reconciliation, the Communist regime's intelligence agents began to make deals with local commanders.[5] Although the Kremlin had restated its commitment to provide military and economic aid to the Kabul regime, the crisis in the Soviet Union was worsening. With future aid looking doubtful, Najibullah changed his strategy from using military confrontations to reaching accommodations with local players from various ethnic and tribal groups. Some local commanders began to cooperate with Najibullah because of war weariness or financial incentives.[6]

One such Mujahideen leader was Zia Khan Nassery, a Pashtun from eastern Afghanistan, who defected with his men.[7] Other rebel gunmen were allowed to visit Kabul freely to buy or sell goods in the market and to meet relatives and friends. This policy contributed to a more relaxed political climate in government-held areas; however, the opposition of exiled Mujahideen leaders and their troops remained as strong as before. The overall effect of Najibullah's compromises created further divisions in Afghan society.

Najibullah's policy of national reconciliation belied the Afghan state's rapid collapse since the Soviet military's retreat from Afghanistan. Although he couched "reconciliation" in a language of reason and patriotism, it amounted to an admission that, as far as he and the Kremlin were concerned, the war was over. The policy also provided a glimpse of how Najibullah's mind worked. A former intelligence officer without much appetite for fighting on the battlefield, he skillfully used inducements and made secret deals to divide the enemy, instead. This goal appeared to be the main thrust of his national reconciliation program, and it suited the Soviet leadership.

In the summer of 1989, Kabul Radio began to address the resistance fight-ers directly and tried to persuade them to discontinue the struggle. Najibullah offered them a cease-fire, bypassing the opposition parties based in Pakistan and Iran. His intelligence network had detected signs of battle fatigue among some internal commanders. His message to them was they had "the right to a considerable share in the government" because they had "suffered for years and remained in the country."[8] Najibullah warned them that foreign players—America, Pakistan, and Saudi Wahhabis—also wanted more power and that removing the PDPA and the armed forces completely would cause Afghanistan to fragment just as Lebanon had in the long civil war that broke out in 1975 and was still continuing in 1989.

Najibullah appealed to the nationalist sentiment of those who had stayed in the country and mocked those who had fled and were fighting from outside. He accused the exiled opposition groups of not having a formal political program that would offer the Afghan people a better future. He claimed that Western supporters, having lost faith in the leaders of external parties, had begun to look to Afghan field commanders. Further, he would welcome contacts with these commanders through emissaries or letters. Najibullah promised to show discre-tion and responsibility and study all ideas carefully.

A number of small political groups emerged in Kabul and other government-held areas. Among them was the National Salvation Society, which was founded in September 1989 by some retired military officers and former ministers who had served under the king almost twenty years before. The society's chairman, Mohammad Asghar, was a former justice minister and rector of Kabul Uni-versity who had been educated at Columbia University in the United States. The society proclaimed that it wanted to create an atmosphere conducive to negotiating a peaceful settlement. It often described itself as the "third force" in Afghanistan.[9]

An unsuccessful coup attempt by the defense minister, Gen. Shah Nawaz Tanai, had come close to overthrowing Najibullah in March 1990. Najibullah took this opportunity to impose his authority, and expelled Tanai and other Politburo members of the Khalq faction from the PDPA. A Second Party Con-gress was held, and the PDPA's name was changed to Watan (Homeland) Party.[10] The members realized that the population would never accept the imposition of communism. "We were supposed to end the exploitation and sufferings of our people," Najibullah said, "but we forced them to take up guns and fight us in the mountains."[11] In an effort to expand his power base, Najibullah imposed changes in which the Pashtun-dominated Khalq faction lost out in the distribution of top positions while other minorities received higher representation.[12]

In a further concession to the opposition, the party amended the Afghan Constitution. Marxism-Leninism was renounced in favor of Islam, and the monopoly of the ruling party was abolished. Afghanistan would instead have political pluralism and a market economy.[13] A greater degree of press freedom was tolerated in Kabul, where some publications took the risk of criticizing the authorities. More non-party figures were brought into the new government, although the ministers of defense, foreign and internal affairs, and state security were still leading party members.[14] The armed forces, however, continued to be under Najibullah's control.

THE COLLAPSE OF AFGHAN COMMUNISM

Najibullah was lucky to have escaped in the bombing of the Presidential Palace in the coup attempt in March 1990. He avoided another possible attempt a month later near the western city of Herat. A Mujahideen group had promised to defect to the regime at a reconciliation ceremony, which Najibullah was scheduled to attend. He pulled out at the last moment and asked Fazle Haq Khaliqyar, then a minister without portfolio, to lead the government delegation. Instead of joining the regime, the guerrillas ambushed the delegation. In the ensuing shoot-out, a number of government officials were killed.[15] Despite these setbacks, Najibullah lifted the state of emergency in May 1990, and France and Italy reopened their embassies in Kabul. The Americans and the British stayed away.[16]

In April 1992 an unexpected and fast-moving chain of events precipitated the overthrow of Najibullah and, as a consequence of the regime's fragilities and contradictions, ended the fourteen-year-old Communist regime in Afghanistan. The collapse of communism was a key moment in the Afghan conflict. Since the 1978 coup the People's Democratic Party had been able to retain its power in Afghanistan only because of its total support from the USSR. In the first five years of the Soviets' occupation, however, Gorbachev had seen how his country's resources were being sucked into Afghanistan. Soon after he became the general secretary of the Soviet Communist Party in 1985, he decided to cut his losses and bring the troops home. As his country sank deeper into crisis, Gorbachev was determined to take whatever steps were needed to restructure the Soviet economy.

Gorbachev's ascent to power was bad news for Afghan Communists. It took another four years to complete the Soviet withdrawal, but the ruling PDPA was on borrowed time. When the Soviet troops retreated, the Afghan armed forces were left with vast quantities of weapons and their soldiers feared for their lives. Some of the units fought doggedly in Jalalabad and elsewhere, but they did so largely to escape Mujahideen acts of vengeance. The 1990 coup attempt was a sign of the nervousness among hard-line Pashtun nationalists in the ruling party and the fragility of the Afghan military without Soviet backing. In the event of a complete breakdown of discipline, it had a vast arsenal of weapons that could be used as an instrument of terror.

The leader of the coup, General Tanai, and some of his close supporters fled to Pakistan, where they found accommodation with the ISI and Hikmatyar. Other Khalqi Pashtuns who stayed in Kabul were purged from the ruling party, or they waited for the right moment to defect to factions that would treat them kindly.[17] Najibullah initially sought to placate the Khalqis in the military, but he also created new units to diversify the security forces at the same time. He set up a new militia, the Special Guard, by drawing troops from the party's youth organization and the armed forces. It was put under the command of the secret service, which Najibullah once headed and trusted.[18] Meanwhile, non-Pashtun ethnic militias were given a much higher profile.[19] Najibullah's strategy had been to counter the adversarial Khalqi-Pashtun forces, but it produced the opposite result. When the regime began to disintegrate, the process was hastened by Pashtun elements defecting to opposition Pashtun nationalist groups and non-Pashtuns to the Tajik forces of Masood.[20]

The short-lived coup against the Soviet leader, Mikhail Gorbachev, in August 1991 triggered the final collapse of communism in Afghanistan. Among the Kremlin hard-liners who led that attempt were senior figures in the KGB and the military.[21] These old-style Communists were dedicated to propping up client regimes abroad. Their removal after the failed coup deprived the Najibullah regime of powerful allies in the Soviet establishment. Within days, Communist Party rule ended in the USSR, the party structure dissolved, and the Kabul regime's support base in the Kremlin collapsed.

Soon after the failed Soviet coup, the Americans and the Soviets signed another agreement in September 1991 to finally stop sending aid to their clients in Afghanistan.[22] In the end, Soviet aid to the Najibullah regime stopped a fortnight before originally planned, on December 15. With their lifeline cut off, various factions of the Najibullah regime rushed to secure their future. Rebellions broke out in the north, where non-Pashtun ethnic groups made deals with the Tajik guerrilla leader, Ahmad Shah Masood. Among the rebel generals was Abdul Momin, commander of the Hairaton garrison, where large quantities of Soviet military and civilian aid were stored. When Najibullah sent a Pashtun general to Hairaton to take over from Momin, he refused to relinquish the command.

The mutiny in northern Afghanistan provoked disaffection among the generals in Kabul, so they made their own deals with the opposition. By April, the Uzbek militia had established control over Kabul Airport. Tajik elements in the regime representing the Parcham faction also supported the rebellion.[23] That shift, in turn, provoked senior Pashtun figures in the party and the secret service to defect to Hikmatyar. Realizing that the end of his regime was near, Najibullah finally announced that he was ready to hand over power to a transitional government under a deal negotiated by the UN special envoy, Benon Sevan.[24]

As the regime collapsed, whatever was left of the state structure and institutions ended as well. Najibullah's subsequent attempt to flee Afghanistan under UN protection failed. On his way to Kabul Airport in a UN car, some of those being left behind prevented his departure. The fallen leader took refuge in a UN building, where he spent the next four years in captivity before being brutally murdered by the Taliban militia.

AFGHANISTAN AND THE FALL OF THE SOVIET UNION

While Afghanistan served as the theater of the last U.S.-Soviet proxy war, which ended with the Soviet Union's defeat, events occurred elsewhere that led first to the end of communism in Eastern Europe and then to the disintegration of the Soviet state itself. The role of the Afghan conflict leading to the USSR's dissolution has often been a topic of discussion and speculation, and some say with conviction that the Soviets' defeat in Afghanistan was the main factor in the ultimate demise of their communist system. The real story is, however, much more complex.[25]

Momentous events such as what transpired in the Soviet bloc between 1989 and 1991 are caused by what Cold War historian John Lewis Gaddis describes as "tectonic forces" of history.[26] These forces, according to Gaddis, are produced by "the interaction of events, conditions, policies, beliefs and even accidents." He suggests three trends combined to produce the effects that ended the Cold War. First, using economic capacity to build military strength proved unsustainable for the Soviet Union. Next, although the Soviet model had a strong appeal among newly independent countries for a period, it simply hid the economic shocks of the energy crisis of the 1970s and did not undertake the same dramatic structural changes that the capitalist system was forced to make. The aging Soviet leadership gave the impression of stability, not stagnation; but eventually it became obvious that economic progress and centralized authority simply did not fit together. The third trend involved a new focus on the way a nation treated its own citizens and those of other countries. In the modern information age, popular rebellion in one country can cause shocks, even monumental political change, in others.

Beneath the veneer of Soviet invincibility, fault lines were developing all over the Communist bloc. The Afghan conflict was an enormous economic and social drain on the Soviet Union, which Gorbachev admitted as early as February 1986, when he called Afghanistan a bleeding wound. Opposition in other countries—Poland and East Germany, in particular—was stretching the Soviet system toward Europe, where the Kremlin had greater interests to protect. The military retreat from Afghanistan in Central Asia was a dramatic symptom of the broader crisis facing the USSR. In the end, it destroyed the image of Soviet invincibility in the eyes of the world. The collapse of the Soviet system and the end of the Cold War resulted from two simultaneous phenomena: Soviet power declined and U.S. confidence increased as the Reagan-Bush administration prosecuted the war against the Soviet empire.[27]

The Soviet army's withdrawal from Afghanistan was completed in February 1989. In October, as Soviet client regimes in Eastern Europe were facing popular revolts, Gorbachev declared that those events concerned only "the peoples and countries of that region" and that the Soviet Union had "no right, moral or political, to interfere."[28] In doing so, he took the policy of disengagement a step further. Its effects were dramatic. Within three months, communism had collapsed in Czechoslovakia, East Germany, Hungary, Poland, and

Romania, and the Soviet Empire in Eastern Europe had all but disappeared. The Soviet Union itself was heading for disintegration.

Meanwhile, the Soviets treated many of their citizens harshly.[29] Dissidents were often kept in terrible conditions. They suffered constant humiliation and deprivation at the hands of the KGB if they were lucky enough not to be executed. The accounts of prominent dissidents like Alexandr Solzhenitsyn[30] and Andrei Sakharov[31] bear testimony to life in Soviet concentration camps and internal exile. Suppression of non-Russian minorities was also widespread and often extreme.

The Soviet state was fundamentally based on social organization by terror, and it tried to impose the same system on millions of Afghans during its occupation. The torture chambers in Communist prisons, the extrajudicial killings, the carpet bombings, and acts of harassment and humiliation, however, reinforced the independent-minded Afghans' belief that the Soviet system was simply unacceptable. Unlike in the Soviet Union, where state terror kept the opposition suppressed for decades, Afghan resistance to the Soviets' occupation was stubborn. Helped by America and its allies, the Afghan resistance generated its own culture of terror, which grew in Afghanistan—and beyond—over time.

11

THE REMAKING OF THE POST-SOVIET WORLD

For almost half a century after the Second World War, the United States was at the forefront in efforts to contain communism. By the advent of the 1990s, the Soviet threat was fast disappearing, and as the only superpower in the world, America searched for a new role. Mikhail Gorbachev's decision to disengage from client regimes meant many Soviet bloc regimes fell.[1] Others were left to find their own accommodations.[2] In the parts of the third world where pro-Moscow rulers were dominant, the absence of Soviet influence created new uncertainties. These rulers' conduct, in the absence of restraint, was a matter of concern and speculation.

After America's proxy war with the Soviet Union in Afghanistan ended, the strategic importance of the Afghan theater had declined. The fall of the Soviet Empire meant that American foreign policy in the 1990s was no longer focused on containing communism. Liberated from the Cold War, opportunities opened for America to advance the cause of freedom and capitalism in countries previously under Soviet influence. It could reshape the world order, but first it had to help dismantle a nuclear power. This chapter looks at America's new priorities in the post-Soviet world.

AMERICA'S RESPONSE TO THE SOVIET UNION'S DEMISE

The USSR was dissolved in December 1991. Within a few weeks, Moscow's new relationship with Washington was on public display at a summit attended by President George H. W. Bush and his Russian counterpart, Boris Yeltsin.[3] The two agreed to a set of principles that would govern the relations between their countries. Further, they declared that as Russia and the United States no longer regarded each other as potential adversaries, they would work to remove "remnants of any Cold War hostility, including taking steps to reduce our strategic arsenals." They would also cooperate to prevent the proliferation of weapons of mass destruction and their associated technology. America and Russia admitted that their "conflicts helped divide the world for a generation" but said that their new alliance as partners would work against the common dangers they faced.

The new relationship was formally described as a strategic partnership, but the reality was very different. Russia was reduced in size and power compared to the Soviet Union and was in a deep economic and political crisis. Bush and Yeltsin's strategic partnership was not an alliance of equals. The term was in recognition of Russia's vestige of a superpower with a sizable nuclear arsenal and military infrastructure. Unless the United States helped Russia transform into a modern democratic society, the world would be a more dangerous place.

American worries that the Soviet Union might disintegrate had grown since the coup attempt against Gorbachev in August 1991. President Bush and his national security adviser, Gen. Brent Scowcroft (Ret.), remained hopeful that the USSR would survive, perhaps as a federation of republics with strong economic and military ties to the center.[4] Otherwise, Scowcroft feared it would succumb to what he described as atomization, accompanied by interethnic conflict, with opposing forces pulling the Soviet system in different directions.

These concerns mounted as the Soviets' central authority rapidly collapsed and non–Russian republics looked ready to break away. Reliable estimates indicated the Soviet Union had about thirty thousand nuclear weapons before the union was dissolved.[5] A third of these were long-range strategic nuclear warheads capable of hitting the United States. In addition, there were thousands of tactical weapons such as short-range nuclear missiles, torpedoes, and sea-launched cruise missiles.

Following the USSR's demise, Russia, Ukraine, Kazakhstan, and Belarus found themselves with almost all long-range strategic weapons.[6] Smaller tactical arms were scattered all over former Soviet territory, and every republic except Kyrgyzstan inherited them. "One nuclear state had suddenly become many," and the danger they posed exceeded "any situation encountered in the Cold War."[7] America's worst fears were coming true. Something radical had to be done.

The United States needed the Russian leadership's cooperation in the project to neutralize the threat from the Soviet era's weapons and to pull Russia out of the crisis—in other words, a strategic partnership.[8] To make it happen, the West had to allow Russia to keep its national pride intact; thus, to achieve this, they entered into a partnership. It could be argued that America's increased involvement in helping Russia with its transformation was among the reasons why America's direct engagement in Afghanistan diminished.

When the Soviet Union dissolved, Gorbachev and Yeltsin assured the Bush administration that "the tight central control of nuclear weapons would remain in place."[9] Yeltsin would replace the Soviet leader at the top of the nuclear command, but the other three successor states with Soviet strategic weapons would not have access to the nuclear codes. Whether this arrangement was indeed the case looked far from certain. Fears persisted after reports indicated that Ukraine wanted operational control over the weapons in its territory.[10] Under pressure to declare their intention, Ukrainian officials denied that they meant control over nuclear weapons; rather, they wanted to establish control over *troops* based on their soil.

Moscow was particularly concerned over Ukraine's fleet of nuclear bombers, which the republic could use to attack Russia if it managed to break the codes on the weapons. A weak and nervous Russia with a vast nuclear arsenal was dangerous, and there was a possibility, too, of one or more of the other nuclear-armed republics resorting to intimidation and blackmail. Further, disgruntled, unpaid scientists could sell enriched uranium and plutonium to a rogue state or group.[11] Or they could be lured by foreign countries trying to develop nuclear weapons of their own. Dealing with such risks became a major U.S. foreign policy priority for the 1990s.[12]

Congress had already laid the foundations for the project to neutralize the nuclear threat in 1991 when it approved a law to prevent the proliferation of weapons of mass destruction.[13] Over the next decade, $7 billion were to be spent on securing the elimination of such weapons, as well as the materials, expertise, and technologies required to make them.[14] Former Soviet republics also returned nuclear warheads to Russia. As a result, Kazakhstan became a non-nuclear state in 1995, and Ukraine and Belarus followed a year later.[15]

All three republics signed the Non-Proliferation Treaty, and with American help programs continued in Kazakhstan and Ukraine to dismantle long-range missiles and aircraft capable of carrying nuclear weapons. To avert the possibility of nuclear materials falling into the wrong hands, in 1993 the United States signed an agreement that allowed it to buy uranium from Russia.[16] The plan would protect, control, and account for nuclear materials, and a secure storage facility was to be built in Russia under a separate deal.

Two further steps were taken in 1994, a year after Bill Clinton succeeded Bush as president. First, the Strategic Arms Reduction Treaty (START 1) came into force on December 5.[17] At the same time, American and Russian laboratories began cooperating with each other to further improve the security of weapons-grade nuclear materials. Under a deal, America would help Russia stop the production of plutonium, and Russian nuclear scientists were given assistance to find jobs in the commercial sector. The other successor states returned the last nuclear warheads to Russia in 1996.

America's Other Crisis: Iraqi Invasion of Kuwait

In August 1990, Iraq's invasion of Kuwait in the oil-rich Gulf caused another crisis for the Bush administration.[18] The occupation of Kuwait gave rise to fears in Washington that the Iraqi army's next move could be into Saudi Arabia, a close ally of the West's and the most important source of oil for the industrialized world. Articulating such fears, President Bush said that what was "at stake was more than one small country."[19] If Saddam Hussein's occupation of Kuwait were allowed to stand, there was a "danger that the world would return to the 1930s," when aggressors ran rampant and started another world war. America's task, therefore, was to liberate Kuwait from Iraqi occupation.

To make it happen, America provided military force and the United Nations the legal basis for its use. Other coalition partners, most notably Kuwait and Saudi Arabia, made substantial financial contributions to the war. Japan and Germany, almost totally dependent on imported oil, were at first reluctant to help for fear of risking their supplies from the Middle East. In the end, though, Bush secured $13 billion from Tokyo and $11 billion from Bonn.[20] By early March 1991, the American-led coalition had liberated Kuwait from Iraqi occupation.

Clinton's Enlargement Agenda in the 1990s

Bill Clinton, the Democratic candidate and former governor of Arkansas, defeated President Bush in the November 1992 election and took the oath of office in January 1993. President Clinton's priority was to revive the U.S. economy after years of decline and vast military expenditures. Initially, National Security Adviser Anthony Lake articulated the mission after Clinton became president.[21] Lake's message was that, in seeking the presidency, Clinton had not only promised a domestic renaissance but also to "engage actively in the world in order to increase our prosperity, update our security arrangements and promote democracy abroad." Lake described the 1990s as an era of unparalleled opportunity and the administration's "big idea" was to enlarge free markets to achieve economic prosperity.

Russia was vital for the Clinton plan to succeed. Since before his inauguration, Clinton had been receiving intelligence briefings on the mounting parliamentary opposition to President Yeltsin's reform program.[22] The U.S. administration was aware that a conservative takeover in Russia could start a new arms race and sink the entire plan for an American renaissance. Yeltsin "needs friends abroad because he's got so many enemies at home" is how Clinton put it and told his advisers "to try to keep Yeltsin going."[23]

The U.S.-Russia collaboration continued throughout the Clinton presidency.[24] However, there were rivalries between them, too. For instance, they competed over who should develop the vast oil and gas reserves in the Caspian Sea. Azerbaijan, Georgia, Kazakhstan, and Turkmenistan—newly independent states emerging from the Soviet era—were known to be rich in resources. American oil companies such as Chevron and Exxon were in the race for big contracts to develop their oil fields and construct pipelines to supply to world markets. The Clinton administration "pushed hard for the pipelines to be built westward through Turkey and the Black Sea" and not through Russia in the north or Iran in the south.[25]

The focus of Clinton's Russia policy was investment, not massive handouts. It continued until an economic crisis in 1998 forced Yeltsin to default on repayments of foreign debt and to devalue the ruble. As billions of dollars were withdrawn from the Russian economy every month, Clinton pushed the International Monetary Fund to support a Russian recovery program. Within two years, Russia's income from oil sales rose substantially, helped by an increase in the world prices, and the crisis subsided.

RESURGENCE OF NEOCONSERVATIVES

While the Clinton administration was busy dealing with the fallout from the Soviet Union's collapse and with the enlargement of free markets, a new current of conservative ideology emerged in America. Known as neoconservatism, it was identified with a hawkish stance in foreign affairs, especially regarding the Middle East. Articulating this ideology, some influential academic and political figures outside the Clinton administration developed an alternative worldview concerning the challenges confronting America by the late 1990s.[26]

The neoconservatives warned of large-scale instability in parts of the Asian and African continents, which they described as the "Arc of Crisis." They also felt the United States should acquire, by military intervention if necessary, a preeminent position in the post-Soviet world. This neoconservatism had figured significantly in the Reagan administration in the 1980s, and it was on the march again. The movement would play an important part in securing George W. Bush's victory in the 2000 presidential election and would rise to prominence during the "war on terror" after the events of September 11, 2001.

The term "Arc of Crisis" was not new. The power of Islamic radicalism had already been recognized in the late 1970s.[27] It was suggested then that at the center of the arc were Central Asia, the Middle East, and parts of Africa. In his State of the Union address in January 1980, President Carter had referred to social and religious, economic, and political change in parts of the developing world. He then cited the Islamic revolution in Iran as an example of the type of future instability the United States would have to face.[28] Carter's national security adviser, Zbigniew Brzezinski, heavily influenced his view of the world. Brzezinski had wanted to harness the power of growing Islamic zeal in the region and use it against the Soviet Union; thus, he had advocated supporting the Mujahideen in the Afghan conflict. Although Brzezinski left the administration following Carter's defeat in November 1980, the policy they had initiated continued into the Reagan-Bush presidency over the next decade.

In the 1990s, President Clinton made a break from that past. His reduced emphasis on militarism encouraged right-wing thinkers outside the administration to push their own vision of the world, one that centered around the theory of the clash of civilizations rather than on democracy and peace, free trade and prosperity. In this vein, Bernard Lewis wrote a historical essay titled "The Roots of Muslim Rage," which explained his view of why so many Muslims resented the West and why their bitterness would be difficult to mollify.[29] Just as it had viewed Soviet communism in its last phase, the U.S. right-wing establishment now saw Islam as the next major threat.

Lewis constructed his analysis on the premise that Muslims, followers of one of the world's great religions, had been left behind by the West as it made advances in science and technology, manufacturing ability, and forms of government—overall, the basis of its wealth and power.[30] Lewis wrote that "at first the Muslim response to Western civilization was one of admiration and emulation—an immense respect for the achievements of the West and a desire to imitate and adopt them." He said that behind this desire was a "growing awareness of the weakness, poverty and backwardness of the Islamic world." He then went on to suggest that generations of Islamic reformers had tried to introduce Western values in their own countries in the hope that they would be able to "achieve equality with the West and perhaps restore their lost superiority."

Reasoning of this type instigated a neoconservative intellectual enterprise that appeared to be aimed at establishing the preeminence of the West over the Muslim world. It made assertions about some indefinable quality in Islam that created a culture of rage and hatred and used kidnapping and assassination in times of upheaval, disruption, and stirred passions.[31] Lewis contended the United States was the "legitimate heir" of European civilization and the "recognized and unchallenged leader of the West." So, in this capacity, Lewis claimed, America also came to inherit the Muslims' resulting grievance, pent-up hate, and anger.

His underlying message was that calm, patience, and order are qualities exclusive to Western civilization, particularly to America while Islam and the Muslims have them to a lesser degree. Lewis views the historic upheaval and realignment of forces in the Muslim-dominated regions, or the Arc of Crisis, as the ultimate struggle of Muslim fundamentalists "against two enemies, modernism and secularism."

Dramatic portrayals of this kind may be attractive to a certain body of opinion in the West, but this picture is simplistic. The views of Lewis and others like him also ignore some of the recent and more basic causes of conflict in the region. For instance, Israel's creation, displacing Palestinians from their homes, and America's alliance with Israel have been a constant source of popular anger and discontent throughout the Muslim world. The contrast between the life of deprivation in Palestinian camps and the affluence in Israeli settlements is also an explosive mix.

In addition, Lewis's analysis ignores internal conditions in many of the Muslim countries, where governments are seen as corrupt and the gap between rich and poor is great. America's relations with the regimes of Egypt, Jordan, and Saudi Arabia bring vast amounts of money into their economies, but this wealth makes little difference to how people live in the slums of Cairo, Amman, or Riyadh. Many slum dwellers view the West as feeding their corrupt rulers, who use Western cash to promote their own lifestyle and to suppress the population. The introduction of unregulated capitalism has left poorer sections in these societies largely untouched. Reality is not the straightforward clash of civilizations, Muslim and Western, that Lewis depicts; rather, his analysis reflects the same kind of "them versus us" mind-set that the Muslim religious fundamentalists have embraced.

The next stage of pushing the "clash of civilizations" theory appeared in an article by Samuel Huntington in 1993.[32] Huntington's hypothesis did not focus on only the Muslims and the West as being on a collision course. He saw a much more turbulent state of affairs in the world, with conflict breaking out along religious and cultural lines. The world, in his view, could be divided into different civilizations, or "the highest cultural grouping of people and the broadest level of cultural identity people have."[33] Huntington argued that, in the coming years, "the world will be shaped in large measure by the interaction among seven or eight major civilizations."[34] The clash of these civilizations will dominate global politics.

Huntington cites the centuries-old military confrontation between the West and Islam before predicting that not only is this conflict unlikely to decline, "it could become more virulent."[35] He presents rhetorical slogans that Saddam Hussein of Iraq and the senior religious leader of Iran, Ayatollah Ali Hoseyni Khamenei, raised against the West during the Gulf War in 1991 as examples of clash of civilizations.[36] But he makes no attempt to examine the historical enmity between Iran and Iraq.[37]

Lewis and Huntington based their analyses fundamentally on religion rather than on the infinitely more complex blend of language, culture, and social evolution that makes a civilization. They fail to take into account the basic realities of the modern world, in which the migration of people has become a standard feature. In the present age of jet aircraft and intercontinental travel, it is common to see in New York, London, or Paris indigenous people living next to Arab, African, Chinese, or Indian neighbors. It is difficult to separate living civilizations in the contemporary world.

Nonetheless, the underlying theme of the clash of civilizations theory galvanized the right-wing political establishment in the United States toward the end of the 1990s. An organization called the Project for the New American Century was set up in 1997 to "rally support for American global leadership."[38] Leading members of the project were, on the one hand, critical of the Clinton administration, which they accused of letting American foreign and defense policies go adrift. On the other hand, the organization was opposed to isolationist tendencies within their own ranks. The group's objectives were to assert the preeminent global position of the United States and to see the country play an interventionist role to shape a twenty-first-century world favorable to American principles and interests, as seen by the leading lights of the project.

Among those who signed the project's manifesto were Jeb Bush, whose brother, George W. Bush, was to win the U.S. presidential election in the year 2000, and Dick Cheney, who would be vice president in the Bush administration.[39] Evoking memories of the Reagan administration, the manifesto emphasized that the nation's leadership should embrace a strong U.S. military and a bold and purposeful foreign policy to promote American principles abroad, and to fulfill America's global responsibilities. The implication was that the Clinton administration was both weak and incoherent.

To ensure the success of their global plan, the project's architects called for a significant increase in U.S. defense spending to enable America to carry out its current global responsibilities and modernize its armed forces. They said that America should strengthen its relations with democratic allies and, at the same time, challenge regimes hostile to American interests and values. Further, America should accept its responsibility in preserving and extending an international order that supports its security, prosperity, and values. The project's manifesto concludes that "such a Reaganite policy of military strength and moral clarity" was necessary to ensure America's security and greatness in the twenty-first century.

As President Clinton's second and final term began in 1997, the Christian right in America was, once again, on the ascendancy. The fundamentalist political ideology of the Reagan era in the 1980s had returned. There was, however, a difference this time. The emerging political right had a new, youthful generation of neoconservative leaders who were much more aggressive, purposeful, and ready to intervene to impose their will. From these neoconservatives emerged George W. Bush, who would defeat the Democratic presidential nominee, Vice President Al Gore, in the November 2000 election. Eight years after Bill Clinton defeated his father for the presidency, George W. Bush arrived at the White House to pursue the neoconservative agenda.

12

THE RISE OF THE TALIBAN

Toward the end of 1994, a little-known militia named the Taliban came to prominence after capturing Qandahar in southern Afghanistan.[1] It had been two years after the fall of the Soviet client regime of Najibullah, and the Afghan state was rapidly disintegrating; the Communist regime in Kabul had collapsed, and the rival Mujahideen factions were engaged in internecine war. The government of President Burhanuddin Rabbani, which was dominated by the Tajik minority, controlled Kabul, its surrounding areas, and the northeast of the country. Another Tajik commander, Ismail Khan, controlled Herat and its neighboring provinces in the west. The Uzbek warlord, Abdul Rashid Dostum, held sway in northern Afghanistan, while a number of Pashtun commanders controlled the eastern and southern provinces close to Pakistan. The domain of Gulbuddin Hikmatyar, Pakistan's favorite, was relatively small.[2]

Although Afghans had longed for peace for more than a decade, their hopes had been shattered by the continuing war among the Mujahideen. The disappointment was all that much greater because many Afghans had expected the Clinton administration to demonstrate the same level of commitment to stabilization and rebuilding that the Reagan administration had shown after confronting the Soviet occupation forces. Instead, U.S. interest in Afghanistan swiftly declined in the 1990s.

WHO WERE THE TALIBAN?

Most of the Taliban were young Afghans who had spent their entire lives as refugees of the war against the Soviet Union. Many were born and grew up in

Pakistan. From early on, they had seen adult male members of their families go to fight the Communists, holding a copy of the Quran in one hand and a gun in the other. Sometimes their fathers, brothers, and uncles returned after months of fighting, only to go back and fight again. Often they returned ill or seriously injured. Many perished in the conflict.

The number of young orphans in Afghan refugee camps ran into hundreds of thousands. Many of these young Afghans had taken part in the final stages of the war. Just before Soviet withdrawal, some in the Taliban leadership had suffered permanent injuries. Their wounds were a constant reminder of the brutal nature of the conflict around Qandahar, their stronghold, in the late 1980s.[3] The nearest medical facilities for the injured were a two-day camel ride from Pakistan's Quetta city.

Most of the senior Taliban leaders came from poor, disadvantaged backgrounds. The supreme leader, Mullah Omar, was born into a landless Pashtun family in Qandahar around 1960. Part of his youth was spent in Uruzgan Province, one of Afghanistan's most backward and inaccessible parts, where Soviet occupation forces rarely went. After the premature death of his father, the responsibility of looking after his mother and extended family fell on him at a young age.

It is, however, known that, toward the end of Soviet occupation, Omar was a member of a Mujahideen faction.[4] He was wounded several times between 1989, when the Soviets retreated, and 1992; he even lost his right eye in an encounter. It was probably his disability and lack of charisma that made him very shy. Most of his early followers said that they joined Omar not because of his military or political skills but because of his piety and belief in Islam.[5]

As many Taliban were born and had lived in Pakistani refugee camps for years, their links with Pakistani society were very close. Their views on social and political issues were shaped during their time in the country's religious schools, where they had found shelter and studied the Quran and Islamic law. After the Mujahideen victory over the Communist regime in 1992, some had returned to their homes in southern Afghanistan. Many had stayed in Pakistan, where they were scattered in Baluchistan and North-West Frontier provinces. They had their identity cards and continued to receive international refugee assistance. Their children received free education in Islamic schools.

These schools were run by the Jamiat-ul-Ulema-i-Islam (JUI), a fundamentalist party that had built up a strong following in Pakistan's border region in the early 1990s. As the JUI expanded its base, other Islamic groups lost support. The teachings, which the Taliban received, included a very strict interpretation of Islam, especially with regard to restrictions on women. It forbade any political role for them, but the Taliban went much further and banned women from education and work as well.[6] Activists of the JUI were extremely hostile to Shi'a Muslims, whom they regarded as unbelievers. The Taliban's attitude was similarly hostile to the Shi'a and other minorities.

The Taliban emerged with promises to end the state of lawlessness and to restore peace and security in Afghanistan. They were eager to expand their control throughout the country and employed extremely coercive measures to suppress all opposition. To legitimize this suppression, they resorted to those parts of the Islamic legal code, Shari'ah, that prescribe severe punishment even for minor offenses. Many Afghans were initially attracted by the Taliban's promises to end banditry and extortion by local warlords. However, broader manifestations of the Taliban regime, including harsh treatment of women and ethnic minorities, emerged later.

Women were forced to stay indoors, and male doctors were refused permission to treat female patients.[7] Female teachers could no longer teach boys even at elementary schools, forcing a large number of institutions to close. Numerous Taliban atrocities took place against Shi'a Afghans, whose loyalty to their country was questioned because of their cultural and spiritual ties with Iran. Relations between the Taliban regime and Iran were severely tested from time to time.

EVOLUTION OF THE TALIBAN–ISI ALLIANCE

Pakistan's military intelligence service, ISI, had backed Hikmatyar throughout the war against the Soviet Union. Even after the communist regime's collapse in Kabul, the agency continued to support Hikmatyar's push against the Tajik-dominated government of President Rabbani. By 1994, however, the prospect of Hikmatyar seizing control of the city was nowhere nearer.

The agency was also under pressure from the civilian government of Benazir Bhutto. She wanted to open up trade routes via Afghanistan to Central Asia, but this aim could not be achieved so long as Afghanistan was fragmented. Bhutto asked her interior minister, Naseerullah Babar, a loyal retired general, to lead an effort to establish whether trade with Central Asia was indeed possible if Afghanistan came under a single authority.[8] Her plan was a direct challenge to the ISI. If Bhutto were to succeed, then the ISI's influence in Afghanistan would be greatly diminished.⁹ The agency's fears were reinforced when Bhutto met two of Afghanistan's northern warlords, Ismail Khan and General Dostum, in Turkmenistan to lobby them for help.¹⁰

Three weeks before the Taliban captured Qandahar in early November 1994, they fought a battle with Hikmatyar's group at a remote border post, Spin Baldak. It was an important refueling stop for the transport mafia and a garrison for Hikmatyar's forces. The emergence of petty warlords and the failure of Hikmatyar to establish order had generated deep resentment in the local population and traders. The transport mafia had given Mullah Omar a large sum of money and promised a monthly retainer if the Taliban could clear the roads for traffic and guarantee security. The offer was too good to refuse.

The Taliban launched an attack on Hikmatyar's garrison and defeated his forces after a brief but intense battle. They then seized a heavily-defended weapons depot. There is evidence that the Taliban were helped by Pakistani frontier troops under the direct command of the interior ministry. Declassified American documents show that Pakistani officers on the scene coordinated the operation and Hikmatyar's base came under artillery fire from Pakistani positions before the Taliban captured the weapons depot.¹¹ Suddenly, the Taliban possessed arms, ammunition, and military vehicles. The battle of Spin Baldak changed the course of the Afghan conflict and had consequences that few anticipated at the time. It was the end of the alliance between Pakistan and Hikmatyar.

The battle of Spin Baldak caused shockwaves among militia commanders, but they continued to quarrel among themselves and openly accused Pakistan of supporting the Taliban. Rivalries and confusion grew in Pakistan, too, as the ISI and the interior ministry competed for influence.¹² While Bhutto was determined to take the lead on Afghanistan, the ISI was not going to be left behind, which explains the "test convoy" that traveled to the Central Asian Republic of Turkmenistan from Pakistan to demonstrate the viability of a trade route through Afghanistan. It was the idea of Benazir Bhutto and Interior Minister Babar, who planned the journey. Ex-Pakistani soldiers specially hired for the purpose drove more than thirty trucks. Diplomats from the United States, Britain, Spain, Italy, China, and South Korea were invited to travel with the convoy to demonstrate to the outside world that the route through Afghanistan was secure and viable. Additionally, a senior officer of ISI, Colonel Imam, was on board and Taliban commanders with their troops provided security escort.¹³

These developments were part of a debate within the ISI for months. While intelligence officers involved in field operations advocated that Pakistan should give more support to the Taliban, those involved in long-term planning and intelligence gathering wanted to keep this support to a minimum. The ISI's high command was short of funds because the usual channels of support from America and Saudi Arabia had dried up and a significant proportion of its resources was being deployed to influence the insurgency in the Indian part of Kashmir.[14]

The debate concluded in mid-1995 when the ISI and the military agreed to support the Taliban. Pashtun army officers played a key role in achieving the consensus.[15] They were concerned that the Afghan government of President Rabbani had become too close to Pakistan's rivals—Russia, Iran, and India. The army had also come to accept that the Taliban were the "only possible alternative" for Pakistan. Because there was deep distrust between the ISI and Rabbani's defense chief, Ahmad Shah Masood, the agency wanted a strong ally to counter him.[16] The Taliban were seen as the solution.

THE TALIBAN AND SAUDI ARABIA

The Taliban did not receive help from Pakistan alone. Saudi Arabia, too, was drawn in to support them. In July 1996, the Saudi intelligence chief, Prince Turki al-Faisal, visited Pakistan's capital, Islamabad, and the Taliban stronghold, Qandahar, where plans to capture Kabul were discussed with the Taliban leadership.[17] Supplies to the Taliban were subsequently increased and the militia turned its attention not to the Afghan capital, but to Jalalabad first. Saudi Arabia and Pakistan helped engineer the surrender and eventual flight of the city's head of the ruling council.[18] He was given cash and safe passage to Pakistan, with a promise that his assets would not be confiscated.

From then on, the Taliban were unstoppable. By late September, their forces had encircled Kabul from three sides and winter was closing in. The city had endured merciless rocket attacks, punctuated by ground assaults, for months. The defenders were well dug-in, but they did not have the numbers to launch counteroffensives and push the Taliban away from the capital. The ISI kept the Taliban supplied with military hardware and fighters. The agency also played a key role in liaising between the Taliban and Saudi intelligence.

It all proved too much for Kabul and its defenders, and on September 26, 1996, President Rabbani's military commander, Ahmad Shah Masood, ordered that his troops evacuate the capital. Within hours, columns of Taliban fighters moved into Kabul. One column entered the UN building where Najibul-lah, the deposed Communist leader, had taken refuge since 1992. He and his brother were beaten, tortured, and hanged outside the Presidential Palace.[19] The shocking manner of their execution served as a pointer to the way in which the Taliban were going to impose their rule.

THE TALIBAN AND THE UNITED STATES

When the Taliban emerged as a force in 1994, the U.S. administration was more of an observer than a player in Afghanistan.[20] American officials in the region were aware of the recruitment of young fighters from Islamic schools in Paki-stan with the help of the Jamiat-ul-Ulema-i-Islam.[21] The fighters had brand-new weapons, which raised a strong suspicion that the Taliban had been created with "the active support" of the Pakistani government. But their long-term in-tentions and policies were not clear. The Taliban were simultaneously described as tools of Pakistan as well as anti-Pakistan, because they were opposed to the anticommunist Afghan factions hitherto supported by Pakistan's military-po-litical establishment and represented an ideology far more radical than most in the ruling elites were comfortable with.

Pakistan supported the Taliban for three strategic objectives: first, to set up a regime of Pashtun clerics in Kabul under its tutelage; second, to open a corri-dor through Afghanistan to Central Asia to earn revenue from trade; and third, to obtain a strategic economic edge over India in the long run.[22] U.S. interests in the Middle East were as important as ever, and the United States had asserted its military presence in the Gulf after driving out the Iraqi occupation forces from Kuwait in 1991. While U.S. relations with Saudi Arabia, a leading oil producer, remained strong, opposition to pro-U.S. regimes in the Middle East was on the rise. Memories of the overthrow of the Shah of Iran and the consequent loss of American influence in the Gulf region were still fresh. America had a long-term need for an insurance policy, a strategic plan, in case Saudi Arabia was lost as an oil supplier and ally.

One such option was to build pipelines from Turkmenistan to the Paki-stani port city of Karachi to carry fuel from oil and gas fields in Central Asia.[23] American oil executives had been in discreet contact with Pakistani and Saudi officials about this idea. After months of lobbying, in 1995 a consortium led by the U.S. corporation, UNOCAL, proposed a plan to build pipelines through Afghanistan.[24] Delta Oil of Saudi Arabia was a partner in the enterprise with an estimated cost of about $2 billion. There was a rival bid from an Argentine corporation, Bridas, but the UNOCAL bid succeeded in the end, and the Turkmen president, Saparmurad Niyazov, signed an agreement with the American-led consortium.[25]

All parties concerned with the pipeline project ignored President Rabbani when his forces were entrenched in Kabul. The Taliban victory in the capital reinforced Pakistan's vision of trade through Afghanistan and encouraged speculation that America was "behind the movement." By August 1998, the Taliban had extended their control as far as the northern city of Mazar-i-Sharif. These advances coincided with growing speculation of American support for the Taliban because they seemed to serve the U.S. policy of isolating Iran by creating a "buffer on Iran's border" and providing "security for trade routes and pipelines that would break Iran's monopoly" on the southern flank of Central Asia.[26] There is no concrete evidence of direct support, military or financial, to the Taliban from the U.S. administration. There is, however, evidence that for a period U.S. diplomats were in contact with the Taliban directly or through Pakistan to secure Osama bin Laden's extradition from late 1998 onward, but without success.[27]

The Clinton administration was clearly worried about the freedom Osama bin Laden enjoyed under Taliban protection in Afghanistan. The administration made discreet attempts to persuade the Taliban regime to cut off ties with bin Laden and hand him over to the Americans. Inducements were used, such as enhanced recognition if the Taliban cooperated, as well as threats, including military strikes against Afghanistan if they continued to provide sanctuary to bin Laden.[28] In the end, all U.S. efforts were frustrated in the face of an uncompromising attitude shown by the Taliban supreme leader, Mullah Omar, on the issue.[29]

Nonetheless, Iran saw the pipeline project, together with the Taliban advances, "as part of a US policy of encirclement," and Iranian foreign minister Ali Akbar Velayati went on a diplomatic offensive in Central Asia in order to gain support for an initiative to convene a meeting of all the states involved in the Afghan crisis, except the United States. Held in Tehran, the meeting condemned foreign interference in Afghanistan. Pakistan and Saudi Arabia predictably stayed away.[30] At the United Nations in New York two weeks later, a junior ministerial-level meeting of member-states concerned with the Afghan conflict was held, but it failed to agree on how to confront the Taliban.

Although the Taliban had succeeded in bringing most of Afghanistan un-der their control by 1998, some northern areas still escaped them.[31] Where they did establish control in the north, a region of non-Pashtun minorities, their hold was fragile. Their brutal tactics against women and minorities meant that they were never able to win the kind of popular support in the north that they had in the south. As international protests against their policies grew louder and peace looked increasingly elusive, UNOCAL announced a suspension of "all activities involving the proposed pipeline project."[32] Soon afterward, at the end of 1998, the company withdrew from the project, citing business reasons and concerns over the treatment of women in Afghanistan.[33]

UNOCAL's decision came at the time when U.S. diplomats had separately yet unsuccessfully attempted to persuade the Taliban to hand over Osama bin Laden. UNOCAL had likely begun to see the project's growing complications and found an opportunity to withdraw. There were other problems with the project from the beginning. The construction of oil and gas pipelines through the length of a mountainous country would have been extremely costly. Even with most of Afghanistan under Taliban control, security would have been a huge issue, both at the construction stage and thereafter in maintenance. The Taliban's unpredictable nature was becoming obvious and the viability of their regime uncertain. President Clinton's priority was to secure access to new mar-kets and to revive the American economy. His administration seemed very re-luctant to invest money or effort in Afghanistan.

TALIBAN RULE, VIOLENCE, AND SOCIETAL ORGANIZATION

The rise of the Taliban happened in a complex set of circumstances. They be-came the dominant force in Afghan society with Pakistan's active support, in reaction to the existing climate of lawlessness, and were propelled forward by a combination of despair and hope among Afghans. Several historical charac-teristics of Afghan society helped the Taliban at first. Afghanistan was a deeply conservative Muslim country, where Shari'ah law, as interpreted by the Afghan tribal custom, had prevailed for centuries.[34] Pashtuns were the most powerful ethnic group, and some 80 percent of Afghanistan's population belonged to the liberal Hanafi school of the Sunni sect.[35]

The system was, therefore, remarkably tolerant of minority faiths and eth-nic groups. Hindus, Sikhs, and Jews had traditionally played an important role in the economy and sectarianism had not been a significant issue. However, the disintegration of the Afghan state system in 1992 created a situation in which ethnic groups were set against each other. Promising to establish order, the Taliban assumed the divine right to control every aspect of life, citing their own ultraconservative brand of Islam. The consequence was a regime based on intolerance and terror.

Young boys and men were taken away and coerced into joining the Taliban militia.[36] Wearing Western-style clothes and shaving became offenses, punishable by flogging and imprisonment. People were detained because they did not pray five times a day or were "suspected of sympathizing with the Taliban's opponents." Taliban courts passed sentences after hearings that lasted only a few minutes. Often, the decisions taken were final and no appeals were allowed. Inside prisons, conditions were extremely harsh and many detainees were given no food.[37] Relatives who visited inmates normally brought them food once or twice a week. Otherwise, they had to ask other prisoners. Corruption was rife, and prisoners were sometimes released after paying bribes.

Some of the worst atrocities were committed against Afghan women. Incidents of beatings for women not covering themselves, even for appearing in public, were common. In Kabul alone, tens of thousands of professional women were, in effect, dismissed from their jobs when the Taliban ordered them not to leave their homes unless they were accompanied by a close male relative. Young girls were prevented from going to school. Islamic courts freely passed sentences of death and amputation.

Many women no longer had access to the most basic medical facilities. Female doctors were few and far between, and male staff at hospitals and clinics could not see female patients. Women and young girls were abducted from minority ethnic communities and forced into marriages, or sent to Pakistan and Gulf states.[38] Premises of international organizations, such as the United Nations and the Red Cross, were raided and female employees prevented from working for them. Aid agencies began to evacuate their staff from Afghanistan.

Within a year of the Taliban takeover of Kabul, the regime had tightened its control over all aspects of society. Torture and ill-treatment had become systematic. A growing number of women were taken away and beaten in detention centers.[39] In the provinces, too, floggings, amputations, and executions were carried out in increasing numbers, but many more cases were believed to be going unreported. Members of ethnic minorities were targeted in the north. The Taliban "deliberately and systematically killed thousands of ethnic Hazara civilians" after seizing control of Mazar-i-Sharif in August 1998.[40] Women, children, and old people were shot as they tried to flee the city.

Taliban militiamen burned homes, destroyed orchards, wheat crops, and irrigation systems, and expelled more than "a hundred thousand mainly Tajik people" from their homes.[41] When the militia captured Bamiyan Province in 1999, many Hazara civilians were killed. Hundreds of men, women, and children, who were separated from their families and taken away, remained unaccounted for. At the end of the year, the regime ordered a campaign against educated Afghans who were not part of the Taliban. Government employees who had won awards during the Soviet occupation of the country between 1979 and 1989 were to be identified. Hundreds of prominent Afghans were detained, and many were tortured or killed.

All Afghan factions were accused by human rights organizations of cruel and ill treatment of innocent civilians, but the most serious protests were over the conduct of the Taliban. It was pointed out that the procedures of Shari'ah courts fell well short of international standards of fair trial, but the courts "continued to impose cruel, inhuman and degrading punishments." People convicted of murder were executed by shooting, usually carried out by relatives of the victims before large crowds. Children as young as five were encouraged or forced to witness these punishments, and fourteen-year-olds were given "the task of displaying the severed limbs of victims to the spectators."

In 1989 the retreat of Soviet forces from Afghanistan was celebrated with euphoria in the region and the West. Afghans were hoping for a better future. However, the end of the U.S.-Soviet conflict left a legacy that caused Afghanistan to sink into anarchy and full-scale civil war. It created a vacuum that destabilized what order remained in the country. The vacuum could only be filled by a new force willing and able to impose order through brutality. The Taliban were that force.

As a result, an untold number of Afghans suffered extreme physical punishments. Those who did not have to endure violence themselves were controlled by fear. The conduct of the Taliban regime caused widespread revulsion in the West. The presence of foreign militants in Afghanistan became a source of growing concern and the American administration began to press the Taliban to act against them.[42] Even then, militants continued to arrive in the country, where they received ideological indoctrination and military training before moving on to distant lands to fight other wars.

13

DIALECTICS OF THE AFGHAN CONFLICT

The last two decades of the twentieth century were a period of intense struggle between competing ideologies—a struggle that played out in the Afghan conflict. Afghanistan was caught up in the Cold War between the United States and the Soviet Union as early as the 1950s. The clash of capitalism and communism, both essentially Western ideologies, magnified the internal divisions in Afghanistan and its tribal system. Such a society has two essential characteristics: an inner weakness born out of social fragmentation and a defensive instinct to react violently against foreign interference. These very characteristics were reinforced as intervention by massive military-economic aid and secret intelligence operations grew in Afghanistan and the country fell under Soviet domination. Afghan Communists became bolder and they seized power in a bloody coup in 1978. The rise of communism radicalized the country's Islamic groups.

THE NATURE OF DIALECTIC

Imposition of a Soviet-style system on a deeply religious people was the beginning of a chain of events that shook the Communist regime in Afghanistan. Rebellions in rural areas, mutinies and desertions in the armed forces, and escalating internal warfare in the ruling People's Democratic Party created a crisis in the country. The deeper the crisis became, the more repressive measures were used by the first Communist regime in 1978–1979.

The nature of such a chain reaction, or *dialectic*, is self-perpetuating.[1] A dialectical process acquires a life of its own by virtue of what is described as the power of *negativity*. Negativity is what comes into being in opposition to the *subject*.[2] The first subject is a thesis in the shape of an event or force that is gradually stripped of its immediate certainty after coming into existence as it embarks on a "pathway of doubt."

Simply put, a thesis is what rises in its environment as a distinct entity, its character imposing itself before reaching a point at which that entity is challenged by the negative force that the original thesis created. In the ensuing struggle between the thesis and its negative, or antithesis, the certainty of the original entity progressively weakens as doubts over its viability are raised. This explanation of the nature of dialectic is based on an acknowledgment that things are multifaceted and always in the process of changing because of the power of negativity.

The conflict between a thesis and its negative is a process that slowly strips the former of properties that determined its certainty and lends the latter contradictory properties. What is obtained in such a process is a reconciliation between the two: a synthesis. While the original and its negative were contrary to one another, their synthesis preserves both and stresses unity once again. The synthesis then transforms itself into another thesis, leading to further contradictions and conflict before reaching another stage of resolution. So the dialectical progression goes on.

We can now begin to understand in dialectical terms the advent of various external and internal forces that eventually conspired to create a culture of violence in Afghanistan. When a small group of Communist sympathizers in the armed forces, representing an ideology that was foreign and contrary to the basic character of Afghan society, seized power in 1978, it was an event that was bound to produce profound consequences. Under the Communist regime, there was a short-lived experiment to restructure Afghan society on the Soviet model—an experiment carried out by coercion through purges, imprisonment, torture, and assassination. The Marxist experiment provoked violent opposition that became progressively more stubborn as measures of the Communist regime acquired greater ruthlessness. The resistance took many forms: Parcham against the Khalq faction, internal dissidents within Khalq, non-Pashtun against Pashtun, anticommunist against communist, and so on. As the conflict escalated, fear and chaos began to take hold and the outcome was the Soviet invasion of Afghanistan in December 1979.

The scale of violence was altogether different during the years of Soviet occupation. The overwhelming war machine of the Communist superpower was at work, and in the final major confrontation of the Cold War, the United States threw its vast resources in support of the anticommunist Mujahideen groups to fight that war machine. All sides used weapons of terror, and the conflict produced millions of victims. The violence the Soviet occupation army committed was answered by Mujahideen opposition on the ground.

The war against the Soviet Union in Afghanistan is often portrayed as one in which the Afghan resistance took on a superpower and won. This view is an oversimplification, because it ignores the dialectical nature of the conflict that triggered intervention by other external powers in opposition to the Soviet Union. The Mujahideen victory could not have been possible without the military and financial support from America and its allies, notably Saudi Arabia, Pakistan, Egypt, and China. American and Pakistani intelligence services were deeply involved in the planning and execution of the war against the Soviet occupation forces. The role of Pakistan in the recruitment and training of anticommunist guerrillas was critical.

State intervention from outside also brought foreign militants to Afghanistan. The military government of Pakistan allowed thousands of Islamic radicals to train and fight in the conflict, which made them battle-hardened and reinforced their fundamentalist ideology.[3] After the defeat of communism, they were left without a cause, and many returned to their own countries to engage in struggles against regimes they regarded as un-Islamic and corrupt.

ISLAM AND THE EXTERNAL DIMENSION

Islam has been a powerful force in modern Afghanistan. It was the main source of resistance to change from above, whether from imperial powers, such as Britain and Russia, or internal regimes such as those of Mohammad Daud and Nur Mohammad Taraki.[4] Religion, interwoven with a tribal system, provided the core of this resistance, as local mullahs who found their position in society under threat endorsed it. The war against the Soviet Union in Afghanistan went beyond this. Islam was used as a political ideology to bind together the disparate factions and their members at the insistence of President Zia of Pakistan and with the active support of the CIA-ISI alliance.

The idea of Islam as a political ideology, not merely a religion, to be used to reshape and control society is sometimes described as "Islamism." While

Afghanistan is a deeply religious country, Islamism had not taken root in the wider Afghan society before the Communists seized power in 1978. In the early 1970s, religious militancy was primarily concentrated in Kabul, where a relatively small number of educated Afghans fought for influence with left-wing groups in student politics and the armed forces. However, the Islamists became isolated in later years. Almost all prominent activists fled to Pakistan by 1975, when an attempt to overthrow President Daud failed.

At this stage, the Islamist movement of Afghans underwent internal turmoil as it prepared to oppose the Daud regime. The movement split into two significant groups: the Hizb-i-Islami, dominated by ethnic Pashtuns and led by Gulbuddin Hikmatyar, and the mainly Tajik Jamiat-i-Islami under the leadership of Burhanuddin Rabbani. The Pashtun-Tajik divide was to prove permanent, but both groups had much in common with their Middle Eastern counterparts. They both recruited members from the intelligentsia. Many activists of these Islamist groups had been students in scientific and technical institutions.[5] They were joined by better-educated Afghans and foreign militants who eventually fought against the Soviet occupation forces. They were Sunni Muslims with a strong anti-Shi'a stance, reflecting the wider trend in the Arab world against Iran. Threatened by the growing Shi'a militancy following the 1979 Islamic revolution in Iran, Sunni Arab regimes wanted to keep Iranian influence in check. Their answer was to support anti-Shi'a forces, whether it meant the Iraqi leader, Saddam Hussein, in his war with Iran or Sunni militants in Afghanistan.

It has been suggested that the ideology of the Afghan Islamists was "borrowed entirely" from two foreign movements: the Muslim Brotherhood, founded in Egypt, and the Jamiat-i-Islami of Pakistan.[6] As with these two movements, the Afghan Islamists opposed secular tendencies and rejected Western influence. Within Islam, they opposed Sufi influence, with its emphasis on love and universality of all religious teachings. Rabbani was among those prominent Afghans who had spent years at al-Azhar University in Cairo and had been active in the Muslim Brotherhood. Hikmatyar, in contrast, was close to Pakistan's Jamaat-i-Islami, which was itself influenced by the Brotherhood and its ideologue, Sayed Qutb.[7] The writings of Qutb were a source of inspiration to many Arabs who fought against the Soviet Union in Afghanistan in the 1980s.

The main appeal of Qutb comes from his assertion that the world is "steeped in jahiliyyah," the Arabic term for "ignorance." He argues that this ignorance originates from the rebellion against God's sovereignty on earth.[8] Qutb attacks communism for denying humans their dignity, and capitalism for exploiting individuals and nations. He claims that the denial of human dignity and exploitation are only consequences of the challenge to God's authority. The solution advanced by Qutb is that Islam acquire a "concrete form" and attain "world leadership," but a movement for its revival must be initiated in order to do so.

Qutb does not openly preach violence, but other ingredients of a revolutionary brand of Islam are present in his writings. He recognizes that there is a significant body of educated people who are disillusioned with the existing order. These people represent a constituency for change in a number of Middle Eastern countries, where economic and social problems, corruption, and a lack of involvement in political processes have created a gulf between governments and their people. Qutb rejects the Communist and capitalist systems alike, asserting that Islam is the only alternative. His vision is idealistic and strongly attracts the alienated who are looking for political adventure.

The Muslim Brotherhood was hostile to successive Egyptian governments and firmly aligned itself with the Palestinian cause after the creation of the state of Israel in 1948.[9] When Anwar El Sadat became president of Egypt in 1970 following the death of Nasir, he promised to implement Islamic law and released all Brotherhood members from jail in an attempt to pacify the movement. But Sadat's decision to sign a peace treaty with Israel in 1979 resulted in a new confrontation, which led to his assassination in October 1981. The Muslim Brotherhood went underground, eventually developing a complex network of more than seventy branches worldwide.[10]

The disintegration of the Afghan state system between 1992 and 1994 and the subsequent rise of the Taliban turned Afghanistan into a haven to which foreign fighters could return without fear of retribution. Many more new Islamic radicals came from the Middle East, North and East Africa, Central Asia, and the Far East to study, train, and fight in Afghanistan during the Taliban period. They developed personal contacts with each other, learned about the Islamist movements in other countries, and planned cross-border activities.

CONFLICT WITHIN AND THE BIRTH OF AL QAEDA

No other veteran of the Afghan conflict has achieved worldwide notoriety like Osama bin Laden.[11] He had his initiation into radical Islam as a student at King Abdul Aziz University in the Saudi city of Jiddah, where he earned a degree in

economics and management. There, bin Laden also developed a deep interest
in the study of Islam and listened to recorded sermons of the fiery Palestinian
academic, Abdullah Azzam. In the 1970s, Jiddah was a center of disaffected
Muslim students from all over the world and Azzam was a leading figure in the
Muslim Brotherhood. His influence encouraged bin Laden to join the movement.[12]

After the Soviet invasion of Afghanistan in December 1979, bin Laden
moved with several hundred construction workers and their heavy equipment
to the Afghan-Pakistan border and set out to "liberate the land from the infidel
invader."[13] He saw a desperately poor country taken over by tens of thousands
of Soviet troops and millions of Muslims bearing the brunt of the military machine of a superpower. Afghans had neither the infrastructure nor manpower
to mount effective resistance to their country's occupiers.

Osama bin Laden created an organization to recruit people to fight the Soviets and began to advertise all over the Arab world in order to attract young
Muslims to Afghanistan.[14] In just over a year, thousands of volunteers, including experts in sabotage and guerrilla warfare, had arrived in his camps. Their
presence clearly suited CIA operations in Afghanistan. Osama's private army
became part of the Mujahideen forces based in Pakistan and supported by the
United States. Military experts with a close understanding of U.S. policy estimated that a "significant quantity" of high-technology American weapons,
including Stinger antiaircraft missiles, reached bin Laden then and were still
with him in the late 1990s.[15]

Osama helped build an elaborate network of underground tunnels in the
mountains near Khost in eastern Afghanistan in the mid-1980s. The complex
was funded by the CIA and included a weapons depot, training facilities, and
a health center for the Mujahideen.[16] Osama set up his own training camp for
Arab fighters, and his following increased among foreign recruits.[17] However,
he increasingly became disillusioned by the continued infighting in the Afghan
resistance after the Soviets left and America's disengagement from Afghanistan
that many saw as abandonment. Osama returned to Saudi Arabia to work for
his family business.

When Iraq invaded Kuwait in 1990 and the security of Saudi Arabia looked
as though it were under threat, he urged the royal family to raise a force from
the Afghan war veterans to fight the Iraqis. Instead, the Saudi rulers invited
the Americans—a decision that greatly angered Osama. As half a million U.S.

troops began to arrive in the region, bin Laden openly criticized the Saudi royal family and lobbied Islamic leaders to speak out against the deployment of non-Muslims to defend the country. It led to a direct confrontation between him and the Saudi royal family.

Osama departed for Sudan, which was going through an Islamic revolution. He was warmly welcomed, not least because of his wealth, in a country devastated by years of civil war between the Muslim north and the Christian south. His relationship with Sudan's de facto leader, Hassan al-Turabi, was close, and he was treated as a state guest in the capital, Khartoum.[18] Returning veterans of the Afghan conflict were given jobs and the authorities allowed bin Laden to set up training camps in Sudan. Meanwhile, he continued to criticize the Saudi royal family. The Saudi authorities finally lost patience and revoked his citizenship in 1994. Osama bin Laden was not to return to his homeland again.

These events had a lasting impact on bin Laden. He had fallen out with the United States and the Saudi ruling establishment, and his freedom of movement was severely restricted. In Khartoum he began to concentrate on building a global network of Islamist groups.[19] His business, Laden International, had a civil engineering company, a foreign exchange dealership, and a firm that owned peanut farms and cornfields. Other business ventures failed, but he had enough money to support Islamic movements abroad. Funds were sent to militants in Jordan and Eritrea, and a network was established in the former Soviet republic of Azerbaijan to smuggle Islamic fighters into Chechnya. He set up more military training camps, where Algerians, Palestinians, Egyptians, and Saudis were given instructions in making bombs and carrying out sabotage.

The ideological nucleus of what became al Qaeda also attracted Ayman al-Zawahiri, regarded as Osama bin Laden's deputy. Al-Zawahiri was born into a leading Egyptian family and fell under the influence of revolutionary Islam at an early age.[20] His grandfather, Rabia'a al-Zawahiri, was once head of al-Azhar Institute, the highest authority of Islam's Sunni branch. His great-uncle, Abdul Rahman Azzam, was the Arab League's first secretary-general. When he was fifteen, al-Zawahiri was arrested for being a member of the Muslim Brotherhood.[21] Although he had trained to be a surgeon, his radical activities led to a rapid advancement in the Egyptian Islamic Jihad. By the late 1970s, when he was still in his twenties, he had taken over the leadership of the group.

In October 1981, al-Zawahiri, along with hundreds of activists, was arrested following the assassination of President Sadat by members of his group

at a military parade. The authorities could not convict him of direct involvement in the murder, but he was sentenced to three years in prison for possessing
weapons. He left Egypt after his release—first going to Saudi Arabia and then
to Pakistan's North-West Frontier Province, where large numbers of foreign
fighters entered Afghanistan during Soviet occupation.

There is evidence that Ayman al-Zawahiri's association with the Afghan
resistance started just before his arrest in Egypt in 1981. He was a temporary
doctor in a Muslim Brotherhood–run clinic in a poor suburb of Cairo, where
he was asked to go to Afghanistan to do some relief work.[22] He thought it was a
"golden opportunity" to familiarize himself with a country that had the potential to be a base for struggle in the Arab world and where the real battle for Islam
was to be fought. On his way to Afghanistan several years later, al-Zawahiri
briefly worked as a surgeon in a Kuwaiti Red Crescent Hospital in the Pakistani frontier city of Peshawar. He frequently visited Afghanistan to operate on
wounded fighters, often with primitive tools and rudimentary medicines. Al-
Zawahiri secured his place in the Afghan resistance as someone who treated
the sick and the wounded just as Osama had secured his as a wealthy Arab who
spent his money and time helping people in an impoverished country that had
been devastated by Soviet forces.

In the years following, al-Zawahiri emerged as an intellectual and the main
ideological force behind Osama bin Laden. He enunciated clear distinctions
between his and other Islamist groups. Al-Zawahiri saw democracy as a "new
religion" that must be destroyed by war.[23] He accused the Muslim Brotherhood
of sacrificing God's ultimate authority by accepting the idea that people are the
source of authority.[24] Other Islamist groups were also condemned for accepting
constitutional systems in the Arab world. In al-Zawahiri's view, such organizations exploit the enthusiasm of young Muslims, who are recruited only to be
directed toward "conferences and elections (instead of jihad)." Subsequently,
al-Zawahiri became even more scathing in his criticism of the Muslim Brotherhood. Those who support democracy are by definition infidels, for "he who
legislates for human beings would establish himself as their god." He argued
that the Brotherhood was guilty of mobilizing the masses of Muslim youth to
the ballot box and extending "bridges of understanding" to the authorities. In
return for a degree of freedom, he said, the Brotherhood was forced to acknowl-
edge the regime's supremacy. Such a relationship, he said, pollutes minds permanently.[25]

The further al-Zawahiri went in his consideration of modern social systems, the more radicalized he became in reaction. He implied that the moral and ideological pollution was worsened by material corruption. He complained that the Muslim Brotherhood had amassed enormous wealth. This material prosperity, he said, was achieved because its leaders had turned to international banking and big business to escape the repressive and secular regime of Nasir in Egypt. Joining the Muslim Brotherhood created opportunities for its members to make a living. Their activities were driven by materialistic, rather than spiritual, aims. These views amounted to a complete rejection by al-Zawahiri and his organization, the Islamic Jihad, of other Islamist groups and brought the Jihad closer to Osama bin Laden and his network.

The influence of the Palestinian-Jordanian academic, Abdullah Azzam, was central in this process. Azzam was only a child when Israel was founded in 1948 and had been active in the Palestinian resistance movement from an early age.[26] He had links with Yasir Arafat, but their association ended when he disagreed with the secular philosophy of the Palestine Liberation Organization, eventually coming to the view that it was far removed from "the real Islam." Azzam's logic was that infidels had drawn national boundaries as part of a conspiracy to prevent the realization of a transnational Islamic state. And he came to the view that his goal was to bring together Muslims from all over the world.

Abdullah Azzam saw in the Afghan conflict an opportunity to realize this ambition. Recruitment of volunteers from across the Muslim world to fight the Soviet occupation forces was to be an important step toward his goal to set up an Islamic "internationale." To achieve this aim, these volunteers would train, acquire battle experience, and establish links with other radical Islamic groups. The Mujahideen resistance in Afghanistan had already established a legendary reputation that would inspire potential followers all over the world. The resistance could eventually become a highly motivated and trained force, ready to destroy the "decadent" West and export the Islamic revolution to other parts of the world.

In November 1989, Azzam and his two sons were assassinated in a bomb attack as they drove to a mosque in Peshawar to pray. The identity of their murderers remained a mystery, but rumors persisted about a link with bin Laden and al-Zawahiri.[27] Reportedly, while they both supported the idea of extending the struggle to overthrow Arab regimes, Azzam wanted to begin in Afghanistan by replacing the Communist regime of Najibullah with a Mujahideen government. Other players, including the Soviet and Afghan secret services, also had an interest in removing Azzam. Whoever was responsible for his assassination, its most significant consequence was that bin Laden and al-Zawahiri gained almost total control of the network of foreign fighters linked to the Afghan conflict.

The split between Osama bin Laden and Abdullah Azzam in the late 1980s was the beginning of al Qaeda. Whereas Azzam insisted on maintaining the focus on Afghanistan, bin Laden was determined to take the war to other countries. To this end, bin Laden formed al Qaeda.[28] His main goal was to overthrow corrupt and heretical regimes in Muslim states and replace them with the rule of Shari'ah, or Islamic law. Al Qaeda's ideology was intensely anti-Western, and bin Laden saw America as the greatest enemy that had to be destroyed.[29]

To understand al Qaeda, we need to consider what conditions led to the creation of its ideology. The two main ideologies to emerge after the Second World War were communism and free-market liberalism.[30] Competition between them during the Cold War obscured the challenge they faced from a third force, radical Islam in the Middle East. The first significant manifestation of this force was the Islamic revolution in Iran in the late 1970s. The Soviet occupation of Afghanistan in the 1980s created an environment in which the challenge from radical Islam was directed against communism. America strengthened it by pouring money and weapons into the Afghan conflict, but failed to recognize that the demise of the Soviet empire would leave the United States itself exposed to assaults from groups like al Qaeda. In time, this failure proved to be a historic blunder.

14

THE NATURE OF AL QAEDA

A l Qaeda is often depicted as a relic, an organization determined to take the world back to medieval times. However, its characteristics are remarkably similar to modern organizations in fact, and imprints of bin Laden's management skills can be found all over its structure. Like any multinational business, it developed as a loose network of groups operating in different parts of the world. Osama became the "emir-general," assisted by a consultative council and four committees: military, religious and legal, finance, and the media. Al Qaeda then extended its presence throughout the Arab world and the Israeli-occupied territories, North and East Africa, South and Southeast Asia, former Soviet territories, China's Xinjiang region, and the Balkans.[1] Its members also set up operational and support cells in Italy, Spain, Germany, the United Kingdom, Canada, and the United States. These cells consisted mostly of suicide bombers, often from educated middle-class backgrounds.

Secrecy was paramount and the "commando" cells often knew little about the rest of the organization. Whether bin Laden was based in Afghanistan, or briefly in Sudan, distances between al Qaeda's leaders and individual units were great. When he returned to Afghanistan in May 1996, his Taliban hosts were closing in on Kabul, though the country was more fragmented and isolated. State institutions and agencies such as the army and the police had disintegrated. Despite the widened gulf between the dominant Pashtuns and other minority groups, the Taliban had established their supremacy in large parts of Afghanistan and subdued the infighting between the old Pashtun warlords.

The new Afghan rulers were intensely anti-U.S. Yet the lack of education and resources made them highly vulnerable to external influences, which were ideal conditions for al Qaeda. The Afghan conflict in the 1980s had prepared the Mujahideen for use of high-technology devices provided by the Americans and their allies. In the 1990s, the inheritors had turned against their old masters.

Al Qaeda and the Taliban's anti-Western ideology was a grotesque mirror image of the Carter and Reagan-Bush administrations' anti-Soviet policy. As far back as 1977, President Carter had made a break with the realpolitik of Nixon and Kissinger, and the United States had begun to project human rights, democracy, and freedom as its core values, which were rooted in Carter's deeply held religious beliefs. Reagan's foreign policy had a far more aggressive moral tone and anticommunism was the essence of his message. In a speech to the National Association of Evangelicals, Reagan called the Soviet Union an evil empire that was armed to the teeth, vicious, expansionist, and racing ahead because of America's self-doubts after the Vietnam debacle.[2] His rhetoric advanced a simple plan: overcome these doubts and rearm in the face of Soviet aggression.

With its fervent anticommunist character, the Reagan-Bush administration identified and armed the Mujahideen to fight the Soviet Union. For years, Reagan and his officials told these anticommunist guerrillas that they were brave freedom fighters who were defending not only their religious and national identity but also way of life from foreign occupation. The CIA supplied weapons and copies of the Quran to both Afghan and Arab groups.

This policy's principal beneficiaries were Islamic radicals whose anti-U.S. ideology had long been known. They represented the opposite of the Christian fundamentalism that had dominated America in the 1980s, and the opposite of the neoconservatism of the 1990s. The neoconservatives, who rose at a time when the Republicans were in opposition, sought to impose Western supremacy over Islam and the rest of the world based on the assertion that Western civilization was superior. Islamic radicalism, intensely hostile to all foreign influence, was the mirror image of that ideology—opposite and even distorted.

After communism, the radical Islamists' mission was to destroy America and its allies (the Saudi royal family in particular), secular regimes in the Arab world, and non-Muslims everywhere. America's assertion of its moral values abroad only strengthened the resolve of Islamic fundamentalists to assert their own ideology. The rise of al Qaeda and its Afghan hosts, the Taliban, was as much a reaction to America's relentless pursuit of an anti-Soviet policy as it was a symbol of the fundamentalists' will to advance their brand of Islam.

By February 1998, the Taliban had extended their grip to most of Afghanistan. Bin Laden's confidence was high. Al Qaeda raised the stakes dramatically by announcing the formation of a new group called the World Islamic Front for Jihad against the Jews and the Crusaders. Published in a London-based Arabic newspaper, *al-Quds*, the announcement was a charter for future activities of al Qaeda.[3] It called on Muslims to kill Americans and their allies, military and civilian, wherever possible, in order "to liberate al-Aqsa Mosque" of Jerusalem and to eject their armies out of "all the lands of Islam, defeated and unable to threaten any Muslim."[4]

The rhetoric was extremely powerful and provocative.[5] It focused on the three biggest grievances in the Middle East: Israeli control over Jerusalem, the Palestinian problem, and Iraq. In a reference to the presence of U.S. troops in the region since the 1991 Gulf War, the declaration spoke of America "occupying the lands of Islam in the holiest of places, plundering its riches, dictating to its rulers, humiliating its people, terrorizing its neighbors and turning its bases into a spearhead" to fight the Muslim peoples.[6] It said that "despite the great devastation inflicted on the Iraqi people" and "the huge number of those killed" by the blockade against Iraq, the Americans were still not content and were "trying to repeat the horrific massacres." America's aims were "religious and economic," and it wanted to serve the interests of Israel by diverting attention from its occupation of Jerusalem and murder of Muslims in the occupied territories.

The proof of these aims, according to al Qaeda's statement, was "the eagerness to destroy Iraq, the strongest neighboring Arab state," and attempts to weaken all other countries in the region to guarantee "Israel's survival and the continuation of the brutal occupation" of the Arab Peninsula. In the view of al Qaeda and its affiliates, these "sins and crimes committed by the Americans are a clear declaration of war on God, his messenger and Muslims." Their assertion was that *ulema*, or "authorities on Islamic law," had "unanimously ruled" over centuries that when enemies attack the Muslim lands, jihad is every Muslim's duty.[7]

This interpretation of Islam by al Qaeda has been described as a distortion of the nature of Islam and jihad.[8] It is often pointed out that the Quran speaks of peace and of war. Islam originates from the same Arabic root as Salaam, which means peace, and is interpreted in various ways: cleansing the body and soul of evil, health, reconciliation, and submission to the authority of God. Jihad is to strive for justice against evil, including one's own failings. The term may mean struggle, armed or otherwise, if the faith, honor, and the homeland are in danger. Or it may involve writing books, making speeches, donating money, and doing humanitarian work in the interests of all. In essence, the instruction to each follower is to do all he can.[9] The need for peace and mutual understanding among different faiths and races is recognized under Islam.[10]

Personal freedom and dignity for men and women are enshrined in the Quran.[11] It does approve of killing enemies, but for specific, not all, times and places.[12] It certainly does not allow killing innocent civilians.[13] Moreover, the Quran explicitly prohibits violence against those who have not attacked.[14] In times of conflict, there is consolation for prisoners of war. For if there is "any good in their hearts," then God will give them mercy and something better than has been taken away from them.[15]

Thousands of teachings are in the Quran. The entire body of Islamic sayings and traditions attributed to the Prophet and interpreted by Islamic authorities in various ways offers a wide range of directions to Muslims, to be followed in accordance with the time and the place. When al Qaeda quotes verses from the Quran to justify its campaign of violence, its choices are very selective and narrow. Armed struggle is only one of jihad's many forms and is recognized as regular warfare against infidels and apostates. The relevant laws prescribe rules about the opening and closing of hostilities and treatment of the innocent and prisoners of war. Islam does not allow torture. Bin Laden and his network adopted few, if any, of these caveats enshrined in the Islamic teachings.

COUNTDOWN TO SEPTEMBER 11, 2001

With the declaration of open warfare against America, al Qaeda had come of age by 1998. It had been linked to a number of high-profile attacks in different parts of the world and its reach had extended to almost every continent. The event that fueled the advance of al Qaeda was the U.S.-led war against Iraq in 1991.[16] Although Saddam Hussein received virtually no support from Arab regimes following his invasion of Kuwait, the arrival of hundreds of thousands of American troops generated popular resentment in the region. The anger was harnessed by al Qaeda. Its long-term consequences were not anticipated by the U.S.-led coalition.

Western intelligence sources estimated that bin Laden had about ten camps in Taliban-controlled parts of Afghanistan and that training in unconventional warfare was provided at several of these.[17] Al Qaeda and its associated groups had training camps in other countries, too, including Sudan, Somalia, and Kenya.[18] The network had set up businesses to generate income and provide cover for "the procurement of explosives, weapons and chemicals and for the travel of al-Qa'ida operatives." Several underground cells had been "detected and neutralized" in Britain, Germany, Italy, Canada, and the United States, but new units had emerged in their place.[19] More cells were active in about fifty other countries. The first generation of al Qaeda militants included men who had fought in Afghanistan in the 1980s, the second generation in Algeria, Egypt, Tajikistan, Chechnya, Nagorno-Karabakh, Kashmir, and Mindanao in the Philippines. There were enough wars going on around the world to supply fighters filled with hatred against America and willing to die for their mission to destroy what the United States stood for.

In October 1993, al Qaeda was involved in attacks on American troops on a humanitarian mission in Somalia, killing eighteen soldiers. Western governments learned afterward that Somali tribesmen had been trained for those attacks earlier that year. Leading al Qaeda figures had visited the country a number of times and reported back to bin Laden in Sudan. Kenya became another stronghold of al Qaeda, which set up businesses there and "began to discuss the possibility of attacking the US embassy in Nairobi."[20] In February 1993, a car bomb attack on the World Trade Center in New York had taken the lives of six people and injured more than a thousand, but its symbolic impact was far more serious, coming as it did in the heart of America's financial capital. The operational leader of the attack was Ramzi Yusuf, a Pakistani Baluch born in Kuwait.[21]

Ramzi had close ties with al Qaeda and often traveled on a fake Iraqi passport. After the Trade Center bombing, he secretly visited Thailand, the Philippines, and Pakistan, where he stayed in a guesthouse run by bin Laden in Peshawar. It is also known that Ramzi spent some time at an al Qaeda training camp on the Pakistan-Afghan border between 1989 and 1991, before leaving for the United States. After his arrest in 1995, he told the FBI that he had spent six months at the camp learning how to make bombs. His arrest was made possible only because the Filipino authorities were alerted in 1994 when an explosives experiment by Yusuf went wrong and started a fire in his Manila apartment. He escaped, leaving behind his computer that had detailed plans to blow up as many as eleven passenger aircraft and to assassinate the Pope. Following a worldwide search, Yusuf was captured a year later in Pakistan's capital, Islamabad, and extradited to America.[22]

Two simultaneous bomb attacks on the American embassies in Nairobi and Dar es Salaam stunned the world in August 1998. More than two hundred people were killed and nearly five thousand wounded in Nairobi. In Dar es Salaam, at least ten died and more than seventy were injured. Within hours, al Qaeda had informed international media by fax that it had carried out the bombings. According to the British government, the faxes were traced to a telephone number that had been in contact with bin Laden's mobile phone.

In an interview with *Time* at a secret location in Afghanistan four months after the embassy bombings, bin Laden was directly asked if he was responsible for the attacks.[23] He responded that "if the instigation for jihad against the Jews" was considered a crime, then "let history be a witness that I am a criminal." He said that his "job is to instigate" and "certain people had responded to this instigation." Those "who risked their lives" were "real men." They "managed to rid the Islamic nation of disgrace," and the organization held them "in the highest esteem."

How could he justify the deaths of Africans? His answer was that he understood the bombers' motives. He claimed that the killing of Muslims was "permissible under Islam" if it became apparent that repelling Americans would be impossible without launching attacks in which Muslims might also die. He played on the U.S. fear that al Qaeda might be trying to acquire chemical weapons. Securing "weapons for the defense of Muslims was a religious duty." If he had "indeed acquired these weapons," then he thanked God for "enabling him to do so."

In October 2000 the American naval destroyer, USS *Cole*, was attacked. A small boat laden with high explosives struck the warship as it was being refueled in Aden harbor. The explosion caused a large hole in the ship, killing seventeen sailors and injuring thirty others.[24] The British government said that several of the perpetrators of the USS *Cole* attack were "trained at Osama bin Laden's camps in Afghanistan." Earlier in January, an attempt to blow up another American vessel was aborted when the boat being used for the attack sank.[25]

The attacks on the World Trade Center and the Pentagon on September 11, 2001, were defining events in a number of ways. Images of hijacked planes striking at the heart of America were the most dramatic illustration of an asymmetric war between the United States and Islamic militants determined to fight the world's only remaining superpower.[26] That day proved that the Soviet Union's demise did not mean that the global challenge to American power had ceased. A new enemy had emerged in the twenty-first century—invisible, unpredictable, and able to strike anywhere. Its most lethal weapons were the suicide bombers who believed that they were destined to go to paradise. Americans had a great deal to lose.[27]

The initial shock felt by America turned into anger and a determination to exact retribution. President George W. Bush described the attacks as "more than acts of terror."[28] He called them "acts of war" and promised a "monumental struggle of good versus evil," a struggle in which "good will prevail." Bush proclaimed America's right to take preemptive military action, unilateral if necessary, in a new "war against terror."[29] And so, more than ten years after turning away from Afghanistan, the United States was back to overthrow the Taliban, successors to the Mujahideen whom it had helped finance with billions of dollars in the war against communism. The idea this time was to destroy al Qaeda, but neither the enemy nor his territory was precisely known and the war on terror seemed to have no end.

It is now possible to deduce what forces and their interplay created a phenomenon of terrorism of such magnitude. The weakness of Afghan institutions, especially after the overthrow of the monarchy in 1973, and the fragmented character of the country's tribal system made possible the society's many ethnic, sectarian, and political groups, who were often at odds with each other. Conflict between these groups was frequent, and as their alienation from the Kabul regime grew, they increasingly looked for external alliances and assistance.

The 1970s were a critical decade for Afghanistan. Communism was on the offensive and Islamic groups were in retreat amid military takeovers and radicalization of society. Ideological conflict between the United States and the Soviet Union fueled this internal upheaval in Afghanistan. Moreover, the growth of radical Islamic movements, which saw the United States and its allies in the region as corrupt and un-Islamic, made certain that Afghanistan became a haven for terrorism after the defeat of communism. It was the 1978 Communist coup that started the dialectic that ultimately gave rise to the terrorism witnessed in the new century.

15

CONCLUSION

Few terms are so contested and encounter so many problems of definition as terrorism. Yet, to understand how Afghanistan turned into a terrorist sanctuary and to find ways of countering the challenge it poses, a definition that is suitable for this study is essential. Despite attempts for almost seventy years, the community of nations has been unable to agree on a universal definition of what constitutes terrorism. Experts, too, all over the world are divided, depending on the politics of those who use force and how they seek to justify it.

Use of force by states is often defended as legitimate in self-defense and the maintenance of international order, whereas violence for political ends by non-state groups is condemned as terrorism. On the contrary, insurgents fighting to overthrow an unfriendly regime, which may itself be accused of employing state terror, are seen as freedom fighters. This was often the case during the Cold War. Even after the demise of the Soviet Union, conflicts in the Middle East, South Asia, and other trouble spots continue to divide opinion on what is terrorism and who are terrorists. Now, as before, groups engaged in opposing foreign occupation see the occupiers as using terror to suppress the local population. However, scholars generally agree that terrorism does relate to the use of violence for political aims. For this study, terrorism is defined as the premeditated use of violence by an individual, group, or state in order to achieve political goals; it is intended to generate shock and panic in the short-term and long-term uncertainty beyond the actual scene of violence, to compel the existing political order to change policy, or to surrender in the face of sudden, disproportionate force. Once the consequences of violence are established, the terrorist's threat of repeating similar acts can be sufficient to terrorize the target.

This definition deals with nuances of the concept in a way that takes into account terrorism's effect on its victims, not the way in which those who use force describe it. The essence of this definition is that all violence involves a degree of terror, whether it is claimed as legal.

But what is the driving force behind terrorism? We considered three main approaches used by scholars—rational choice, psychological approach, and structural analysis—to explore this question. Rational choice explains terrorist behavior as being driven by deliberate decisions in which a group concludes that violence would bring more advantages than disadvantages in achieving its political aims. The psychological approach seeks to show that certain emotional forces compel people to commit violence. These approaches are sometimes described as two sides of the same coin.

Counterterrorism experts associated with law-enforcement agencies in the West tend to portray terrorists as mad or irrational people, although it remains an assertion rather than a credible conclusion based on proper data analysis. What is sometimes described as new terrorism today claims that al Qaeda represents a threat that is "old madness, new methods."[1] Advocates of new terrorism explain terrorist acts in terms of their characteristics—lethality and suddenness, for example—but do not put forward anything new about what motivates people or groups to commit such acts.

New terrorism sheds no light on what motivates a terrorist in addition to what has already been discussed in previous studies—rational choice, psychological forces, and structural factors. Studies on new terrorism also pose other problems. If al Qaeda's tactics represent new terrorism today, how long are they to remain "new" and at what point does new terrorism become old? And how are we to define the next generation of terrorist activity? Because of questions such as these, other experts have made the point that new terrorism is not new at all. State and non-state groups that practice violence for political purposes will always find means that are available to them at the time.

The third approach to explain terrorism examined earlier in this study is structural analysis. It seeks to demonstrate the phenomenon as a product of external causes in the environment, such as political, economic, social, and cultural factors. We could have applied any of these three approaches mentioned above to study terrorism's growth during the Afghan conflict, but there were considerations in support of all three. It led us to an alternative that was more appropriate for this study: the concept of a violent culture. It is defined as a condition in which violence permeates all levels of society and becomes part of human thinking, behavior, and way of life.

A culture of violence takes years or more to establish itself and has the following characteristics:

- It is dialectical and replicates itself once established.
- It is prompted and shaped by external intervention, which upsets the balance of forces locally, resulting in disorder and conflict.
- It develops along with the breakdown of institutions such as security forces, judiciary and legislature.
- Law is superseded by violence.
- Expectations are altered and adapted to force as a way of life.
- The cycle of violence distorts the culture and creates a climate of fear that drives human behavior and lifestyle.

Next this study explored the nature of dialectic to establish how the war in Afghanistan could be viewed in those terms. We examined how conflict between a force or event and its opposition makes a dialectical process. Each stage in the process concludes with a resolution of contradictions and something new (synthesis) emerges. All of this activity can be simply stated as violence breeds more violence and human behavior adapts to the escalating use of force in society. This is how a culture of terror matures.

Our conclusion now looks at the Afghan conflict in the context of an escalating dialectic of terror. When a small group of Communist sympathizers in the armed forces, representing an ideology that was foreign and contrary to the basic character of Afghan society, seized power in April 1978, it was an event of profound consequences. The Marxist experiment to restructure Afghan society following the coup provoked violent opposition, which became progressively more stubborn each time the regime resorted to greater coercion. Imposition of communism provoked resistance not only in wider society, but also within the regime. It came in many forms: factional opposition to Khalq from Parcham and internal conflict within Khalq; ethnic resistance to Pashtun domination over non-Pashtun groups; ideological opposition to communism from religious groups, and so on. As conflict escalated between these contradictions, fear and chaos began to take hold and the outcome was the Soviet invasion of Afghanistan in December 1979.

Afghanistan's vulnerability to external forces has been a fact of life throughout the long history of great power rivalries in the region. Afghanistan had been part of the Cold War theater in the Middle East and South Asia, but America had lost the race for influence in the country by the early 1970s. The 1978 Communist coup and the Soviet invasion a year later had a deep effect on Afghan society. These events created their opposite in the form of greater intervention by other powers.

American secret aid to the anticommunist Afghan opposition had started several months before the Soviet invasion. America's reaction to the invasion was fierce. It attracted other regional powers to the United States: Pakistan, China, Saudi Arabia, Egypt, and smaller Gulf states. American and Pakistani intelligence became the main players in prosecuting the war against Soviet occupation, but Iran was also involved. Ronald Reagan's arrival in the White House in January 1981 stiffened the opposition's resolve, and as the number of Soviet occupation troops in Afghanistan rose, the CIA-ISI war machine poured vast amounts of weaponry and money into the conflict.

More anticommunist fighters were recruited, trained, and sent to fight the Soviets. Religious indoctrination whipped up Islamic radicalism, and a new generation of zealots was created in refugee camps in Pakistan and Iran. Mujahideen fighters were relentless in their attacks: they planned and executed ambushes and assassinations, sabotaged bridges, roads, and power plants; and intercepted supply convoys. Heavy rocket bombardment of civilian areas caused panic in Soviet-held parts of Afghanistan, causing shortages of essential supplies. Kabul and other towns became more and more dependent on handouts and many residents became increasingly desperate. The country underwent further fragmentation as the culture of terror was reinforced.

By the end of the U.S. proxy war against the Soviets, more than a million people had been killed and one-third of the entire Afghan population was forced to leave the country. Inside the country, life under fear had become the norm in government-held areas, as well as rebel territory. Afghanistan was a country devastated by war, its institutions frail, millions of people destitute and hardened to violence. Guns were plentiful and the mind-set of Afghans had become geared toward violence.

A state of flux existed in Afghanistan after the Soviet military retreat, with Moscow's client regime trying to forge new alliances in attempts to end the conflict and to gain acceptability abroad. These attempts were unsuccessful, and as a result, the Kabul regime of President Najibullah became even more dependent on Soviet help. By the end of 1991, the Soviet Union had collapsed and the Afghan regime was helpless. The consequent decline in American interest in Afghanistan created a void that was filled by other forces.

Loss of aid from Moscow sparked rebellions in Najibullah's army and spread to the Afghan capital. Defections by senior military officers to the Tajik guerrilla commander, Ahmad Shah Masood, in the north made officers in the capital fearful about whether the regime could survive. These events triggered the collapse of Afghanistan's military structure, and various disaffected soldiers began to make their own deals with resistance groups. Within a few weeks, the regime had disintegrated.

The internal conflict in the Najibullah regime produced contradictions that caused deep splits in Afghan society along ethnic and tribal lines. While nationalism of an ethnic character emerged as the overriding force and Islam replaced communism, Islamic groups were more divided than the regime they had defeated. Two more years of civil war followed, prompted by a total institutional collapse. It was in this climate of anarchy that the Taliban rose in the early 1990s as Afghanistan's new dominant force. Helped by Pakistan and Saudi Arabia, the Taliban had seized control of most of Afghanistan, including Kabul, by 1996.

Hence the cycle of violence that began with the 1978 Communist coup had come full circle. The culture of terror had matured and become pervasive in Afghan society. Like Communist rule in its early years, the Taliban regime was based on a system of institutionalized punishment, but the degree of coercion used by the Taliban was extreme. Severe penalties were imposed for conduct normally taken for granted, such as dressing, girls going to school, women going to work, and practicing one's faith. Public beatings of men and women happened every day for conduct deemed to be in violation of the Taliban Islamic code. Summary trials leading to amputations and death by stoning and firing squad were used to control Afghan society.

The manner of their rise from the ruins of civil war made the Taliban look like a homegrown phenomenon. In fact, it was much more than a consequence of the anarchy after the collapse of communism. We know that the Taliban were encouraged and sustained by Sunni religious establishments of Pakistan and Saudi Arabia. In fact, the phenomenon was a product of wider external and internal forces drawn to Afghanistan.

Internally, the Taliban represented an extreme form of Pashtun nationalism in Afghan society, but their harsh treatment of women and other minorities displayed influence of Pakistan's fundamentalist ideology of Jamiat-i-Islami. The anticapitalist ideologies of the Muslim Brotherhood and its offshoot, the Islamic Jihad, had been somewhat dormant during the war against the Soviets, but once that war was over, violent opposition to America and what it stood for came to the fore.

Before al Qaeda turned its fury on the West, radical Islam in the Middle East had undergone its own internal conflict and a new brand of Islam had emerged—fierce and durable, with many of its fighters willing and ready to die in suicide bombing attacks. Afghanistan under the Taliban regime became a sanctuary for al Qaeda, not only because their ideologies were intensely anti-Western, but also because their survival depended on each other.

So the dialectic that began in April 1978 with a Communist coup by young military officers in Afghanistan finally created a culture that attracted radical Islamists from distant countries to train and to plan acts of violence against their enemy. The most dramatic of these attacks were on the World Trade Center in New York and the Pentagon in Washington on September 11, 2001. These events defined the U.S. response to the new threat, and a decade after victory over communism, America decided to intervene in Afghanistan again. The aim this time was to overthrow the Taliban and establish a friendly government in Kabul.

The U.S.-led invasion of Afghanistan in 2001 was the beginning of an experiment to create a Western-style democracy, inclusive of different ethnic groups and resilient enough to counter the possibility of Afghanistan becoming a sanctuary for terrorists again. However, defeating the Taliban regime was the easy part in President George W. Bush's war on terror. Subsequent events lay bare the difficulties in prosecuting an open-ended war against an invisible enemy.

Overwhelming military force is not enough to defeat terrorism as shown by the resurgent power of the Taliban and al Qaeda in Afghanistan. In the next stage of the dialectical process, they reinforced their control over large parts of southern Afghanistan and Pakistan's frontier. The U.S.-led invasion ousted the Taliban regime in Kabul at the end of 2001. However, it is a myth that the Taliban ever lost their roots in Afghanistan and Pakistan, and al Qaeda the sanctuary it had long possessed. In Iraq the abrupt dissolution of the state structure in early 2003 created an environment in which terror under Saddam Hussein was replaced by new terror caused by violence far greater in scale. The dismantling of the state institutions left a void that other external and homegrown armed groups moved in to fill.

Effective counterterrorism efforts require an understanding of the culture, society, and local conditions, together with an institutional arrangement that enjoys broad consent in society. Unless effective institutions are there to provide citizens with security and ways of earning their livelihood, other players will appear and impose rules far more arbitrary and inconsistent. In the absence of a coordinated strategy, the thought of victory in the war against terror is a triumph of hope over reality.

Parallels can be seen in Palestine, Lebanon, and other places where social and institutional frailties, combined with outside intervention, fuel a dialectic of violence that, in time, becomes part of the culture. Violent players and their victims become used to coercion, their thinking and behavior driven by the perceived justification for, or expectation of, force to resolve matters. Players and victims may be different in each place. What triggers a cycle of violence is unique and where events will lead may be unknown. Still, where the appropriate agents are present, a violent dialectic and terror are close companions.

AFTERWORD

The last two decades of the twentieth century were a period of exceptional savagery in Afghanistan. First came the violence of the Soviet occupation and the U.S.-Soviet proxy war in the 1980s. What followed was the West's neglect of Afghanistan and the outbreak of a "war of all against all" following the collapse of communism in the Soviet Union and Afghanistan. The culture of violence to which outside powers great and small, as well as Afghan factions, had contributed became deeply ingrained in Afghan society. Violent human behavior was revealed in more frightening ways than ever.

The first decade of our new century opened with the horror of September 11, 2001, and ended reminiscent of the Soviet decade in Afghanistan and the American military era in Vietnam before the 1975 withdrawal. In late 2009, the total number of American and allied troops in Afghanistan approached 110,000—reminding one of the Soviet presence in Afghanistan twenty years earlier. It was the bloodiest year for the U.S.-led occupation forces. After well-orchestrated leaks, President Obama's senior general, Stanley McChrystal, openly demanded 40,000 extra soldiers, warning his commander in chief that without the additional troops, the mission would fail.[1]

In his August 2009 report, General McChrystal presented the Obama administration with a list of new objectives for Afghanistan. Among them were goals to: "discredit and diminish insurgent and their extremist allies' capability"; "promote the capability of, and confidence in, the Afghan National Security Forces"; and "maintain and increase international and public support for ISAF goal and policies" in Afghanistan.[2] Those keeping a keen eye on the

Afghan War might ask what the international occupation force had been doing there for the preceding eight years and what was new about McChrystal's objectives? His assessment further stated that ISAF was not adequately executing the basics of counterinsurgency warfare.[3] Therefore, in his view more military (with civilian) resources must be committed.

General McChrystal's remedy bore a striking resemblance to a letter written by Soviet colonel K. Tsagolov to his defense minister Dmitry Yazov in August 1987.[4] At a time when Soviet leader Mikhail Gorbachev had decided to withdraw from Afghanistan after a failed invasion and occupation, Colonel Tsagolov, using Marxist jargon, wrote, "A deep political crisis of the Afghan society is obvious. . . . The coalition of social forces continues to change in favor of the counter-revolution. The state regime is not capable of stopping the counter-revolution on its own."[5]

Colonel Tsagolov criticized the policy of national reconciliation being pursued by then–president Najibullah at the Kremlin's behest. Tsagolov observed that "our efforts over the last eight years have not led to the expected results"; national reconciliation "has not led to a breakthrough in the military-political situation, and will not lead to one." The "counter-revolution will not be satisfied with partial power today, knowing that tomorrow it can have it all." Colonel Tsagolov's recommended solution was to "help the progressive political forces" to preserve the "democratic content" of the country and to "ensure future development of social processes" in Afghanistan "in the direction of our long-term interests."[6]

Two decades later in 2009, and with the support for America's war in Afghanistan diminishing in the United States and Europe, President Obama hesitated and his national security team was divided over what to do. Zbigniew Brzezinski, the national security adviser to President Carter and the architect of the American policy that gave the Soviets their "Vietnam" in Afghanistan, cautioned the leaders. He said, "We are running the risk of replicating —obviously unintentionally—the fate of the Soviets."[7] He also backed the idea of a new international conference and development strategy with the help of the military to ensure that America's European allies did not leave Washington in the lurch.

How did the war in Afghanistan become so brutal, betraying the first impressions of an easy victory in overthrowing the Taliban regime? The answer must be in the particular character of the Afghan conflict after the American-led invasion. Unlike the Cold War of bygone years, the new confrontation between the United States and its enemies was not a match of equals, both aware of the certainty of mutual destruction in the event of an all-out war. When combatants are not equals and mutual destruction is not certain, the dominant side becomes vulnerable in other ways. Overwhelming power often leads to impudence and disregard for law, reason, and morality. With too much power comes the belief that it is easy to crush the enemy and the gates to atrocities open on all sides.

From the outset, one side in the new Afghan conflict possessed overwhelming power and acquired impudence. But the underdog had strength in numbers, opposition fighters prepared to make the ultimate sacrifice. Fear lost its deterrent quality; death was no more an unwelcome prospect, life was to be endured, not enjoyed; and the rationality in martyrdom began to replace the rationality in survival. Human beings are at their most dangerous when they no longer fear death. Such state of mind begins to explain the conduct of the suicide bomber.

Along with its allies, the United States became consumed in the fortification of the Western world following September 11, 2001. One fundamental aspect of its militaristic approach was the remaking of West Asia, resulting in the Iraq War and aggressive intent elsewhere in the region. Amid ceaseless media coverage of real or perceived threats to the West, the proliferation of the culture of violence throughout Pakistan and in Iran, India, and other distant places received much less attention. In October 2009, a suicide bomb attack in Iran's Sistan-Baluchistan province near the Pakistani border killed dozens of people. A Sunni resistance group, Jundullah, admitted responsibility for the attack, in which tribal leaders and senior commanders of the Iranian Revolutionary Guards were assassinated. Jundullah had been involved in a long-running insurgency in Sistan-Baluchistan, a Sunni-majority province in Shi'a-dominated Iran. Some experts believed the group was linked to al Qaeda and the Taliban.[8]

The Council for Foreign Relations, a New York–based research institution, acknowledged the existence of local terrorist groups in the Indian section of the disputed region of Kashmir. However, CFR pointed out that "most of the recent terrorism has been conducted by Islamist outsiders who seek to claim Kashmir for Pakistan."[9] According to the organization, many militants involved in attacks across the border in India received training in the same madrasahs where Taliban and al Qaeda fighters had studied since the 1980s. Some received training in Afghanistan when the Taliban ruled the country. Many represented an indigenous phenomenon in Pakistani society.

Militant bases multiplied from the Afghan-Pakistan frontier to locations throughout Pakistan. Under American pressure, Pakistan's armed forces launched operations against militant hideouts. The Taliban–al Qaeda alliance retaliated with increasing frequency against military and civilian targets across Pakistan.[10] These attacks raised questions about whether militants might have infiltrated the nuclear-armed military of Pakistan. How had things reach this point?

EXPLAINING THE CONTEXT

With the advent of the 1990s, the rationale for arming Islamist militants to fight the Soviet Union had lost its effect. The Cold War was over, the Soviet state had disintegrated, and the Najibullah regime in Kabul had collapsed by 1992. By the mid-1990s, the phenomenon of terrorism had mutated into something far more serious with the emergence of the Pakistan-backed Taliban. After years of active intervention, the West had moved on to other priorities, leaving the Afghan chaos to its regional allies, Pakistan and Saudi Arabia.

True, there was not another September 11, 2001–type attack on mainland America during the administration of George W. Bush. But this "success" must be examined in its context. Historically, attacks by external forces on the United States are rare. Even so, the Oklahoma City bombing of 1995 and activities of anti-state private militias pointed to a domestic phenomenon of terrorism in parts of America. Beyond U.S. shores, the terrorist bombings in Madrid in 2004, and those in Bali and London a year later, meant that the West continued to be targeted in Europe and elsewhere and that thousands of American and allied soldiers continued to be wounded or die in America's foreign wars.

In Pakistan, the conversion of local Taliban supporters to an indigenous umbrella group under the name Tehrik-i-Taliban Pakistan was the most significant development responsible for the proliferation of violence.[11] It began between 2002 and 2004 when Pakistan's armed forces were busy capturing "foreigners" to hand over to the Americans for money and to carry out military operations in areas linked to al Qaeda. Many of these operations were against groups in Baluchistan and North-West Frontier Province not allied to al Qaeda or the Taliban. These groups opposed Pakistan's central government demanding more autonomy and a greater share of income from local resources, principally Baluchistan's gold, copper and coal mines, and vast reserves of natural gas. Washington compensated the military regime of Gen. Pervez Musharraf for prosecuting so-called antiterrorism operations inside Pakistan. Missile attacks by unmanned aircraft operated by the United States from June 2004 killed some suspected militants but also killed many innocent civilians in tribal areas. These attacks raised questions about Pakistani sovereignty and caused anger in the population.[12]

The anti-American sentiment had devastating consequences. Local militant groups in Pakistan started to join ranks to create a separate movement instead of merging into the Afghan Taliban. They developed their own distinct identity, sometimes launching attacks, other times cutting deals with the authorities. According to the Council for Foreign Relations, the Taliban of Pakistan had become an effective fighting force between 30,000 and 35,000 strong by 2008.[13]

They would network among themselves, as well as with the Afghan Taliban and al Qaeda when it suited them. Their aim was to oppose Pakistan's military and civilian government and to confront the U.S.-led forces in the region. The Pakistani Taliban developed close affiliations with Jamiat Ulema-i-Islam, a religious party that insisted on the strict enforcement of Islamic law.

The leadership of Pakistan based Kashmiri militants had connections with al Qaeda since before the advent of the Pakistani Taliban following the U.S. invasion of Afghanistan in 2001. Farooq Kashmiri Khalil, the leader of the Harakat-ul-Mujahideen group, was a signatory to al Qaeda's 1998 declaration of war. Quoting American and Indian officials, the Council for Foreign Relations stated that Maulana Masood Azhar, leader of the Jaish-e-Muhammad group founded in 2000, was suspected of receiving money from al Qaeda. And yet another group, Lashkar-e-Taiba, had been active in the region since 1993.

In December 2001, barely three months after September 11, the Indian Parliament was attacked. The Indian authorities blamed Lashkar-e-Taiba and Jaish-e-Muhammad for the attack, in which more than a dozen people were killed, including all five militants. A series of other attacks followed, the most audacious of which was the three-day carnage in Mumbai, India's main commercial city, in November 2008. Some 170 people of many nationalities died and over 300 were wounded in a coordinated orgy of violence; all but one of the ten gunmen were killed. Evidence was provided by experts and media reports in the United States, India, even Pakistan, that the attackers came from Pakistan and were said to have belonged to Lashkar-e-Taiba. After vehement denials of

Pakistani involvement in the Mumbai attack, Islamabad, against mounting evidence, admitted that the lone surviving gunman, twenty-one-year-old Ajmal Kasab, was a Pakistani citizen.[14]

THE DYNAMIC OF A CULTURE OF VIOLENCE

The monster of terrorism in Pakistan has grown as a result of policies followed over decades. At the heart of these policies has been a tendency to pursue high-risk strategies while existing in a state of denial. When the Pakistani state was established in 1947, the idea of a separate nation for the peoples of the Muslim faith of British India was not universally supported. Pashtuns under the leadership of Abdul Ghaffar Khan opposed partition.

For years after the establishment of Pakistan, the Pashtuns and other minorities continued to challenge the domination of the most populous province, Punjab, at the center. The response of Pakistan's ruling military-political elite has been suppression of the country's minorities. This was achieved via two avenues: by adopting coercive military methods and by playing the "Islamic card" in national politics. When minorities made demands for greater autonomy, they were portrayed as working against Islam and encountered military force.

The fear of internal collapse is one of the main forces that determines the conduct of the military-political elite of Pakistan. The other is the perceived fear of India. Internal suppression at the expense of the rule of law and a national accord fuels resistance. And violence is diverted toward external threats—India on one side, Afghanistan on the other. For decades, this has been the essence of the high-risk strategy of Pakistan's military-political establishment, especially its military intelligence organ, Inter-Services Intelligence Directorate.

The crisis for Pakistan thus became the crisis for the region and beyond. Islamic fundamentalists encouraged by the military ruler, General Zia, to fight America's war in Afghanistan in the 1980s were devastatingly effective in defeating the Soviet Union and its client regime in Kabul. But the phenomenon undermined the rule of law and inflamed religious and sectarian violence. It had a corrosive effect on national institutions, making Pakistan a failing state.

The election in November 2008 of Barack Obama, the first African American in history to become America's president, was a revolutionary event. A man of undoubted intellect, Obama was victorious despite enormous odds and thanks to a strong desire among Americans for change. A leader who emerges in such conditions faces opposing demands. Like the end of the Vietnam era in the mid-1970s and the Cold War in the 1990s, the world's pre-eminent power looked for peace in order to recover and rebuild. But the United States could not beat a hasty retreat. The exit strategy had to be structured to end the war gradually while adopting a more intensive diplomatic policy. The task proved to be a greater challenge in practice than in theory, as events after Obama's inauguration in January 2009 would demonstrate.

The Taliban in Afghanistan and Pakistan are a varied group, some easier to bring on board than others. However, if too many are left out, there will be little peace. The political manipulation and opportunism that have infected Pakistan must be rooted out. Peace and stability require the United States to engage with Pakistan's political and military leaders, to pursue tough diplomatic policies, and to exercise close scrutiny and control over corrupt behaviors. It is a battle of a different kind.

The people of Pakistan have lived through long spells of military rule and interludes of democratically elected civilian governments that have collapsed before fulfilling their promises. Each time the country has been under direct military rule, this repression has resulted in widespread discontent among its citizens. In the end, popular revolt has forced the military to recede into the background and allow a civilian government to come to the fore. Before long, the civilian government, too, has become discredited by its own corruption and abuses of power. Chaos has inevitably ensued and Pakistan's armed forces have returned to center stage. This cycle must end if the region is to experience any long-term peace and security. Within the first hundred days of the Obama presidency, which began on January 20, 2009, he was drawn into Pakistan and Afghanistan because of escalating violence. By the end of 2009, while Washington struggled to find a way forward, the cycle had only worsened.

The Afghanistan crisis has deteriorated in the absence of a credible strategy. Its roots go back to the beginning of the Cold War. Years after the 2001 U.S.-led invasion, the loss of more innocent lives than those of terrorists plainly demonstrates the futility of counterinsurgency. In order to succeed, a strategy must be not about destruction, but about rebuilding. It should attract support rather than inspire alienation. Its foundations must be based on a thorough understanding of the cultures and sensitivities of others and on reasons of human pride. Only through such understanding is it possible to gather reliable intelligence and to work on stabilization. That military occupation, coercion, and the forced submission of the populous to external value systems and lifestyles are all methods that provoke conflict is a historical fact. A superpower that employs pilotless drones and high altitude bombers to control people will unavoidably struggle to gain the confidence of the population at large.

Hints like these offer a contribution toward creating a credible strategy for dealing with the Afghanistan–Pakistan crisis. At its heart are the failures of institutions and processes (to varying degrees) in both countries. The origins of this crisis are rooted in self-serving corruption and internal conflict on one hand, and self-seeking outside intervention on the other. The consequences are fragmented societies and violence that threatens peace far beyond their own borders. The scale of fraud in the 2009 Afghan election, which forced President Hamid Karzai into a second round of voting, was an example of the mismatch between the ambitious goals set by the occupying powers and the meager commitments made from the outset. Resistance to occupation seemed to have become irreversible by then.

Karzai's only opponent in the second round, Abdullah Abdullah, made a number of demands, including the dismissal of the head of Afghanistan's Election Commission, to ensure the fraud was not repeated. Karzai's government refused and Abdullah announced his boycott less than a week before the second round was to take place.[15] The Election Commission cancelled the second round of voting amid mounting concern from the occupying powers that more of their soldiers would die in a fruitless election with a single candidate left. The legitimacy of the entire election process and Karzai's presidency lay in tatters.

Was Afghanistan approaching the endgame insofar as America's experiment in imposing democracy was concerned—just as the attempt of Sovietization of the country in the decade of Soviet occupation in the 1980s? The omens were not good. Eight years after the Taliban regime had been overthrown, corruption and mismanagement had infected the U.S.-installed system in Afghanistan; poppy fields and heroin financed the insurgency. It would be far better—and cheaper—for the United States to buy the entire poppy crop from Afghan peasants every year and therefore deprive the insurgency of money while Afghanistan is rebuilt. In Pakistan, the military's stubborn domination continued to distort the equilibrium in national life.

In order to guide the international efforts, the choices that must be made are clear: persuade Pakistan's military to relax its hold, allow and encourage the proper development of democratic institutions and processes, fight corruption, and encourage the rule of law. Additionally, to save both Afghanistan and Pakistan from future generations of militants build effective systems of education that provide modern schools instead of religious madrasahs. The United States has a responsibility to play a vital role in all this at a time when the region's need for stability has never been greater. But it may only be possible if Washington can accept the idea that a coercive enterprise to remake a traditional society rarely succeeds.

However, events in 2010 took the opposite and a chaotic turn. With President Obama bowing to General McChrystal's plan, the number of foreign troops rose to nearly 140,000 by the middle of the year. Taliban attacks on the occupation forces increased, resulting in more casualties. Then General McChrystal and his team were quoted making disparaging comments about the Obama administration in a *Rolling Stone* article in June 2010.[16] Obama dismissed McChrystal and replaced him with Gen. David Petraeus.[17]

Soon after, the release of more than ninety thousand secret files on actions taken by the U.S.-led occupation forces in Afghanistan depicted a frightening pattern of extrajudicial killings, kidnappings, and torture of suspected insurgents and civilians, as well as manipulation and misrepresentation of news.[18] The disclosures turned the focus back on the conduct of the war, including in the first year of the Obama administration.

I close here remembering something the Russian philosopher and writer Leo Tolstoy once said: "In all history there is no war which was not hatched by the governments, the governments alone, independent of the interests of the people, to whom war is always pernicious even when successful."

APPENDIX A
Chronology (Summary)

WAR TO OVERTHROW THE TALIBAN IN AFGHANISTAN, 2001

September 11   Hijackers crash planes into the World Trade Center in New York and the Pentagon in Washington. A fourth plane crashes into a field near Shanksville in Pennsylvania after some passengers and members of the crew attempt to retake control from the hijackers; all aboard killed.

October 7   American and British forces attack Afghanistan.

October 9   Al Qaeda issues a statement calling for a holy war.

October 10   FBI releases a list of twenty-two most wanted terrorists.

October 19   Pakistan allows U.S.–coalition forces to use its air base.

November 4   Egypt says the battle is between bin Laden and the world.

November 7   The Italian Parliament votes to deploy troops.

November 9   Northern Alliance forces capture Mazar-i-Sharif.

November 13   Northern Alliance forces capture Afghanistan's capital, Kabul, as Taliban forces retreat.

November 16   France sends troops to Uzbekistan to support U.S.-led coalition.

November 18   Television station in Kabul reopens after five years.

November 25   Anti-Taliban forces seize airfield at Qandahar, where U.S. troops set up a base.

December 3   At the UN talks in Bonn, Afghan groups agree to establish a twenty-nine-member interim ruling council to govern Afghanistan under Pashtun leader Hamid Karzai.

| December 18 | U.S. secretary of defense Donald Rumsfeld tells a North Atlantic Treaty Organization (NATO) meeting that the war on terrorism must be extended beyond Afghanistan. |
| December 22 | New interim government under Hamid Karzai takes office in Afghanistan. |

THE AFGHAN CONFLICT (1978–2001)

1973	Gen. Mohammad Daud Khan overthrows King Zahir Shah and declares a republic.
1978	President Daud and his family are assassinated in a military coup known as the Saur Revolution. The PDPA is installed in power with Nur Mohammad Taraki as the new leader.
1979	Taraki is murdered in September by forces supporting Hafizullah Amin, who becomes the new leader. In December, Soviet forces invade Afghanistan and install Babrak Karmal. Amin is killed.
1980	Refugees pour into Pakistan and Iran as the Afghan army disintegrates. Opposition groups launch guerrilla war against Communist rulers in Kabul.
1985	Mikhail Gorbachev takes over Soviet leadership, calls Afghanistan a bleeding wound.
1986	Najibullah replaces Karmal. With Soviet encouragement, he talks about reconciliation.
1988	UN-sponsored Geneva accords signed, paving the way for a Soviet military withdrawal from Afghanistan. Osama bin Laden and his associates form al Qaeda.
1989	Soviet military completely withdraws.
1990	Defense Minister Shah Nawaz Tanai leads an attempted coup in Kabul but fails. Tanai escapes to Pakistan.
1991	The Soviet Union is dissolved. Aid to the Najibullah government stops.
1992	When government collapses, Najibullah takes refuge in a UN building in Kabul. Mujahideen take power, but bitter factional fighting breaks out. Almost fifty thousand people are killed in Kabul between 1992 and 1994.

Pakistan loses patience with Gulbuddin Hikmatyar and begins to support new fundamentalist Islamic group, the Taliban.

1993   The World Trade Center is attacked. The United States accuses Osama bin Laden.

1994   Taliban forces rapidly conquer Afghan provinces. Government forces retreat.

1996   Taliban forces capture the capital, Kabul. Execute former president Najibullah. Impose draconian Islamic laws.

2001   Taliban flee Kabul and their southern stronghold, Qandahar, as opposition forces supported by the U.S.-led coalition take over. Osama bin Laden and the Taliban leader, Mullah Omar, escape.

APPENDIX B

U.S. and Soviet/Russian Leaders (1978–2009)

UNITED STATES

Jimmy Carter	1977–1981
Ronald Reagan	1981–1989
George H. W. Bush	1989–1993
Bill Clinton	1993–2001
George W. Bush	2001–2009
Barack Obama	2009 (assumed presidency)

SOVIET UNION

Leonid Brezhnev	1964–1982
Yuri Andropov	1982–1984
Konstantin Chernenko	1984–1985
Mikhail Gorbachev	1985–1991

RUSSIA

Boris Yeltsin	1991–1999
Vladimir Putin	1999–2008 (acting president December 31, 1999; inaugurated president May 7, 2000)
Dmitry Medvedev	2008 (assumed presidency)

APPENDIX C

Afghan Opposition Parties in the Cold War

PAKISTAN-BASED SUNNI MUSLIM PARTIES
(IN A LOOSE ALLIANCE OF SEVEN)

FUNDAMENTALIST/ISLAMIST	LEADER
Hizb-i-Islami (Islamic Party)	Gulbuddin Hikmatyar
Hizb-i-Islami	Yunis Khalis
Jamiat-i-Islami (Islamic Society)	Burhanuddin Rabbani
Ittihad-i-Islami (Islamic Union for the Liberation of Afghanistan)	Abdul Rabb Rasul Sayyaf

CONSERVATIVE/NATIONALIST	LEADER
Mahaz-i-Melli (National Islamic Front of Afghanistan)	Pir Ahmad Gailani
Jabha-i-Nejat-i-Melli (National Liberation Front of Afghanistan)	Sibghatullah Mujaddidi
Harakat-i-Inqilab-i-Islami (Islamic Revolution Movement)	Mohammad Nabi Mohammadi

Eight Shi'a Parties Based in Iran

MAJOR GUERRILLA FORCES	LEADER
Harakat–i–Islami (Islamic Movement)	Ayatollah Mohsini
Sazman–i–Nasr (Organization for Victory)	Sheikh Abdul Karim Khalili
Pasdaran–i–Jihad–i–Islami (Guardians of Islamic Holy War)	Regional leaders inside Afghanistan

SMALLER PARTIES WITH REGIONAL FOLLOWING	REGION
Nahzat–i–Islami (Islamic Movement)	Hazarajat
Dawat–i Ittihad–i Islami (Invitation to Islamic Unity)	Ghazni Province
Niru–i–Islami (Islamic Force)	Jowsjan
Hizb–i–Islami Rad–i–Afghanistan (Party of Islamic Thunder)	
Jebh–i–Mutahed (United Front)	Bamiyan, formed in 1988

APPENDIX D

Osama Bin Laden's Statement, October 7, 2001[1]

I bear witness that there is no God but Allah and that Mohammed is his messenger. There is America, hit by God in one of its softest spots. Its greatest buildings were destroyed, thank God for that.

There is America, full of fear from its north to its south, from its west to its east. Thank God for that. What America is tasting now is something insignificant compared to what we have tasted for scores of years. Our nation (the Islamic world) has been tasting this humiliation and this degradation for more than 80 years. Its sons are killed, its blood is shed, its sanctuaries are attacked, and no one hears and no one heeds.

When God blessed one of the groups of Islam, vanguards of Islam, they destroyed America. I pray to God to elevate their status and bless them. Millions of innocent children are being killed as I speak. They are being killed in Iraq without committing any sins and we don't hear condemnation or a fatwa from the rulers.

In these days, Israeli tanks infest Palestine—in Jenin, Ramallah, Rafah, Beit Jalla, and other places in the land of Islam, and we don't hear anyone raising his voice or moving a limb. When the sword comes down (on America), after 80 years, hypocrisy rears its ugly head. They deplore and they lament for those killers, who have abused the blood, honour, and sanctuaries of Muslims. The

1 Statement broadcast in Arabic on Al-Jazeera television. Bin Laden expresses delight at the attacks on America on September 11, 2001. See translated text provided by the Associated Press, *The Guardian,* October 7, 2001, available on http://www.guardian.co.uk/world/2001/oct/07/afghanistan.terrorism15.

least that can be said about those people is that they are debauched. They have followed injustice. They supported the butcher over the victim, the oppressor over the innocent child. May God show them His wrath and give them what they deserve.

I say that the situation is clear and obvious. After this event, after the senior officials have spoken in America, starting with the head of infidels worldwide, Bush, and those with him. They have come out in force with their men and have turned even the countries that belong to Islam to this treachery, and they want to wag their tail at God, to fight Islam, to suppress people in the name of terrorism.

When people at the ends of the earth, Japan, were killed by their hundreds of thousands, young and old, it was not considered a war crime, it is something that has justification. Millions of children in Iraq is something that has justification. But when they lose dozens of people in Nairobi and Dar-es-Salaam (capitals of Kenya and Tanzania, where US embassies were bombed in 1998), Iraq was struck and Afghanistan was struck. Hypocrisy stood in force behind the head of infidels worldwide, behind the cowards of this age, America and those who are with it.

These events have divided the whole world into two sides. The side of believers and the side of infidels, may God keep you away from them. Every Muslim has to rush to make his religion victorious. The winds of faith have come. The winds of change have come to eradicate oppression from the island of Muhammad, peace be upon him.

To America, I say only a few words to it and its people. I swear by God, who has elevated the skies without pillars, neither America nor the people who live in it will dream of security before we live it in Palestine, and not before all the infidel armies leave the land of Muhammad, peace be upon him. God is great, may pride be with Islam. May peace and God's mercy be upon you.

APPENDIX E

September 11, 2001, Hijackers[1]

AMERICAN AIRLINES FLIGHT 11, BOSTON–LOS ANGELES

(Crashed into the North Tower, World Trade Center)

NAME	NATIONALITY	AGE
Mohammad Atta (pilot)	Egyptian	33
Abd al-Aziz al-Umari	Saudi	22
Ustam bin al-Mohammad al-Saqami	Saudi	25
Wail Mohammad al-Shehri	Saudi	28
Walid Mohammad al-Shehri	Saudi	22

UNITED AIRLINES FLIGHT 175, BOSTON–LOS ANGELES

(Crashed into the South Tower, World Trade Center)

NAME	NATIONALITY	AGE
Marwan Yusuf al-Shehhi (pilot)	UAE[2]	23
Ahmad Saleh Said al-Ghamdi	Saudi	22
Fayez Rashid Banihammad	UAE	24
Hamzah Saleh al-Ghamdi	Saudi	20
Mahanid Mohammad al-Shehri	Saudi	22

---

1 See "DCI Testimony Before the Joint Inquiry into Terrorist Attacks Against the United States," June 18, 2002, CIA document "11 September 2001 Hijackers."
2 United Arab Emirates.

AMERICAN AIRLINES FLIGHT 77, WASHINGTON, D.C.–LOS ANGELES

(Crashed into the Pentagon)

NAME	NATIONALITY	AGE
Hani Saleh Hasan Hanjur (pilot)	Saudi	29
Khalid bin Mohammad al-Mihdhar	Saudi	26
Majid Muqid bin Ghanim	Saudi	24
Nawaf bin Mohammad al-Hazmi	Saudi	25
Salim Mohammad al-Hazmi	Saudi	20

UNITED AIRLINES FLIGHT 93, NEWARK, NEW JERSEY–SAN FRANCISCO

(Crashed in the Pennsylvania countryside)

NAME	NATIONALITY	AGE
Ziad Samir Jarrah (pilot)	Lebanese	26
Ahmad Abdullah al-Nami	Saudi	23
Ahmad Ibrahim al-Haznawi	Saudi	20
Said Abdullah al-Ghamdi	Saudi	21

APPENDIX F
Bibliographic Essay

I have consulted a vast amount of primary and secondary sources in writing this book. Its first distinctive feature deals with the definitional inconsistencies that have made the word "terrorism" so contested. The definition of terrorism arrived at in this volume does not differentiate between state and non-state players or among ideological camps. The book's second distinctive feature is its focus on the concept of culture as it is used to explain how terrorism grows.

Martha Crenshaw's academic work on the rational choice theory, Jerrold Post on the psychological approach, and Jeffrey Ian Ross on the structural analysis of terrorism have been helpful in discussing the three main themes around which previous studies are organized. Their work is complemented by those of other authors who have alluded to one or more of the three approaches. Among these writers are Jack Gibb, E. V. Walter, Lawrence Davidson, Paul Wilkinson, David Lake, Mark Harrison, Clark McCauley, Lawrence Freedman, Gary Gambill, Leonard Weinberg, Edward Muller and Erich Weede, Magnus Ranstorp, and Ted Gurr.

For an overview of the concept of culture, I began with E. B. Tylor's definition contained in Robert Murphy's *Culture and Social Anthropology: An Overview.* Resources of the University of Manitoba in Canada, the University of North Carolina, and A & M University in Texas were also useful to explain the meaning of the term and its features. Establishing these elements was essential in developing the second stage of the concept and understanding how, in a culture, violence replicates itself, creates a climate of fear, and becomes part of human behavior and lifestyle.

Aspects of Islamic militancy and its internal conditions that led to the birth of al Qaeda are drawn from works by Fred Halliday—*Two Hours that Shook the World: September 11, 2001: Causes and Consequences*, "The Arc of Crisis and the New Cold War," and "The Communist Regime in Afghanistan"—and Ruth Wedgwood, especially "Al Qaeda, Terrorism and Military Commissions." The sources on HAMAS, particularly its manifesto and covenant, are from the Middle East Consultations and Research Analysis group and the Federation of American Scientists.

As well as news sources and academic works, I consulted primary source material from U.S. government documents found in the National Security Archive in Washington, D.C., and various presidential archives to build the survey of the world in 1978. John Dumbrell's *American Foreign Policy: From Carter to Clinton* was particularly helpful to gain a broad understanding of U.S. policy between 1976 and 2000. The discussion on the Cold War and Afghanistan begins with citations from "U.S.-Soviet Relations and the Turn Towards Confrontation," a collection in the Cold War International History Project (CWIHP) of the Woodrow Wilson International Center for Scholars in Washington and from the Congressional Research Service.

This book is distinctive in another respect. It sheds light on new material, contained in two document collections and published for the first time by the CWIHP after the events of September 11, 2001, that have been vital in discussing the Soviets' role in Afghanistan. The first is *The Soviet Invasion of Afghanistan*, which includes material obtained from the Russian and East German archives and released in November 2001. It reveals the inside story of Soviet thinking and decision-making from the first Communist coup in Afghanistan in 1978 through the Soviet invasion a year later, and the subsequent proxy war with the United States in the 1980s to the Soviets' military retreat in 1989. The collection also contains minutes of many important Politburo meetings and memorandums and reports by Soviet leaders. This evidence brings to light how decisions were made in the Kremlin in the 1970s and 1980s.

The other manuscript made available by the CWIHP is *The KGB in Afghanistan* written by KGB archivist Vasili Mitrokhin, who defected to Britain with a large volume of handwritten notes from the files of the Soviet secret service. This manuscript, published in February 2002, reveals the length and depth of the KGB's involvement in Afghanistan during the Cold War. The two collections together demonstrate that the KGB's role in Afghanistan was far more adventurist than that of other Soviet state agencies. Mitrokhin also provides an authoritative inside account of events surrounding the Soviet's invasion of Afghanistan, President Hafizullah Amin's assassination, and Babrak Karmal's installation as the head of the Soviet client regime in Kabul in December 1979.

For the American proxy war against the Soviet Union in the 1980s and the rise of the Taliban regime in the early 1990s, the National Security Archive has been particularly useful. Available in March 1991, *Afghanistan: The Making of U.S. Policy, 1973–1990*, contains declassified documents that have been helpful in this book's sections that deal with the U.S. proxy war, the role of the CIA, and Pakistan, Egypt, and China as America's allies. The documents also help construct a picture of U.S. motives in the Cold War and where Afghanistan fit in with America's anti-Soviet strategy. In addition, I found the NATO-Russia Archive, published by the Berlin Information-Center for Transatlantic Security, useful to understand America's changing relationship with Russia and other successor states following the dissolution of the Soviet Union in 1991.

Another new collection from the National Security Archive is *The Taliban File*, which contains declassified documents on the Taliban and U.S. policy regarding them. The briefing book indicates a relatively uncritical, even positive reaction of the American administration in the early period of Taliban advances, but the Americans' attitude hardens as the Taliban regime's excesses increase. By 1998, the Clinton administration is clearly worried about Afghanistan and even tries to persuade the Taliban to hand over or expel Osama bin Laden, who had made Afghanistan his base.

Other primary sources were also useful. For an enhanced understanding of the American view of the Afghan conflict during the Cold War, I consulted memoirs of ex-U.S. administration officials. Examples I wish to mention are Zbigniew Brzezinski's *Power and Principles: Memoirs of the National Security Adviser, 1977–1981*, and Cyrus Vance's *Hard Choices: Critical Years in America's Foreign Policy*. Both men discuss policy disputes in the Carter administration and how the hard-line approach to the Soviet Union that Brzezinski advocated prevailed over a more moderate approach. Also figuring in my research were Richard Clarke's *Against All Enemies: Inside America's War on Terrorism* and, for a Pakistani perspective of America's proxy war against the Soviets in Afghanistan, *Afghanistan: The Bear Trap: The Defeat of a Superpower* by Brig. Mohammad Yousaf of Pakistan's military agency, Inter-Services Intelligence. The ISI, as it is commonly known, was the CIA's partner in supplying and training the anti-Soviet guerrilla forces, as well as in planning and directing Mujahideen operations in Afghanistan.

Two other works are particularly useful to learn more about the war tactics of the opposing sides—*The Other Side of the Mountain: Mujahideen Tactics in the Soviet-Afghan War* by Col. Ali Ahmad Jalali and Lt. Col. Lester Grau and the Russian General Staff's own postmortem, *The Soviet-Afghan War: How A Superpower Fought and Lost*. Lester Grau and Michael Gress translated and edited the latter volume.

Understanding the complex tribal and ethnic mix of Afghan society in that vast country is essential when studying how a dialectic of violence developed and created a culture in which terror grew. Experts have produced numerous major works that enhanced my understanding of Afghan society. Prominent among them are *The Fragmentation of Afghanistan* by Barnett Rubin, *Afghanistan Under Soviet Domination* by Anthony Hyman, *Afghanistan: The Soviet Invasion and the Afghan Response* by Hasan Kakar, and *Taliban: The Afghan Warlords* by Ahmed Rashid. On human rights, reports by Amnesty International and Human Rights Watch were useful. Their works helped me make sense of what I learned from people in private conversations, which are noted in the bibliography. Particularly useful were the private views of President Najibullah; Politburo members Abdul Wakil, Farid Mazdak, and Mahmood Baryalai; and representing the moderate opposition inside Afghanistan, Professor Mohammad Asghar and retired general Abdul Hakim Katawazi.

After the demise of the Soviet Union, the Clinton administration's strategies represented a major turning point in U.S. foreign policy. For an appreciation of America's challenge to pacify the Soviet nuclear arsenal and Clinton's drive toward an enlargement of free markets, I turned to *At the Highest Levels: The Inside Story of the End of the Cold War* by Michael Beschloss and Strobe Talbott and *The Russia Hand: A Memoir of Presidential Diplomacy* also by Talbott. Among other useful sources were *Nuclear Weapons in the Former Soviet Union* by Amy Woolf of the U.S. Congressional Research Service and "The Legacy of Nuclear Weapons" by Jeremiah Sullivan and published by the Program in Arms Control, Disarmament, and International Security of the University of Illinois. From these latter two I gathered information about the scale of the former Soviet Union's nuclear arsenal and how the United States dealt with it.

The regrouping of America's political right wing during the Clinton presidency was also a significant phenomenon, as demonstrated by George W. Bush's presidential victory in the year 2000 and in the determined response of the United States to the events of September 11, 2001. Reading the Project for the New American Century's manifesto, or "Statement of Principles," enhanced my discussion of the rise of America's neoconservatives and their ideas. I also consulted other works identified with the American Right, such as "The Arc of Crisis: Its Central Sector" by George Lenczowski, "The Roots of Muslim Rage" by Bernard Lewis, and Samuel Huntington's "Clash of Civilizations." My study of the above-mentioned literature led to the portrayal of radical Islam as a grotesque mirror image of the Christian fundamentalist right in the United States in the 1980s and 1990s.

Illustrating the growth of a culture of terror in Afghanistan required a basic understanding of dialectics and of how that violent culture replicated to a level where the country became a safe haven for terrorism. Here, I found the works of Kim O'Connor on Hegel, Daniel Berthold-Bond, and the Digital Text Project of Columbia University useful. The entire study of the Afghan conflict between 1978 and 2001—and beyond—then fits into the dialectical model.

NOTES

Chapter 1. The Concept of Terror

1. World Trade Center Disaster, BBC News, September 11, 2001.
2. "'Shock and Awe' Campaign Underway in Iraq," CNN.com, March 22, 2003, http://edition.cnn.com/2003/fyi/news/03/22/iraq.war/.
3. Transcript of the second televised debate between Al Gore and George W. Bush in the 2000 presidential election campaign. The debate was held on October 11, 2000, at Wake Forest University, Winston-Salem, North Carolina.
4. For an account of these difficulties, see "Definitions of Terrorism" (UN Office on Drugs and Crime).
5. Debate in the Sixth Committee of the Sixtieth General Assembly, October 7, 2005.
6. Among the characteristics usually highlighted is a sudden and often spectacular action using extreme and illegal force intended to weaken the will of the other side to achieve some political goal. See, for example, Jack Gibbs, "Conceptualization of Terrorism," *American Sociological Review* 54, no. 3 (June 1989): 330; E. V. Walter, "Violence and the Process of Terror," *American Sociological Review* 29, no. 2 (April 1964): 248; Lawrence Davidson, "Terrorism in Context: The Case of the West Bank," *Journal of Palestinian Studies* 15, no. 3 (Spring 1986): 111.
7. See, for example, Paul Wilkinson, "Trends in International Terrorism and the American Response" in Lawrence Freedman et al., *Terrorism and International Order* (London: RIIA/Routledge, 1986), 37; Albert Bandura, "Mechanisms of Moral Disengagement" in *Origins of Terrorism: Psychologies, Ideologies, Theologies, State of Mind*, ed. Walter Reich (Washington, DC: Woodrow Wilson International Center/Cambridge University Press, 1990), 162; Geoffrey Levitt, *Democracies Against Terror* (Washington, DC: Center for Strategic and International Studies/Praeger, 1988), 6.
8. It may be a controversial point to make, but the effect of the nuclear bombing of the Japanese cities of Hiroshima and Nagasaki and the bombing of Dresden and Berlin in Germany was pure terror for civilians. The attacks were admittedly part

of the Allied attempts to bring about a swift resolution for World War II. Nevertheless, the impact of the bombings on the civilian populations was unmistakable.

9. The two terms, "terrorism" and "political violence," are subsumed in this study, because the motive in both cases is political—to break civil morale, change public opinion, and force the other side to surrender its position or alter its policy.

10. Martha Crenshaw, "The Logic of Terrorism: Terrorist Behavior as a Product of Strategic Choice" in Reich, *Origins of Terrorism*, 7–24; David Lake, "Rational Extremism: Understanding Terrorism in the Twenty-first Century," *International Organization* (Spring 2002): 15–29; Robert Pape, "The Strategic Logic of Suicide Terrorism," *American Political Science Review* 97, no. 3 (August 2003): 1–19; Lawrence Freedman, "Terrorism and Strategy" in Freedman et al, *Terrorism and International Order*, 56–76.

11. Jerrold Post, "Terrorist Psycho-logic: Terrorist Behavior as a Product of Psychological Forces" in Reich, *Origins of Terrorism*, 25–40; Randy Borum, "Understanding the Terrorist Mind-Set," *The FBI Law Enforcement Bulletin* (July 2003): 7–10.

12. Freedman, "Terrorism and Strategy,"; Christopher Harmon, "Terrorism: A Matter for Moral Judgement," *Terrorism and Political Violence* 4 (Spring 1992): 3.

13. They were from middle-class Arab families and had been educated in the West. See Appendix E.

14. Mark Harrison, "An Economist Looks at Suicide Terrorism," *Security Management,* June 5, 2003), 2.

15. Crenshaw, "The Logic of Terrorism," 7.

16. See Gary Gambill, "The Balance of Terror: War by Other Means in the Contemporary Middle East," *Journal of Palestine Studies* 28, no. 1 (Autumn 1998): 53–54; Leonard Weinberg, "Turning to Terror: The Conditions Under Which Political Parties Turn to Terrorist Activities," *Comparative Politics* 23, no. 4 (July 1991): 423.

17. Crenshaw concedes that the benefits of taking part in terrorist organizations are partly psychological but leaves that consideration to those interested in the study of the psychological causes of terrorism. See "The Logic of Terrorism," 7.

18. Martha Crenshaw, "The Causes of Terrorism," *Comparative Politics* 13, no. 4 (July 1981): 385.

19. Edward Muller and Erich Weede, "Cross-National Variation in Political Violence: A Rational Action Approach," *The Journal of Conflict Resolution* 34, no. 4 (December 1990): 625.

20. Magnus Ranstorp, "Hizbollah's Command Leadership: Its Structure, Decision-Making and Relationship with Iranian Clergy and Institutions," *Terrorism and Political Violence* 6 (Autumn 1994): 203–39.

21. Such as the Palestinian hijackers of Air France Flight 139 in July 1976. More than a hundred Israeli Jewish hostages were rescued in a surprise raid by Israeli commandos at Entebbe airport in Uganda. All seven hijackers were killed.

22. Al Qaeda statement that "there are no innocent victims in Western societies," cited in Ruth Wedgwood, "Al-Qa'ida, Terrorism and Military Commissions," *American Journal of International Law* 96 (April 2002): 328–29; also, al Qaeda statement, February 23, 1998, taken from Fred Halliday, *Two Hours that Shook the World* (London: Saqi Books, 2002), 217–19.

23. Such as Palestinian militants launching attacks inside Israel.

24. Lake, "Rational Extremism," 19.

25. For example, Paul Wilkinson, *Terrorism & the Liberal State* (London: Macmillan, 1986), 93; also Scott Atran, "Genesis and Future of Suicide Terrorism;" Post, Interview with NBC, 2001; Gambill, "Balance of Terror," 53; David Pion-Berlin and George Lopez, "Of Victims and Executioners: Argentine State Terror, 1975–1979," *International Studies Quarterly* 35, no. 1 (March 1991): 63–65. Harry Eckstein uses the term "internal war" to describe changing the rulers, policies, or constitution of a political order. See Eckstein, "On the Etiology of Internal Wars," *History and Theory* 4, no. 2 (1965): 133–63.

26. Post, "Terrorist Psycho-logic" in Reich, *Origins of Terrorism*; Post, interview with NBC Australia, October 22, 2001; Ted Gurr, "Psychological Factors in Civil Strife," *World Politics* 20, no. 2 (January 1968): 245–78; Gurr, "A Causal Model of Civil Strife: A Comparative Analysis Using New Indices," *The American Political Science Review* 62, no. 4 (December 1968):1104–24.

27. Post, "Terrorist Psycho-logic" in Reich, *Origins of Terrorism*, 25.

28. See Gurr, "Psychological Factors in Civil Violence," 277.

29. Post, interview with NBC Australia, October 22, 2001.

30. Post, "Terrorist Psycho-logic," in Reich, *Origins of Terrorism*, 27.

31. Borum, "Understanding the Terrorist Mind-Set," 7.

32. Ibid., 10.

33. Many reasons are cited for joining an organization: unemployment, social alienation, lack of education, or, among the educated, genuine political and religious convictions or even boredom. See "The Process of Joining a Terrorist Group" in *The Sociology and Psychology of Terrorism: Who Becomes A Terrorist and Why?"* (Washington, DC: The Federal Research Division, Library of Congress, September 1999), http://www.loc.gov/rr/frd/pdf-files/Soc_Psych_of_Terrorism.pdf.

34. For example, Bruce Hoffman discusses the sources of power for religious and secular organizations in "Responding to Terrorism Across the Technological Spectrum," *Terrorism and Political Violence* 6 (Autumn 1994): 366–90; also, Paul Wilkinson, "Terrorism: International Dimensions" in *The New Terrorism*, ed. William Gutteridge (London: Mansell Publishing, 1986), 29–56.

35. Post, "Terrorist Psycho-logic," in Reich, *Origins of Terrorism*, 27–29.

36. Jerrold Post argues that "individuals become terrorists to join terrorist groups and commit acts of violence." See "Terrorist Psycho-logic," 35.

37. For Mao, the victory over the Nationalists and the establishment of a Communist state on the Chinese mainland was not enough. Mao launched the Great Leap Forward in 1958 and the Cultural Revolution in 1966; both campaigns were used to target opponents. Che Guevara left Cuba in 1965—six years after the Communist victory there—to continue the revolution in other parts of Latin America. Guevara was killed in Bolivia in 1967.

38. For a detailed study, see Jeffrey Ian Ross, "Structural Causes of Oppositional Political Terrorism: Towards a Causal Model," *Journal of Peace Research* 30 (August 1993): 317–29. Mohamed Suliman, citing the example of Sudan, gives poverty,

environmental degradation, scarcity of farming land, non-productive urbaniza-
tion, and uneven development as relevant structural causes. See Suliman's analysis, "Oil and the Civil War in Sudan" (*Institute of African Alternatives*). Timo Kivimaki and Liisa Laakso divide structural causes into economic grievances (poverty, deprivation, and lack of opportunities) and political grievances (humiliation,
political deprivation, and lack of non-violent channels of protest). See Kivimaki
and Laakso, "Causes of Terrorism," *Development Cooperation as an Instrument in
the Prevention of Terrorism* (Copenhagen: Nordic Institute of Asian Studies, July
2003), 86–89. Tore Bjorgo cites reasons such as hegemony and inequality of
power, social injustice, external actors sustaining illegitimate governments, and
repression by foreign occupiers or weak governance. See Bjorgo, "Issues for Discussion" (paper presented at the UN conference Fighting Terrorism for Humanity, New York, September 2003).

39. Ross, "Structural Causes of Oppositional Political Terrorism," 318.
40. Crenshaw, "The Causes of Terrorism," 382; also, Lawrence Hamilton and James
Hamilton, "Dynamics of Terrorism," *International Studies Quarterly* 27 (May
1983): 40.
41. Kivimaki and Laakso, "Causes of Terrorism," 85. The term *terrorist constituency*
means the environment in which a group is based and the people on whose behalf
it claims to fight.
42. Tore Bjorgo identifies this limitation in "Issues for Discussion," although he does
not cover state terror on its own people. He sees state sponsorship of international
terrorism as a foreign policy tool. See "Issues for Discussion," 2.

Chapter 3. Afghanistan in the Cold War

1. Anthony Hyman, *Afghanistan under Soviet Domination, 1964–1991,* 3rd ed. (London: Macmillan, 1992), 50.
2. Hyman, *Afghanistan under Soviet Domination*, 51; also, Barnett Rubin, *The Fragmentation of Afghanistan*, 2nd ed. (New Haven: Yale University Press, 2002), 74.
3. Before the 1973 Arab-Israel conflict, U.S. and Israeli intelligence thought there
was no imminent threat of a surprise attack on Israel by Egypt and Syria. See "Secretary's Staff Meeting, Tuesday, October 23, 1973 – 4:35 pm," National Security
Archive, http://www.gwu.edu/~nsarchiv/NSAEBB/NSAEBB98/octwar-63.pdf.
4. Before the Islamic revolution, Iran and Israel were allies in the Middle East and
there was substantial trade between the two countries, including sales of Iranian
oil to Israel. See "Iran: A Country Study," Federal Research Division, Library of
Congress, http://lcweb2.loc.gov/frd/cs/pdf/CS_Iran.pdf.
5. The royal family finally left Iran in January 1979 and the monarchy was overthrown a month later.
6. Soviet naval presence in the Indian Ocean had been increasing since the early
1970s and it had acquired the rights to use air and naval bases in Umm Qasr in
Iraq, Berbera in Somalia, and Aden in the People's Republic of Yemen. For an in-
depth analysis, see Alexander Ghebhardt, "Soviet and U.S. Interests in the Indian
Ocean," *Asian Survey* 15 (August 1975): 674–75.

7. The aim of the doctrine was to defend Pakistan from its bigger adversary, India. The two countries had fought wars in 1947, 1965, and 1971. In the 1971 conflict, Pakistan lost its eastern part, which became the independent nation of Bangladesh.

8. Ahmed Rashid, a Pakistani author with a wide knowledge of his country's military concerns, discusses this in a conversation with Harry Kreisler, "Islam in Central Asia: Foreign Intervention and Fundamentalism" (Berkeley: Institute of International Studies, University of California, March 26, 2002), p 4.

9. Rubin, *The Fragmentation of Afghanistan*, 62.

10. Zulfiqar Ali Bhutto was executed in April 1979 after being convicted of involvement in an opponent's murder.

11. Information about the military regime in this section is drawn from "Zia-ul Haq and Military Domination, 1977–1988" in *Pakistan: A Country Study*, Federal Research Division, Library of Congress, http://memory.loc.gov/frd/cs/pktoc.html

12. The Muslim League and Jamaat-i-Islami.

13. Pakistan joined the South-East Asia Treaty Organization (SEATO) in 1954 and Central Treaty Organization in 1959. See *Pakistan: A Country Study*.

14. Started by Bhutto after India tested a nuclear device in 1974.

15. In some places, the corridor is less than 10 miles (15 km) wide.

16. Hyman, *Afghanistan under Soviet Domination*, 50.

17. The two countries finally established full diplomatic relations on January 1, 1979.

18. SEATO members were Australia, New Zealand, the Philippines, Thailand, France, Britain, the United States, and Pakistan, which left after its defeat in its 1971 war with India. The organization was dissolved in 1977.

19. CENTO had been inactive since 1974, when Turkey invaded Cyprus. It was disbanded after the withdrawal of Pakistan, Turkey, and Iran following the fall of the Iranian monarchy in 1979, leaving only Britain in the organization.

20. Gerald Ford, an unelected vice president, became president when Nixon resigned in August 1974. A month later, Ford granted Nixon a full pardon for any crimes the former president may have committed when in office. The decision was deeply unpopular. In the 1976 presidential election, Ford was defeated by the Democratic candidate, Jimmy Carter.

21. John Dumbrell, *American Foreign Policy: Carter to Clinton* (London: Macmillan, 1997), 17–21.

22. David Skidmore, "Carter's Foreign Policy," *Political Science Quarterly* 108 (Winter 1993–1994), 715.

23. For a general discussion on the differing approaches of Brzezinski and Vance in 1977, see Dumbrell, *American Foreign Policy*, 15.

24. In his memoirs, Cyrus Vance provides a detailed account of his view of U.S.-Soviet relations during the Carter administration and his differences with Brzezinski. See *Hard Choices: Critical Years in America's Foreign Policy* (New York: Simon and Schuster, 1983), 423.

25. Afghan historian Hasan Kakar has written one of the best books on the early years of the crisis. See the introductory chapter in *Afghanistan: The Soviet Invasion and the Afghan Response, 1979–1982* (Berkeley: University of California Press, 1995).

26. Hyman, *Afghanistan under Soviet Domination*, 11; also, Rubin, *The Fragmentation of Afghanistan*, 26.
27. Enclaves of Pashtun, however, were scattered among other ethnic groups throughout Afghanistan as a consequence of forced or voluntary migration caused by political expediency or economic opportunities. There were also tiny minorities of Afghan Hindus, Sikhs, Christians, and Jews, but many of them fled abroad during the war.
28. Rubin, *Fragmentation of Afghanistan*, 26.
29. "Islamic Expression in Afghanistan" in *Afghanistan: A Country Study*, Federal Research Division, Library of Congress, http://lcweb2.loc.gov/frd/cs/aftoc.html.
30. Ibid.
31. For more on this perspective, see Pervaiz Iqbal Cheema, "The Afghanistan Crisis and Pakistan's Security Dilemma," *Asian Survey* 23 (March 1983): 8–9; also, Rasul Bakhsh Rais, "Afghanistan and the Regional Powers," *Asian Survey* 33 (September 1993): 906.
32. See *Background Notes on Afghanistan* (Washington, DC: U.S. Department of State, March 1977), p 7, cited in the National Security Archive, 1991.
33. *Policy Review* (Kabul: U.S. embassy, March 1977), pp 3–4.
34. *Policy Review* (Kabul: U.S. embassy, 1977)
35. Both Hyman in *Afghanistan under Soviet Domination*, 27–31, and Rubin in *Fragmentation of Afghanistan*, 64–70, discuss Afghanistan's dependence on foreign aid and the difficulties encountered during the period under discussion.
36. See, for example, Hyman, *Afghanistan under Soviet Domination*, 31 and 47.
37. Among them were Abdul Qadir and Mohammad Aslam Watanjar. They were also among the leaders of the 1978 communist coup that brought the PDPA to power in Afghanistan. Daud appointed some communists in his cabinet after the 1973 takeover—for instance, Faiz Mohammad as minister of interior and Pasha Gul Wafadar as minister of frontier affairs.
38. U.S. embassy cable from Kabul, "Afghan coup: Initial assessment," sent to the secretary of state, Henry Kissinger, on July 17, 1973. American diplomats in Kabul were consistent in their view that the United States was falling behind the Soviet Union in the race for influence in Afghanistan.

Chapter 4. Afghanistan under Communism

1. See Henry Bradsher, *Afghan Communism and Soviet Intervention*, 2nd ed. (Karachi, Pakistan: Oxford University Press, 2000), 2; also, Hyman, *Afghanistan under Soviet Domination, 1964–1991,* 29. Hyman says a total of 7,000 Afghan military officers were trained in the USSR and Czechoslovakia by 1970 while fewer than 600 went to the United States.
2. President Eisenhower approved the first aid package to Pakistan in February 1954. In December of that year, U.S. secretary of state John Foster Dulles refused Afghanistan's request for military assistance. See Rubin, *The Fragmentation of Afghanistan*, 65.
3. New evidence of Soviet involvement in Afghanistan is revealed in a manuscript

written by ex-KGB agent, Vasili Mitrokhin, who worked for several years at the central archive of the agency and took detailed notes from files on foreign intelligence operations before defecting to Great Britain in 1992. See Vasili Mitrokhin, *The KGB in Afghanistan* (Washington, DC: The Cold War International History Project, Woodrow Wilson Center, 2002).

4. Ibid., 19–20.

5. Ibid., 20.

6. Ibid., 23.

7. David Gibbs, "Does the USSR Have a Grand Strategy? Reinterpreting the Invasion of Afghanistan," *Journal of Peace Research* 24 (December 1987): 370; also, Hyman, *Afghanistan under Soviet Domination*, 51.

8. Afghan historian Hasan Kakar gives this account of the clash between Daud and Brezhnev, days before the communist coup in which Daud was assassinated. See his introductory chapter in *The Soviet Invasion and the Afghan Response, 1979–1982* (Berkeley: University of California Press, 1995).

9. Khyber was the main ideologue and organizer of the Parcham faction within the People's Democratic Party. See Hyman, *Afghanistan under Soviet Domination*, 72–77; also, Bradsher, *Afghan Communism and Soviet Intervention*, 22–23.

10. Private conversations with prominent Afghans.

11. Kakar advances this in the introductory chapter of *The Soviet Invasion and the Afghan Response*.

12. Taraki's representative is named by Mitrokhin as Saleh. See *The KGB in Afghanistan*, 28.

13. Ibid., 29.

14. Soviet ambassador's report, May 31, 1978, in *Documents on the Soviet Invasion of Afghanistan* (The Cold War International History Project, Woodrow Wilson Center, Washington, DC, November 2001), 28–29.

15. Message from the Central Committee of the Soviet Communist Party to the East German leader, Erich Honecker, about a visit to Kabul by Politburo representative, Boris Ponomarev, dated October 13, 1978. See *Documents on the Soviet Invasion of Afghanistan*, 30.

16. Record of the meeting on June 18, 1978. See *Documents on the Soviet Invasion of Afghanistan*, 29.

17. These tensions came to the fore after the overthrow of the king in 1973 and again following the communist coup in April 1978.

18. For example, Najibullah, a Pashtun who was later to become head of the Afghan secret service, KHAD, and then president, was a leading member of the Parcham faction.

19. Private conversations with Afghans.

20. Mitrokhin, *The KGB in the Afghanistan*, p 39.

21. Ibid., 33.

22. Bradsher, *Afghan Communism and Soviet Intervention*, 35; Hyman, *Afghanistan under Soviet Domination*, 84; and Mitrokhin, *The KGB in Afghanistan*, 39.

23. Mitrokhin, *The KGB in Afghanistan*, 43.

24. Taraki's news conference in Kabul on May 6, 1978, cited by Alexander Dastarac and M. Levant, "What Went Wrong in Afghanistan," *Middle East Research and Information Project Report*, no. 89 (July–August 1980): 4.

25. The November 28, 1978, announcement said the implementation was to begin in January 1979.

26. Dastarac and Levant, "What Went Wrong in Afghanistan?," 4.

27. The State Department, "The Kidnapping and Death of Ambassador Adolph Dubs: Summary of Report of Investigation" (Washington, 1979), 2–3. The report accused Soviet diplomats and advisers of involvement in the bungled attempt to rescue the ambassador. See 8–9.

28. U.S. embassy cable, "Taraki's news conference on the effects of the death of Adolph Dubs," April 30, 1979.

29. Text of Taraki's news conference, 9; also, Bradsher, *Afghan Communism and Soviet Intervention*, 47.

30. Bradsher, *Afghanistan and the Soviet Union* (Durham, NC: Duke University Press, 1985), 100.

31. There are several authoritative accounts of the Herat uprising. See, for example, Raja Anwar, *The Tragedy of Afghanistan: A First-Hand Account* (London: Verso, 1988), 155–56; Hyman, *Afghanistan under Soviet Domination*, 100–101; Bradsher, *Afghanistan and the Soviet Union*, 101–2.

32. Telephone conversation between Taraki and Soviet Premier Alexei Kosygin on March 17 or 18, 1979. For transcript, see *Documents on the Soviet Invasion of Afghanistan*, 40–41.

33. Taraki's meeting with Brezhnev on March 20 1979. See *Documents on the Soviet Invasion of Afghanistan*, 15.

34. See U.S. embassy cable, "An initial evaluation of the Bala Hisar mutiny," dated August 6, 1979, 1–5; also Hyman, *Afghanistan under Soviet Domination,* 149–53.

Chapter 5. Toward Distintegration

1. The four were Aslam Watanjar, Abdul Qadir, Sayed Mohammad Gulabzoi, and Mohammad Rafi. The first three belonged to Khalq. Only Rafi was a Parcham member.

2. Many rural Pashtuns in the armed forces sympathized with the Khalq faction of the PDPA; Parcham was a minority faction in the military, but had a high profile among educated Afghans in Kabul and a few other towns.

3. Main among them were the Tajiks, Uzbeks, Turkmen, and Aimaks, as well as Hazaras in Central Afghanistan.

4. At the Bala Hisar fort.

5. For an account of the revolt on August 4, 1979, see Raja Anwar, *The Tragedy of Afghanistan: A First-hand Account* (London: Verso, 1988), 163–64. Anthony Arnold, who served as an American intelligence analyst in Afghanistan, has also written on the Bala Hisar mutiny. See his book, *Afghanistan: The Soviet Invasion in Perspective* (Stanford: Hoover Institution Press, 1985), 80.

6. Secret report sent to Moscow from Kabul by Soviet party official, Boris Pono-

marev, on July 19, 1979 following talks with Taraki and Amin. See *Documents on the Soviet Invasion of Afghanistan*, 48.

7. Record of the meeting between the Soviet ambassador, Alexander Puzanov, and Amin on July 21, 1979. See *Documents on the Soviet Invasion of Afghanistan*, 48.

8. General Pavlovsky had commanded the Soviet invasion of Czechoslovakia in 1968. See Arnold, *The Soviet Invasion in Perspective*, 48.

9. General Pavlovsky's meeting with Amin on August 25, 1979. See *Documents on the Soviet Invasion of Afghanistan,* 49.

10. Mitrokhin, *The KGB in Afghanistan*, 13. Only 125 KGB troops were sent, which raises the question about what kind of support they were there to offer the Kabul regime as it tried to overcome rebellions.

11. The term *airborne* refers to troops being dropped by parachute or taken by helicopter to the area of deployment. Their deployment took place between June 29 and early July 1979. According to Kabul residents at the time, even the Afghan regime seemed unaware of the deployment at Bagram, which was, in effect, a Soviet base.

12. The civilian-military air base in Kabul was much smaller.

13. State Department memorandum, "Soviet-Afghan Relations: Is Moscow's Patience Wearing Thin?," May 24, 1979, 2.

14. Mitrokhin, *The KGB in Afghanistan*, 45.

15. Ivanov, a senior KGB official with the rank of Lieutenant General, was stationed in Kabul from spring 1979. See Mitrokhin, *The KGB in Afghanistan*, 44.

16. Ibid., 45.

17. At the forefront of the anti-Amin campaign was the "gang of four," including Aslam Watanjar, Asadullah Sarwari, Sherjan Mazdooryar, and Sayed Mohammad Gulabzoi. All four had been sidelined in the July reshuffle. For an account, see Anwar, *The Tragedy of Afghanistan*, 165–66.

18. Anwar in conversation with Mrs. Taraki in Kabul in 1983.

19. Mitrokhin, *The KGB in Afghanistan*, 52–53.

Chapter 6. The Second Communist Coup

1. Mitrokhin, *The KGB in Afghanistan*. In addition to Mitrokhin, various other authors have given written accounts of Taraki's Moscow stopover, during which he also met with the exiled Parcham leader Babrak Karmal. See, for instance, Hyman, *Afghanistan under Soviet Domination*, 154; Anwar, *The Tragedy of Afghanistan*, 167–68; Henry Bradsher, *Afghanistan and the Soviet Union* (Durham, NC: Duke University Press, 1985), 110–11.

2. The report was prepared by the Soviet ambassador, Alexander Puzanov; senior KGB officer in Kabul, Boris Ivanov; and head of the Soviet military experts, Lev Gorelov.

3. Aslam Watanjar (interior minister), Asadullah Sarwari (head of state security), Sherjan Mazdooryar (minister for frontier affairs), and Sayed Mohammad Gulabzoi (minister of communications).

4. Minutes of the Soviet Politburo meeting on September 13, 1979. See *Documents on the Soviet Invasion of Afghanistan*, 49.

5. Mitrokhin, *The KGB in Afghanistan*, 14.

6. Mitrokhin says they were briefly given shelter in the official residence of a KGB agent who was working undercover as a third secretary in the Soviet embassy. On September 19, 1979, Watanjar, Sarwari, and Gulabzoi were secretly flown to Tashkent in the Soviet republic of Uzbekistan. After extensive debriefing, the three were taken to Bulgaria. See *The KGB in Afghanistan*, 77–83.

7. Mitrokhin, *The KGB in Afghanistan,* 60–61.

8. Gromyko and Ustinov took the lead in the preparation of the report, which was discussed by the Politburo on September 15, 1979. See *Documents on the Soviet Invasion of Afghanistan*, 49.

9. *Documents on the Soviet Invasion of Afghanistan*, 50.

10. Some of these meetings are described in the personal notes of Puzanov, the Soviet ambassador in Kabul during the period. See Mitrokhin, *The KGB in Afghanistan*, 61-68.

11. Message from the Kremlin to the East German leader, Erich Honecker, on September 16, when Taraki was removed from all his posts and expelled from the People's Democratic Party of Afghanistan.

12. Minutes of the Politburo meeting on September 20, 1979. See *Documents on the Soviet Invasion of Afghanistan*, 51.

13. Brezhnev's speech at the Soviet Politburo meeting on September 20, 1979. See *Documents on the Soviet Invasion of Afghanistan*, 51.

14. Mitrokhin, *The KGB in Afghanistan*, 85. The author says that Amin was being advised by his close associates to "adopt a more reasonable attitude towards the United States and other Western countries."

15. The depth of animosity between Amin and Puzanov is revealed in the Soviet ambassador's diary, from which Mitrokhin quotes at length. See, for example, *The KGB in Afghanistan*, 73–74.

16. Amin's ally was the foreign minister, Shah Wali.

17. Puzanov was replaced by Fikrat Tabeyev, who at fifty one was a relatively young member of the Central Committee of the Soviet Communist Party.

18. Mitrokhin, *The KGB in Afghanistan*, 85–86.

19. A message entitled "Khalqis possibly waving olive branch to Washington?" from the American embassy in Kabul on September 22, 1979, seemed to confirm this. Referring to contacts with Afghan officials, it informed the State Department that Amin wanted to improve relations with the United States.

20. Report by Andrei Gromyko, Yuri Andropov, Dmitri Ustinov, and Boris Ponomarev. It was submitted to the Central Committee of the Soviet Communist Party on October 29, 1979. See *Documents on the Soviet Invasion of Afghanistan*, 52–53.

21. Minutes of the meeting between Amin and Puzanov on November 3, 1979.

22. Hyman, *Afghanistan under Soviet Domination,* 157; Bradsher, *Afghanistan and the Soviet Union*, 120. According to Bradsher, the main cause of the Rishkor mutiny was anger at the treatment of Aslam Watanjar, who was among those purged along with Taraki.

23. Cable from the American embassy, "Reflections on the Afghanistan political crisis," September 1979.

24. It was noted that there had been twenty-three cabinet reshuffles between the first communist coup in April 1978 and September 1979. The number of changes among lower-ranking ministers was even higher—thirty-four. See American embassy cable, "Reflections on the Afghanistan political crisis."

25. In addition to the above, see Bradsher, *Afghan Communism and Soviet Intervention*, 61–62. In February 1980, the regime of Babrak Karmal, installed after the Soviet invasion, gave a figure of twelve thousand dead during the period when Taraki and Amin were in power. See Olivier Roy, *Islam and Resistance in Afghanistan*, 2nd ed. (Cambridge: Cambridge University Press, 1990), 95–97. However, this "official" figure included only those who had "disappeared" from detention in the Pul-i-Charkhi prison, where prisoners were routinely tortured and executed. Roy points out that the numbers of people missing or executed in the countryside were much higher and received less publicity.

26. Taraki was murdered on October 8, 1979.

27. For further explanation of this connection, see Bradsher, *Afghanistan and the Soviet Union*, 120.

28. According to some accounts, the Soviet Union had been in talks with Etemadi in the summer of 1979. Bradsher, *Afghan Communism and Soviet Intervention*, 50; also Bradsher, *Afghanistan and the Soviet Union*, 105–6.

29. Balkh and Badakhshan provinces in the north, through Hazarajat in the central highlands, to Ghazni, Farah, and Uruzgan provinces in the south.

30. Tahir Amin, "Afghan Resistance: Past, Present and Future," *Asian Survey* 24 (April 1984): 380–81. In a number of provincial capitals, military garrisons were besieged and could only be supplied by air. Defections from these units to local guerrilla commanders were common.

31. See Mitrokhin, *The KGB in Afghanistan*, 14. According to Mitrokhin, the appeals for Soviet troops to defend Kabul were made on December 2, 3, 12, and 17, 1979.

32. Minutes of the Brezhnev-Honecker summit in East Berlin on October 4, 1979. See *Documents on the Soviet Invasion of Afghanistan*, 52.

33. Logar province, east of the capital, at the end of September 1979. See Mitrokhin, *The KGB in Afghanistan*, 88–89.

34. For more on these Soviet concerns, see minutes of the Brezhnev-Honecker summit on October 4, 1979, *The Soviet Invasion of Afghanistan*, 52.

35. Their report, dated October 29,1979, has already been cited.

36. This evidence suggests that the real objective of the above report to the Central Committee of the Soviet Communist Party was to keep the plan to invade Afghanistan secret from the general membership, in order to buy time for preparations that would be required for a military invasion of Afghanistan and to keep Amin unaware of what was about to happen.

37. For an explanation of the internal organization of the KGB, see Christopher Andrew and Vasili Mitrokhin, Appendix C, in *The Sword and the Shield: The Mitrokhin Archive and the Secret History of the KGB* (New York: Basic Books, 2001), 568.

38. See Mitrokhin, *The KGB in Afghanistan*, 89–90. According to him, the KGB envoy to Karmal was Lieutenant-Colonel Petrov, who went to Czechoslovakia on

October 25 for negotiations with him on future Soviet operations in Afghanistan. Petrov departed four days before the report was submitted to the Communist Party Central Committee.

39. Among them were Karmal himself, Watanjar, Gulabzoi, and Sarwari.
40. "Personal memorandum: Andropov to Brezhnev," *Documents on the Soviet Invasion of Afghanistan*, 54.
41. They were Karmal, Gulabzoi, Watanjar, Sarwari, and Abdul Wakil. See Mitrokhin, *The KGB in Afghanistan*, 91.
42. American embassy cable, "Soviet airlift to Kabul," December 26, 1979.
43. Mitrokhin, *The KGB in Afghanistan*, 101–2; Kakar, *The Soviet Invasion and the Afghan Response*, chapter 1; Bradsher, *Afghan Communism and the Soviet Intervention*, 97–100.
44. Daud (1978), Taraki (1979), and Amin (1979).
45. King Zahir Shah, who was ousted by his cousin in 1973, had abdicated and was living in Italy.

Chapter 7. Let Battle Commence

1. The Jimmy Carter Library, Atlanta, Georgia.
2. Ali Ahmad Jalali and Lester W. Grau, *The Other Side of the Mountain: Mujahideen Tactics in the Soviet-Afghan War* (Quantico, VA: Military Press, 2000), vii.
3. Brigadier Mohammad Yousaf and Mark Adkin, *Afghanistan: The Bear Trap* (Barnsley, UK: Leo Cooper, 2001), 26.
4. Rubin, *The Fragmentation of Afghanistan*, 184.
5. The U.S. embassy was stormed by Islamic militants on November 4, 1979. About half of the original hostages were gradually released, but fifty-two Americans remained captive until the end. The crisis ended as soon as Carter, having lost the 1980 election, handed over the presidency to Ronald Reagan in January 1981.
6. See John Dumbrell, *American Foreign Policy: Carter to Clinton* (London: Macmillan, 1997), 47–50; also, Fred Halliday, "The Arc of Crisis and the New Cold War," *Middle East Research and Information Project* 0, special anniversary issue 100/101 (Oct–Dec 1981): 15–16.
7. Francis Fukuyama, "The Soviet Threat to the Persian Gulf," (paper prepared for the Security Conference on Asia and the Pacific [SECAP], Tokyo, January 1980).
8. Diego Cordovez and Selig Harrison, "Overview: Afghanistan and the End of the Cold War," in *Out of Afghanistan: An Inside Story of the Soviet Withdrawal* (New York: Oxford University Press, 1995).
9. Summary of President Carter's briefing for members of the U.S. Congress on January 8, 1980.
10. See Dumbrell, *American Foreign Policy*, 49; Dennis Ross, "Considering Soviet Threats to the Persian Gulf," *International Security* 6 no. 2 (Autumn 1981): 176–80; Robert Wirsing and James Roherty, "The United States and Pakistan," *International Affairs* 58, no. 4 (Autumn 1982): 588–89. The policy of containment was announced by President Truman in early 1947, when he called on the American Congress to approve an aid program for Greece and Turkey to encourage them to resist Soviet ambitions in the region. See "President Harry S. Truman's Address

Before a Joint Session of Congress, March 12, 1947," The Avalon Project, Yale Law School, http://avalon.law.yale.edu/20th_century/trudoc.asp.

11. Norman Podhoretz, "The First Term: The Reagan Road to Détente," *Foreign Affairs* 63, No. 3 (1984).

12. On October 1, 1979.

13. The announcement was made on February 19, 1980. More than fifty countries, including the United States, Canada, West Germany, Japan, and most Islamic nations, boycotted the Moscow Olympics, held in July and August that year.

14. Robert Gates, a career CIA officer, served as the agency's Director between 1991 and 1993. See his memoir, *From the Shadows: The Ultimate Insider's Story of Five Presidents and How They Won the Cold War* (New York: Simon & Schuster, 1997), 143–49.

15. The Special Coordinating Committee, under the chairmanship of the National Security Adviser, oversaw policy issues that cut across several departments, including intelligence, evaluation of arms control, and crisis management.

16. Gates, *From the Shadows*, 144.

17. Carter's presidential order was described as a "finding" in the administrative jargon. Carter himself has never spoken about the order.

18. Brzezinski interview, "The CIA's Intervention in Afghanistan," *Le Nouvel Observateur*, January 15–21, 1998. (English version posted on October 15, 2001 by the Center for Research on Globalization, http://www.globalresearch.ca/articles/BRZ110A.html.

19. These remarks were made by Brzezinski in 1998. The events of September 11, 2001, were yet to unfold, but there had been a number of attacks on American targets in the 1990s.

20. Gates, *From the Shadows*, 146.

21. The Inter Services Intelligence (ISI), the most secretive of Pakistan's intelligence organs, soon took charge of training the Afghan guerrillas and channeling weapons and funds to them.

22. Based on his contacts in the CIA, John Cooley provides an account of how the American-led operation to help the Afghan insurgents was forged in *Unholy Wars: Afghanistan, America and International Terrorism* (London: Pluto Press, 2002), 41–43.

23. The officer mentioned here is Brigadier Mohammad Yousaf, head of the Afghan Bureau in the Pakistani military intelligence service from 1983 to 1987. See Yousaf and Adkin, *Afghanistan: The Bear Trap*, 97.

24. The two holiest places in Islam being the Saudi Arabian cities of Mecca and Medina.

25. Gates, *From the Shadows*, 148.

26. When Sadat made his momentous visit to Jerusalem, which led to the 1978 Camp David agreements and subsequent peace treaty with Israel.

27. Gates, *From the Shadows*, 178.

Chapter 8. The Reagan Offensive

1. See Ronald Reagan's speeches: welcoming the British prime minister, Margaret Thatcher, in the White House on February 26, 1981; the state banquet for President Zia-ul Haq of Pakistan on December 7, 1982; radio address on defense

spending on February 19, 1983; address on foreign policy on October 20, 1984; and welcoming King Fahd of Saudi Arabia in the White House on February 11, 1985, which are available from the Ronald Reagan Presidential Library.

2. Gates, *From the Shadows*, 197.

3. U.S.-Pakistani joint statement on June 15, 1981, at the end of a visit by Undersecretary of State for Security Assistance James Buckley.

4. Statement by James Buckley to the Senate Foreign Relations Committee on November 12, 1981. See "U.S. Cooperation with Pakistan" (Washington, DC: State Department, Current Policy No. 347), 4.

5. See, for example, Cooley, *Unholy Wars*, 46–47; and Janette Rainwater, "Afghanistan, 'Terrorism,' and Blowback: A Chronology," Progressive Politics Online, September 19, 2002, http://www.janrainwater.com/htdocs/afghan2.htm.

6. For Casey's role in CIA operations during the Reagan presidency, see Gates, *From the Shadows*, 199. Also, for Brigadier Yousaf's account of encounters with Casey both in Pakistan and the United States, see Yousaf and Adkin, *Afghanistan: The Bear Trap*, 63, 95, 115–16, 197.

7. Casey's leadership of the CIA came under severe criticism in the late 1980s following revelations about the Iran–contra affair. In this operation, the CIA was involved in secret and illegal weapons sales to Iran, which was under a U.S. arms embargo, in order to finance the anti-Sandinista campaign being waged by the right-wing contra rebels in Nicaragua. Shortly after the affair became public, Casey suffered a stroke and died in May 1987.

8. Gates, *From the Shadows*, 251.

9. Ibid., 200.

10. See "The Development of Soviet Military Power: Trends Since 1965 and Prospects for the 1980s" (Washington, DC: Center for the Study of Intelligence, CIA, 2001), 308.

11. The Soviet leadership was in a state of paralysis during this period. Three leaders had died in less than three years: Brezhnev in November 1982; his successor, Yuri Andropov, in February 1984; and Konstantin Chernenko in March 1985. Chernenko's death cleared the way for the appointment of Mikhail Gorbachev, at fifty-four the youngest member of the Politburo, as the General-Secretary of the Soviet Communist Party in May of that year.

12. See the section about Soviets' Cold War setbacks in the CIA report entitled "A Cold War Conundrum: The 1983 Soviet War Scare" (Washington, DC: Central Intelligence Agency, 1997).

13. One of these new programs was the Strategic Defense Initiative, also known as the Star Wars antimissile program.

14. Sadat's remarks were broadcast on NBC on September 22, 1981. For details, see "Sadat on Arms to Afghan Freedom Fighters" (Washington, DC: Joint Chiefs of Staff Message Center, U.S. Defense Department, September 23, 1981).

15. For corroboration, see Cooley, *Unholy Wars*, 21.

16. See U.S. Embassy cable, "Soviet Media on Sadat's Statement," (Moscow, September 24, 1981).

17. See the text of the State Department's news briefing in Washington: "U.S. Response to Soviet Criticism after Sadat Interview: A Summary of the News Briefing." Cable No. 254629 to U.S. Missions, September 23, 1981. Telegram number 254629 went to relevant U.S. missions for guidance.

18. Brown was in China January 4–13, 1980. See Cooley, *Unholy Wars*, 51–52; and "Rainwater, Afghanistan, "Terrorism," and Blowback."

19. See "Chronology of China-U.S. Relations," China Internet Information Center, http://www.china.org.cn/english/china-us/26890.htm.

20. Cooley, *Unholy Wars*, 52. See also "China SIGINT Capabilities," *Weekly Intelligence Notes* #15-01 (McLean, VA: Association of Former Intelligence Officers, April 16, 2001).

21. "China and the Afghan Resistance," Weekly summary of the U.S. Defense Intelligence Agency, March 6, 1981.

22. Ibid., 2.

23. Russian General Staff, *The Soviet-Afghan War: How A Superpower Fought and Lost*, trans. and ed. Lester Grau and Michael Gress (Lawrence: University Press of Kansas, 2002), 12.

24. The revolt in Qandahar happened on January 1, 1980. See ibid., 31.

25. Most notably in the Panjshir Valley and Kunar Province north of Kabul, Ghazni, and Paktia in the east.

26. Casualty estimates are not available, but the Russian General Staff gives an account of what happened. See *The Soviet-Afghan War*, 20–24. The author also heard similar accounts in 1990–1991 during private briefings with senior military officers in the Communist army of Afghanistan, Gen. Mohammad Afzal Lodin and Gen. Nabi Azimi.

27. See Directorate for Research, Defense Intelligence Agency, "Afghan Resistance," November 5, 1982.

28. U.S. intelligence report, "USSR-Afghanistan," quoting Pakistani officials and Afghan resistance leaders on March 1, 1980.

29. See "Afghanistan: Eighteen Months of Occupation," Special Report No. 86 (Washington, DC: State Department, August 1981), 2. Ten years later, this author visited Paghman numerous times as a war correspondent in 1990–1991 and found the area devastated and largely depopulated. Active resistance fighters used the mountains as their bases, from which they launched attacks on the capital.

30. Russian General Staff, *The Soviet Afghan War*, 26.

31. "Afghanistan: Two Years of Occupation," Special Report No. 91 (Washington, DC: State Department, December 1981), 2.

32. Mitrokhin, *The KGB in Afghanistan*, 118.

33. Report from Secretary of State George Shultz to Congress and UN member states, "Chemical Warfare in Southeast Asia and Afghanistan: An Update," Special Report No. 104 (Washington, DC: State Department, November 1982), 4–5. See also the BBC report broadcast "Chemical Weapons in Afghanistan?" on World Service Newsreel, 1500 GMT, April 23, 1980, cited in "Reports of the Use of Chemical Weapons in Afghanistan, Laos and Cambodia," compiled by the U.S. State Department in 1980.

34. Attributed to Brigadier Yousaf. See Yousaf and Adkin, *Afghanistan: The Bear Trap*, 1.
35. Brigadier Yousaf says that he personally selected these advisers and briefed them before sending them with Mujahideen units into Afghanistan. See ibid., 113–14.
36. See Jalali and Grau, *The Other Side of the Mountain*, 67. This three-volume study, commissioned by the U.S. Marine Corps, is a reliable source of information about resistance tactics in the battlefield.
37. Yousaf and Adkin, *Afghanistan: The Bear Trap*, 117.
38. Brigadier Yousaf was head of the Afghan Bureau of Pakistan's ISI during this period.
39. Yousaf and Adkin, *Afghanistan: The Bear Trap*, 98. Although Gates is less specific, he confirms that "the CIA's covert program to the Mujahideen increased several times over." See *From the Shadows*, 321.
40. Yousaf and Adkin, *Afghanistan: The Bear Trap*, 98.
41. Gates, *From the Shadows*, 321. The order President Reagan signed was the National Security Decision Directive 166, per page 349. Its title was "U.S. Policy, Programs and Strategy in Afghanistan." See "National Security Decision Directives: Reagan Administration" (Washington, DC: Federation of American Scientists, http://www.fas.org/irp/offdocs/nsdd/index.htm1). 1985. The release of the document was denied.
42. This distribution included both U.S. and Arab aid. According to Brigadier Yousaf, the main recipients in 1987 were Gulbuddin Hikmatyar (18–20 percent), Burhanuddin Rabbani (18–19 percent), Abdul Rasul Sayyaf (17–18 percent), and Yunis Khalis (13–15 percent)—all fundamentalist Islamist leaders. See Yousaf and Adkin, *Afghanistan: The Bear Trap*, 105.
43. The Stinger is a lightweight, shoulder-fired antiaircraft weapon. Its infrared homing device and fire-and-forget capability made it a highly effective system against low-flying aircraft and helicopters. See "Stinger: One Year of Combat," prepared by the U.S. Central Command, October 26, 1987. From time to time the Soviet and Afghan state media acknowledged their losses. See, for example, the Tass report "Afghan Transport Plane Shot Down by Stinger," Tass, August 13, 1987, which quotes the Afghan news agency Bakhtar. For a Pakistani military perspective, see Brigadier Yousaf's account in Yousaf and Adkin, *Afghanistan: The Bear Trap*, 178–80.
44. Gates, *From the Shadows*, 349–50.
45. Analysis by French scholar Olivier Roy, after spending more than two months in Afghanistan, in an interview with Agence France-Presse on September 27, 1987. The Russian General Staff acknowledges in *The Soviet-Afghan War* (212–13 and 222) that the Stinger system forced the Soviet command to severely limit its use of helicopters, and jet bombers were forced to fly high-altitude, and less accurate, missions.
46. Some do challenge the view that Stinger missiles changed the complexion of the Afghan conflict. See, for example, Alan Kuperman, "Stinging Rebukes," *Foreign Affairs* 81, no. 1 (January–February 2002). Kuperman asserts that "Soviet technical and tactical counter-measures had nullified the effect" within a short period and

that Gorbachev had, in fact, decided to withdraw from Afghanistan in 1985. However, the Soviet armed forces' changed behavior after the introduction of Stinger missiles indicates that their impact was considerable, and they at least hastened the Soviets' retreat from Afghanistan. During his reporting assignment in Afghanistan in 1990–1991, this author witnessed the extent to which Afghan and Soviet aircraft went to avoid the weapon and the fear of which seemed to dominate the pro-Soviet government in Kabul.

47. In his speech at the Twenty-seventh Soviet Communist Party Congress.

48. Minutes of the Politburo meeting on November 13, 1986, in the *Documents on the Soviet Invasion of Afghanistan*, 73–74.

49. Ibid., 76. The timing of Gorbachev's speech is worth noting. It was made just two months after the Afghan resistance began using American-supplied Stinger missiles.

50. The Russian General Staff, *The Soviet-Afghan War*, 1.

51. The governments of Afghanistan and Pakistan signed the accords in May 1988. The U.S. and Soviet representatives served as guarantors.

52. Russian General Staff, *The Soviet Afghan War*, 13.

53. Reagan was succeeded by his vice president, George H. W. Bush, in January 1989. The Soviet occupation forces completed their retreat from Afghanistan a month later.

Chapter 9. Consequences of the U.S.-Soviet War

1. See "The Soviet View" in Jalali and Grau, *The Other Side of the Mountain*, 126–27.

2. Ibid., 126.

3. The British imperial army in India fought three wars with the Afghans: First Anglo-Afghan War (1839–1842), Second (1878–1880), and Third (1919). In addition, there were numerous border skirmishes.

4. See Jalali and Grau, *On the Other Side of Mountain*, vol. 3, 127. The figures put the Soviet losses at 13,833 dead and almost 470,000 wounded and sick. More than 100,000 contracted hepatitis while 30,000 suffered from typhoid. Some 10,000 Soviet citizens became permanently disabled.

5. Tad Daley, "Afghanistan and Gorbachev's Global Foreign Policy," *Asian Survey* 29, no. 5 (May 1989): 506–7.

6. Jalali and Grau, *On the Other Side of the Mountain*, vol. 1, iii.

7. For example, the Soviets confronted unrest in the Republic of Georgia; coal miners' strikes in Siberia, Ukraine, and Central Asia; pro-independence demonstrations in the Baltic republics; civil war between Armenia and Azerbaijan; and the collapse of the Berlin Wall.

8. At Ojhri camp, outside the Pakistani city of Rawalpindi, in April 1988. See Yousaf and Adkin, *Afghanistan: The Bear Trap*, 220–21. His reaction was, "If it was deliberate sabotage, it was a masterstroke." Brigadier Yousaf had retired from the army in 1987.

9. Ibid., 223.

10. Critics have described the ISI as a state within the state, answerable neither to the leadership of the Pakistani military nor to the president or prime minister. See

"Directorate for Inter-Services Intelligence (ISI)" (Washington, DC: Federation of American Scientists, July 2002).

11. Hikmatyar is a staunch Pashtun nationalist from the Tajik-dominated northern province of Baghlan.

12. A Pashtun from eastern Afghanistan, Khalis was educated in Afghan and Pakistani religious schools.

13. Sayyaf studied Arabic in Mecca and was closely identified with the Saudi conservative Wahhabi sect of Islam.

14. Masood and Hikmatyar, the ISI's favorite guerrilla leader, were also bitter enemies.

15. Pakistani military intelligence spread the word that Hikmatyar commanded the largest guerrilla organization and that it was "the best-organized and militarily most effective group." See, for example, Bradsher, *Afghan Communism and Soviet Intervention*, 185.

16. They were going to a military demonstration, where an American M-1 battle tank was to be shown in action. All thirty-one people on board died, including at least eight other Pakistani generals, U.S. ambassador Arnold Raphel, and U.S. defense attaché Brig. Gen. Herbert Wassom. See Yousaf and Adkin, *Afghanistan: The Bear Trap*, 8–9.

17. U.S. intelligence described him as "a real fire-breather" on religious matters. See the biographic sketch the U.S. Defense Intelligence Agency prepared of Lt. Gen. Hamid Gul (Washington, DC: U.S. Defense Intelligence Agency, January 1989), 2.

18. Jalalabad was an attractive target. One of the largest cities in Afghanistan, its proximity to Pakistan made it easier for the ISI to plan and execute an attack. See Hyman, *Afghanistan Under Soviet Domination*, 257.

19. "The Geneva Accords of 1988 on Afghanistan," Institute of Afghan Studies, http://www.institute-for-afghan-studies.org/Accords%20Treaties/geneva_accords_1988_pakistan_afghanistan.htm.

20. Yousaf and Adkin, *Afghanistan: The Bear Trap*, 215; and Hyman, *Afghanistan Under Soviet Domination*, 256. This author personally witnessed giant Soviet transport planes with military and economic aid landing at Kabul airport virtually every day. Regarding CIA aid to the Mujahideen, also see Rubin, *The Fragmentation of Afghanistan*, 255.

21. Yousaf and Adkin, *Afghanistan: The Bear Trap*, 217; and Rubin, *The Fragmentation of Afghanistan*, 247.

22. William Maley, *The Afghanistan Wars* (Basingstoke, UK: Palgrave Macmillan, 2002), 159.

23. Yousaf and Adkin, *Afghanistan: The Bear Trap*, 228–30. The village was Samarkhel.

24. Brigadier Yousaf suggests that brutal killings of surrendering Afghan government troops was a mistake. See ibid., 230.

25. Ibid. Brigadier Yousaf says the number of refugees was twenty thousand, but it did not include those who fled west, in particular, to Kabul.

26. Bradsher, *Afghan Communism and Soviet Intervention*, 345–46. According to Brigadier Yousaf, the losses on the Mujahideen side "exceeded 3,000 killed and wounded." See Yousaf and Adkin, *Afghanistan: The Bear Trap*, 231.

27. General Gul's replacement, Shamsur Rahman Kallu, was a retired general and an ally of Prime Minister Benazir Bhutto's.

28. For an insider's account, see Riaz Mohammad Khan, *Untying the Afghan Knot: Negotiating Soviet Withdrawal* (Durham, NC: Duke University Press, 1991), 304. A career Pakistani diplomat, he was a member of the Pakistani negotiating team at the Geneva talks on Afghanistan and served from 1986 to 1988 as director-general in the Foreign Office.

29. Zalmay Khalilzad, "Testimony before the U.S. House Subcommittee on Asian and Pacific Affairs," June 14, 1989, 1–9. Khalilzad, an Afghan American academic, had been closely involved in the U.S. decision-making process regarding Afghanistan since the 1980s.

Chapter 10. The Final Days of Communism

1. "Report on Afghanistan" by Eduard Shevardnadze (foreign minister), Dmitri Yazov (defense minister), Vladimir Kryuchkov (KGB chairman) et al., dated January 23, 1989, and submitted to the Communist Party Politburo of the Soviet Union. See the minutes of the Politburo meeting that approved the report on January 24, 1989, in the *Documents on the Soviet Invasion of Afghanistan*, 76–79.

2. For instance, President Najibullah and Lt. Gen. Shah Nawaz Tanai, a fellow Pashtun, had a rocky relationship. Their hostility exploded when Tanai led a military coup on March 6, 1990. When it failed, Tanai fled with military secrets to Pakistan, where he began collaborating with the ISI and Hikmatyar.

3. Author's private conversations with Afghan leaders.

4. Shevardnadze et al. "Report on Afghanistan."

5. The discussion here on Najibullah's strategy of making deals with internal commanders draws mainly on Hyman, *Afghanistan Under Soviet Domination*, 257–60.

6. Documentary evidence of Najibullah's incentives to field commanders is difficult to find, because deals were made through secret and often indirect negotiations using the Afghan secret service. The results, however, were obvious to the author and other observers. Some commanders and their troops would suddenly emerge in public and be given accommodations, vehicles, and reportedly monthly allowances to live in government-held areas. In return, they declared their support for the Kabul regime.

7. Nassery was rumored to be a U.S. citizen, and his defection to the Najibullah regime led to bitter criticisms from fundamentalists. See Rubin, *The Fragmentation of Afghanistan*, 291.

8. Summary of Najibullah's speeches in summer 1989, quoted by Hyman, *Afghanistan Under Soviet Domination*, 258.

9. Private meetings with Professor Mohammad Asghar and his deputy, Gen. Abdul Hakeem Katawazi (Ret.), in Kabul during 1990–1991. They always insisted that the National Salvation Society had no intention of cooperating with Najibullah; moreover, they would not accept a post in the Afghan government as long as Najibullah was in power.

10. On June 26–29. See Rubin, *The Fragmentation of Afghanistan*, 152. The Homeland

Party had an Executive Committee and a Central Council, replacing the Politburo and the Central Committee.

11. Deepak Tripathi, *From Our Own Correspondent*, BBC World Service, first broadcast on August 5, 1992.

12. The three PDPA secretaries were replaced by four vice presidents. President Najibullah and First Vice President Suleiman Laiq of the Homeland Party were Pashtuns from the Parcham faction. Among the other three vice presidents—Najmuddin Kawiani, Farid Mazdak, and Nazar Mohammad—Kawiani and Mazdak were Parchami Tajiks. Nazar Mohammad, a Pashtun, was a Khalq member.

13. "Afghan Constitution of 1990," Afghanistan Online, http://www.afghan-web.com/history/const/const1990.html.

14. The prime minister was Fazle Haq Khaliqyar, a dignitary from Herat Province. While not a PDPA member, he had previously served in Najibullah's government as a minister without portfolio.

15. The most senior Afghan official to be killed was Deputy Defense Minister Lt. Gen. Jalal Razminda. Khaliqyar took several bullets in his abdomen and was paralyzed. This author was with the official party and reported on the massacre. Refer to his reports broadcast on the BBC World Service, April 6–8, 1990. For a Mujahideen perspective, see "Najib suffers major setback in Herat," (Peshawar, Pakistan: AFGHANews, vol. 6, no. 8, April 15, 1990, available http://www.scribd.com/doc/29565597/Afgha-Newspaper).

16. The Turkish Embassy remained open during the conflict.

17. Pashtun members who waited until the Najibullah regime's final moments before defecting included Defense Minister Gen. Aslam Watanjar, Interior Minister Raz Mohammad Paktin, and Vice President Gen. Mohammad Rafi. Together, they took the main Khalqi military and the Sarandoy militia, which came under the interior ministry.

18. For an authoritative look at the last days of Najibullah's rule, see Fred Halliday and Zahir Tanin, "The Communist Regime in Afghanistan, 1978–1992: Institutions and Conflicts," *Europe-Asia Studies* 50 (December 1998): 1367–80.

19. For example, Gen. Abdul Rashid Dostum assumed control of the Uzbek militia, and the Ismaili Hazara force was under Gen. Sayed Jaffar Nadiri.

20. Dostum, Nadiri, and Maj. Gen. Abdul Momin. See Halliday and Tanin, "The Communist Regime in Afghanistan," 1370; Rubin, *The Fragmentation of Afghanistan*, 269–70; and Bradsher, *Afghan Communism and Soviet Intervention*, 377.

21. KGB chief Vladimir Kryuchkov, Defense Minister Dmitri Yazov, Vice President Gennady Yanayev, and Prime Minister Valentin Pavlov were removed from their posts and arrested. Interior Minister Boris Pugo committed suicide.

22. The agreement, which was announced on September 13, 1991, said that U.S. and Soviet aid would end on January 1, 1992. See Mitrokhin, *The KGB in Afghanistan*, 17.

23. For example, Foreign Minister Abdul Wakil and former deputy prime minister Mahmood Baryalai were the cousin and half-brother, respectively, of Babrak Karmal, whom Najibullah had replaced as the leader of Afghanistan in 1986. Also

included were Tajik members of the ruling party's Executive (previously the PDPA Politburo) Farid Mazdak and Najmuddin Kawiani, as well as the deputy defense minister and commander of the Kabul garrison, Gen. Nabi Azimi.

24. Benon Sevan later became the executive director of the Oil-for-Food Program for Iraq.

25. Interpretations of the end of the Cold War range from the West's preparation with its nuclear weapons and alliance system to the failure of Communist ideology. See Charles Kegley, "How Did the Cold War Die? Principles for an Autopsy," *Mershon International Studies Review* 38, no. 1 (April 1994): 12. All of these assertions are challenged in the article. For the full text, see 11–41.

26. See John Lewis Gaddis, *The United States and the End of the Cold War: Implications, Reconsiderations, Provocations* (New York: Oxford University Press, 1992), 156–67.

27. William Wohlforth, "Realism and the End of the Cold War," *International Security* 19, no. 3 (Winter 1994–1995): 96.

28. Arnold Beichman, *The Long Pretense: Soviet Treaty Diplomacy from Lenin to Gorbachev* (Piscataway, NJ: Transaction, 1991), 205.

29. Economic pressures and a low quality of life for Soviet citizens are among the factors cited for the Soviet Union's slow demise. See Walter Laqueur, "Gorbachev and Epimetheus: The Origins of the Russian Crisis," *Journal of Contemporary History* 28, no. 3 (July 1993): 389–416.

30. This Russian author wrote such works as *The Gulag Archipelago*, depicting life in Soviet labor camps, and *One Day in the Life of Ivan Denisovich*, recounting a prisoner's typical day of forced labor, deprivation, and suffering while in a labor camp under Stalin. Alexandr Solzhenitsyn won the 1970 Nobel Prize for Literature.

31. A nuclear scientist who was regarded as the father of the Soviet hydrogen bomb, Sakharov turned against the excesses of the Soviet system. He spent six years in internal exile in Gorky until his release on Gorbachev's orders in 1986. He was awarded the Nobel Peace Prize in 1975.

Chapter 11. The Remaking of the Post-Soviet World

1. The collapse of the Berlin Wall and the fall of Communist regimes in Poland, Bulgaria, Romania, and Czechoslovakia all occurred in late 1989.

2. For example, Afghanistan, Iraq, Syria, Libya, and Ethiopia.

3. "Joint Declaration," first U.S.-Russia summit between President Bush and President Yeltsin at Camp David, *NATO-Russia Archive* (Berlin Information-Center for Transatlantic Security, February 1, 1992).

4. Michael Beschloss and Strobe Talbott, *At the Highest Levels: The Inside Story of the End of the Cold War* (Boston: Little, Brown, 1993), 443.

5. For two authoritative estimates, see Amy F. Woolf, *Nuclear Weapons in the Former Soviet Union: Location, Command and Control*, Issue Brief 91144 (Washington, DC: Congressional Research Service, 1996); and Jeremiah Sullivan, "The Legacy of Nuclear Weapons," *Swords and Ploughshares* 7, no. 2 (Winter 1992).

6. Their inventories were: Russia, 7,327; Ukraine, 1,568; Kazakhstan, 1,360; and Belarus, 54.

7. Sullivan, "The Legacy of Nuclear Weapons."

8. The term *strategic partnership* also suggested that there would continue to be areas of competing interests for both Russia and the United States.

9. Sullivan, "The Legacy of Nuclear Weapons."

10. Woolf, *Nuclear Weapons in the Former Soviet Union.*

11. Additional information that came to light in 1993 suggested that Russia had twelve hundred tons of enriched uranium, or more than twice the amount originally thought.

12. See the "Joint Russian-American Declaration on Defense Conversion," after the second Bush-Yeltsin summit, Washington, DC, June 17, 1992.

13. The Soviet Threat Reduction Act, sponsored by Senator Sam Nunn and Senator Richard Lugar, was renamed after the USSR's collapse as the Cooperative Threat Reduction Program.

14. "A Short History of Threat Reduction," *Arms Control Today,* June 2003.

15. Susan Koch, "Cooperative Threat Reduction: Reducing Weapons of Mass Destruction," *USIA Electronic Journal* 3, no. 3 (July 1998).

16. "A Short History of Threat Reduction."

17. The original parties to START 1, signed on July 31, 1991, were the United States and the Soviet Union. On May 23, 1992, America and the four nuclear-capable successor states to the USSR—Russia, Ukraine, Belarus, and Kazakhstan—concluded the Lisbon Protocol, which made all five nations party to START 1. See Arms Control Association, "START 1 at a Glance," *Fact Sheets.*

18. Iraq invaded Kuwait in August 1990, and a U.S.-led military campaign liberated the emirate in early 1991. Thereafter, containing Iraq in the region became a greater U.S. priority.

19. See the text of George W. Bush's State of the Union address January 1991.

20. Walter LaFeber, *America, Russia, and the Cold War, 1945–2000,* 9th ed. (New York: McGraw-Hill, 2002), 359.

21. See the text of Anthony Lake's speech, "From Containment to Enlargement," School of Advanced International Studies, Johns Hopkins University, Washington, DC, September 21, 1993, http://www.mtholyoke.edu/acad/intrel/lakedoc. html.

22. See Strobe Talbott, *The Russia Hand: A Memoir of Presidential Diplomacy* (New York: Random House, 2003), 38. A former Rhodes scholar who had attended Oxford with Clinton, Talbott was appointed ambassador-at-large and later deputy secretary of state by President Clinton.

23. Ibid., 38.

24. See, for example, "The Vancouver Declaration" after the first Clinton-Yeltsin summit in Canada, *The NATO-Russia Archive* (Berlin Information-Center for Transatlantic Security, April 3–4, 1993); "Joint Declaration on Common Security Challenges at the Threshold of the Twenty-First Century," seventh Yeltsin-Clinton summit in Moscow, September 2, 1998; and "Strengthening Transatlantic Security—A U.S. Strategy for the Twenty-First Century" (Washington, DC: Department of Defense, December 2000).

25. The preference, therefore, was to build a pipeline between Baku in Azerbaijan and Ceyhan in Turkey, a NATO ally of the United States. See Stanley Kober, "The Great Game, Round Two," *Foreign Policy Briefing* no. 63 (Washington, DC: Cato Institute, October 31, 2000).

26. See, for example, "Statement of Principles," Project for the New American Century, June 3, 1997, http://www.newamericancentury.org/statementofprinciples.htm.

27. See George Lenczowski, "The Arc of Crisis: Its Central Sector," *Foreign Affairs* (Spring 1979).

28. President Jimmy Carter, "State of the Union Address," January 23, 1980.

29. Bernard Lewis, "The Roots of Muslim Rage," *Atlantic Weekly*, September 1990, http://www.theatlantic.com/magazine/archive/1990/09/the-roots-of-muslim-rage/4643/1/.

30. Ibid. See the subsection titled "A Clash of Civilizations."

31. Ibid. The line of argument pursued here seems powerful to many in the West, but it completely fails to recognize that hatred, kidnapping, and murder are not exclusive to Islam. Examples of civil conflicts in Northern Ireland (Roman Catholic versus Protestant), Sri Lanka (Tamils, both Hindu and Muslim, versus Sinhala of the Buddhist faith), and Yugoslavia in the same period are omitted.

32. Samuel Huntington, "The Clash of Civilizations?" *Foreign Affairs* (Summer 1993), 22–49.

33. Ibid., 24. He defines a civilization as "both by common objective elements, such as language, history, religion, customs, institutions, and by the subjective self-identification of the people."

34. Huntington identified them as Western, Islamic, Hindu, Confucian, Japanese, Slavic-Orthodox, Latin American, and possibly African.

35. Huntington, "The Clash of Civilizations?," 31–32.

36. Ibid., 35–36.

37. From 1980 to 1988, Iran and Iraq had fought one of the most vicious wars the world had seen in the twentieth century.

38. Project for the New American Century, "Statement of Principles."

39. Some of the others were Donald Rumsfeld, the defense secretary under President George W. Bush; Paul Wolfowitz, later to be Rumsfeld's deputy; Zalmay Khalilzad; Fred Ikle; Francis Fukuyama; Dan Quayle; and Elliott Abrams.

Chapter 12. The Rise of the Taliban

1. Qandahar's population in 1994 was about 250,000. An important market town, it has road links to the Afghan capital, Kabul, and Herat, near the Iranian border, and the Central Asian republics of the former Soviet Union. Qandahar and Peshawar in Pakistan's North-West Frontier Province (renamed Khyber Pakhtunkhwa) are regarded as the principal cities of the Pashtun people.

2. Pakistani journalist, Ahmed Rashid, has written extensively on the Taliban. For example, see *Taliban: The Story of the Afghan Warlords* (London: Pan Books, 2001), 21; "Pakistan and the Taliban," *The Nation (Lahore-Pakistan)*, April 11, 1998, http://

www.rawa.org/arashid.htm; "Afghanistan: Ending the Policy Quagmire," *Journal of International Affairs* 54, no. 2 (Spring 2001); and "The Taliban: Exporting Extremism" *Foreign Affairs* 78, no. 6 (November/December 1999).

3. The Taliban's supreme leader, Mullah Omar, lost his right eye; one-time foreign minister Mohammed Ghaus also had one eye; the governor of Qandahar, Mullah Mohammad Hasan, and the mayor of Kabul, Abdul Majid, both had lost a leg. See Rashid, *Taliban*, 17–18.

4. The Hizb-i-Islami (Khalis), one of the more hard-line factions.

5. See U.S. Embassy cable, "Finally A Talkative Talib: Origins and Membership of the Students' Movement," Islamabad, February 20, 1995, 4–5, in *The Taliban File*, Electronic Briefing Book no. 97 (Washington, DC: National Security Archive, September 11, 2003); see also Rashid, *Taliban*, 23–24.

6. Rashid, "Pakistan and the Taliban."

7. U.S. Embassy cable, "The Taliban: What We've Heard," Islamabad, January 26, 1995, cited in *The Taliban File*.

8. In October 1994, Babar accompanied the ambassadors of six countries (the United States, Britain, Spain, Italy, China, and South Korea) in a land convoy that traveled from Pakistan to Herat in western Afghanistan. Pakistani officials from the departments of Railways, Highways, Telecommunications, and Electricity were with them. According to Ahmed Rashid, the journey was undertaken without the Kabul government's knowledge. See *Taliban*, 27, 251.

9. Conscious of the need to establish its own role, ISI officers discreetly traveled to Herat in September 1994 to "survey" the road.

10. See Rashid, *Taliban*, 27.

11. Rashid, who has proven contacts in the Pakistani military, quotes his sources as saying that the Spin Baldak dump had approximately 18,000 Kalashnikov rifles and 120 artillery pieces, as well as ammunition. See "Pakistan and the Taliban," 81, and *Taliban*, 27; see also U.S. Embassy cable, "[Excised] Believe Pakistan Is Backing Taliban," Islamabad, December 6, 1994, in *The Taliban File*.

12. Then head of the ISI, Lt. Gen. Javed Ashraf Qazi, was said to have told the Americans that his agency had "no role in supporting the Taliban." He said he had "strongly recommended to Prime Minister Bhutto" that the group should not be supported in any way, but that the interior minister had become the "principal patron of the Taliban." See U.S. Embassy cable, "[Excised] Believe Pakistan Is Backing the Taliban."

13. Colonel Imam was described as the region's most prominent ISI field officer, operating under cover as Pakistan's consul-general in Herat. The Taliban commanders who were with the convoy were Mullah Borjan and Mullah Turabi. See Rashid, *Taliban*, 28.

14. For a summary of the ISI's problems at the time, see Rashid, "Pakistan and the Taliban".

15. The army chief, Gen. Abdul Waheed; the head of military intelligence, Lt. Gen. Ali Kuli Khan; and all ISI field officers collaborating with the Taliban were Pashtuns.

16. Rabbani and Masood were both Tajik.

17. Rashid, *Taliban*, 48.
18. Haji Abdul Qadir. His surrender brought the collapse of Jalalabad city's ruling council representing the Mujahideen administration in Kabul.
19. Najibullah's brother, Shahpur Ahmadzai, was chief of security at the Presidential Palace before his fall.
20. See U.S. diplomatic cables from Pakistan to Washington. For example, American Consulate "New Fighting and New Forces in Qandahar," Peshawar, November 3, 1994; also, U.S. Embassy cable, "[Excised] Believe Pakistan Is Backing Taliban."
21. American Consulate, "New Fighting," 5–6.
22. Olivier Roy provides an authoritative analysis on this strategic objective. See "Rivalries and Power Plays in Afghanistan: The Taliban, the Shari'a and the Pipeline," *Middle East Report* no. 202 (Winter 1996): 38.
23. Turkmenistan had vast gas and oil reserves, as well as a government eager to do business with the outside world, and was close to the oil-rich Caspian region.
24. Unocal, "Suspension of activities related to proposed natural gas pipeline across Afghanistan," news release, August 21, 1998. The pipelines would also carry oil from the Caspian, where American companies, including Chevron, had invested heavily.
25. It was seen as a move by the Turkmen leader to engage a big American company and the Clinton administration in his country. See Rashid, *Taliban*, 160. The author provides a detailed analysis of the battle for pipelines in chapters 12 and 13. Olivier Roy points out that the American political adviser to Unocal, Charles Santos, was close to the Clinton administration. See "Rivalries and Power Plays in Afghanistan," 39.
26. Barnett Rubin, "Women and Pipelines: Afghanistan's Proxy Wars," *International Affairs* 73, no. 2 (April 1997): 292.
27. U.S. Embassy cable, "Ambassador raises bin Laden with Foreign Secretary, Shamshad Ahmad," Islamabad, October 6, 1998; "Coordinating our efforts and sharpening our message on Osama bin Laden," Islamabad, October 19, 1998; "Osama bin Laden: Charge reiterates U.S. concerns to key Taliban official, who sticks to well-known Taliban positions," Islamabad, December 19, 2000, in *Update: The Taliban File Part IV* (Washington, DC: National Security Archive, August 18, 2005).
28. U.S. Embassy cable, "Coordinating our efforts."
29. U.S. Embassy cable, "Osama bin Laden."
30. On October 30, 1996. See Rubin, "Women and Pipelines," 293.
31. For example, President Rabbani moved his headquarters to Badakhshan Province in the northeast after being forced out of Kabul.
32. Unocal, "Suspension of activities."
33. Unocal statement on withdrawal from the proposed Central Asia Gas (CentGas) pipeline project, December 4, 1998.
34. Rashid, "The Taliban," 24.
35. Shi'a predominate the Hazara and Tajik communities in central Afghanistan.
36. Amnesty International, *Amnesty International Report 1997 - Afghanistan*, January 1, 1997, http://www.unhcr.org/refworld/country,,AMNESTY,,AFG,4562d8cf 2,3ae6a9fd40,0.htm.

37. U.S. State Department, *Afghanistan Report on Human Rights Practices for 1996*, released by the Bureau of Democracy, Human Rights, and Labor, January 30, 1997, http://www.state.gov/www/global/human_rights/1996_hrp_report/afghanis. html; see also U.S. State Department reports for subsequent years.
38. Country Report on Human Rights Practices: Afghanistan, 2002.
39. Amnesty International, *Amnesty International Report 1998 - Afghanistan*, January 1, 1998, http://www.unhcr.org/refworld/country,,AMNESTY,,AFG,4562d8cf2, 3 ae6a9fa54,0.htm.
40. In addition to the 1998 Amnesty International report, see Human Rights Watch, *Human Rights Watch World Report 1999 - Afghanistan*, January 1, 1999, http://www. unhcr.org/refworld/country,,HRW,,AFG,4562d8cf2,3ae6a8b520,0.html.
41. Amnesty International, *Amnesty International Report 2000 - Afghanistan*, June 1, 2000, http://www.unhcr.org/refworld/country,,AMNESTY,,AFG,4562d8cf2,3 ae6aa121f,0.htm.
42. For example, the secretary of state, Warren Christopher, wrote to the Taliban as early as in 1996, seeking their cooperation to "expel all terrorists and those who support terrorism" from Afghanistan. See U.S. State Department, "U.S. Engagement with the Taliban on Usama bin Laden," declassified on September, 8, 2003, in *The Taliban File*.

Chapter 13. Dialectics of the Afghan Conflict
1. According to German philosopher, Georg Hegel, dialectic is a process in which an event or force, a delineated concept (thesis), produces contradictions (antithesis), and thesis and anti-thesis eventually merge to form a synthesis. See Kim O'Connor, "dialectic," (Winter 2003), http://csmt.uchicago.edu/glossary2004/ dialectic.htm; Daniel Berthold-Bond, "The Nature of Dialectic," in *Hegel's Grand Synthesis: A Study of Being, Thought, and History* (New York: Harper, 1993), 81–91; "Hegel," Digital Text Projects (New York: Columbia University Press, 1991), http://www.ilt.columbia.edu/publications/digitext.html.
2. See Berthold-Bond, "Dialectic and Negativity," in *Hegel's Grand Synthesis*.
3. Estimates differ considerably, but according to Ahmed Rashid, who has closely followed events in Afghanistan, the number was over 25,000. See "Pakistan: Trouble Ahead, Trouble Behind," *Current History* (April 1996): 161.
4. French scholar Olivier Roy makes this point in a study of Islam in Afghan society. See "Has Islamism a future in Afghanistan?" in *Fundamentalism Reborn? Afghanistan and the Taliban*, ed. William Maley (London: Hurst & Company, 2001), 199–211.
5. For instance, Hikmatyar and Rabbani's senior commander, Ahmad Shah Masood, had been an engineering student.
6. Roy, "Has Islamism a future in Afghanistan?," 201. The founder of the Muslim Brotherhood was Hasan al-Banna, who started the movement in 1928. Today, it inspires organizations such as HAMAS and the Egyptian Jihad, and there are branches of the Brotherhood in other Arab states.
7. Sayed Qutb was an American-educated Egyptian, who worked in the Ministry of Public Instruction in Cairo. His association with the Islamic Brotherhood led

him to leave the civil service, and he became the most influential theorist in the movement. Qutb spent years in jail. In 1965 he wrote his most controversial book, *Milestones*, after which he was accused of conspiring against the government of President Nasir, rearrested, and executed in August 1966.

8. See the introductory chapter, *Milestones*, available on http://majalla.org/books/2005 /qutb-nilestone.pdf.

9. See *Muslim Brotherhood* (Washington, DC: Federation of American Scientists).

10. Organizations such as al-Jihad, al-Gama'at al-Islamiyya, HAMAS, and Islamist groups in Afghanistan.

11. For his family history and transformation, see Peter Bergen, *Holy War Inc.: Inside the Secret World of Osama bin Laden*, 2nd ed. (London: Phoenix, 2002), 44–65.

12. Maha Azzam, *Al-Qa'ida: the misunderstood Wahhabi connection and the ideology of violence* (London: Royal Institute of International Affairs, Briefing Paper no. 1, February 2003), 2.

13. See Yael Shahar, "Osama bin Laden: Marketing Terrorism" (Herzliya, Israel: International Policy Institute for Counter-Terrorism, August 22, 1998). Osama's father, Mohammad Awad bin Laden, a naturalized Saudi citizen of Yemeni origin, had made his fortune from a huge empire of construction firms. He was close to the Saudi royal family.

14. The name of the organization was Makhtab al-Khidmat, meaning "the House of Auxiliaries," which bin Laden created with Abdullah Azzam. The fighters it trained usually joined the Hizb-i Islami group of Gulbuddin Hikmatyar.

15. Shahar, "Osama bin Laden."

16. Ahmed Rashid, "Osama bin Laden: How the U.S. Helped Midwife a Terrorist," in *Taliban: Militant Islam, Oil, and Fundamentalism in Central Asia* (New Haven, CT: Yale University Press, 2000).

17. Arab fighters also set up bases in the provinces of Badakhshan, Kunar, and Nuristan.

18. Hasan al-Turabi was head of the Islamic Liberation Front and speaker of the Sudanese Parliament.

19. See Jason Burke's authoritative article, "The making of the world's most wanted man," *The Observer*, October 28, 2001.

20. There are many sources of information and analysis on his place in the hierarchy. See, for example, Nimrod Raphaeli, "Ayman Mohammad al-Rabi' al-Zawahiri: The Making of an Arch-Terrorist," *Terrorism and Political Violence* (Washington, DC: The Middle East Media Research Institute, Winter 2002); also Ed Blanche, "Ayman al-Zawahiri: attention turns to the other prime suspect," *Jane's Intelligence Review*, October 3, 2001, and the U.S. Federal Bureau of Investigation.

21. Blanche, "Ayman al-Zawahiri."

22. Raphaeli, "Ayman Mohammad al-Rabi' al-Zawahiri."

23. Raphaeli examines these views, in particular, in a discussion of al-Zawahiri's two books, *The Bitter Harvest* and *Knights under the Banner of the Prophet*.

24. This appears to be a reference to the Muslim Brotherhood directly or indirectly taking part in elections in Egypt.

25. Raphaeli, "Ayman Mohammad al-Rabi' al-Zawahiri."

26. He was born in 1941 near Jenin on the West Bank. He was a member of the Palestinian Muslim Brotherhood and the Palestinian Jihad. See Trevor Stanley, *Abdullah Azzam: The Godfather of Jihad*, Perspectives on World History and Current Events, 2003–2005, http://www.pwhce.org/azzam.html; and Colonel Jonathan Fighel, "Sheikh Abdullah Azzam: Bin Laden's spiritual mentor" (Herzliya, Israel: International Institute for Counter-Terrorism, September 27, 2001).

27. See, for example, Fighel, "Sheikh Abdullah Azzam"; Lawrence Kudlow, "Iraq and al-Qa'ida" and "al-Qa'ida" (Herzliya, Israel: International Policy Institute for Counter-Terrorism).

28. Sometime during 1988–1989. See Kudlow, "al-Qa'ida," and "Timeline: Al-Qaeda," BBC News, September 4, 2006, http://news.bbc.co.uk/2/hi/3618762.stm.

29. A statement by al Qaeda, first published in 1996, held America, Israel, and the Saudi royal family responsible for the 1991 Gulf War and the Lebanon conflict. The statement called it a duty of every tribe in the Arab Peninsula to fight "in the cause of Allah and to cleanse the land from those occupiers." It promised young Muslims "paradise after death" in the war. See "Declaration of War against the Americans occupying the Land of the two Holy Places," Mid-East Web, http://www.mideastweb.org/osamabinladen1.htm.

30. For a thought-provoking analysis of Soviet communism, National Socialism, and Islamic fundamentalism, described as the three assaults on the West in the twentieth century, see John Gray, *Al-Qaeda and What It Means to Be Modern* (London: Faber and Faber, 2003), 5–27.

Chapter 14. The Nature of al Qaeda

1. For a fuller list, refer to Phil Hirschkorn, Rohan Gunaratna, Ed Blanche, and Stefan Leader, "Blowback," *Jane's Intelligence Review* 13, no. 8 (August 1, 2001), special report.

2. John Dumbrell, *American Foreign Policy: Carter to Clinton* (London: Macmillan, 1997), 69.

3. "Text of World Islamic Front's Statement Urging Jihad Against Jews and Crusaders." It was signed by Osama bin Laden, Ayman al-Zawahiri (the Egyptian Jihad), Rifa'i Ahmad Taha (the Islamic Group of Egypt), Sheikh Mir Hamzah (the Jamiat-ul Ulema-i-Pakistan), and Fazlul Rahman (the Jihad Movement of Bangladesh). See Mid-East Web quoting Al-Quds Al-Arabi, February 23, 1998, 3.

4. The term *edict* is preferred here instead of *fatwa* (ruling) in order to describe the call to kill non-Muslims, because bin Laden and his associates had no religious authority to issue such rulings.

5. The statement begins by quoting a particularly militant verse from the Quran and swiftly goes on to the message of its signatories.

6. To end the Iraqi occupation of Kuwait.

7. "Text of World Islamic Front's Statement Urging Jihad Against Jews and Crusaders."

8. For an illuminating analysis, see Bernard Lewis, "License to Kill: Osama bin Laden's Declaration of Jihad," *Foreign Affairs* 77, no. 6 (November/December 1998): 14–19.

9. Quran (9:41), which the Muslims believe to be the word of God as revealed to the Prophet Mohammad in Arabic. For three different translated versions of the Quran, see the University of Southern California website, http://www.usc.edu/schools/college/crcc/engagement/resources/texts/muslim/quran/.

10. All people are "one community" (Quran 2:213); "If the enemy leans towards peace, then incline to it" (Quran 8:61).

11. "We have honored the sons of Adam, provided them with transport on land and sea, given them things for sustenance good and pure and conferred on them special favors" (17:70); "We have created you male and female, made you into nations and tribes, so you may know (and not despise) each other" (Quran 49:13).

12. See, for example, 9:5, 9:28–29 of the Quran for instructions on how to deal with the unbelievers, or the pagans, during the time of the Prophet Mohammad, especially the references to "the forbidden months" and "after this year."

13. "Whoever killed a human being—unless it was for murder or mischief in the land—it would be as though he killed the whole people" (Quran 5: 32); "We must punish those from the enemy who did us harm and treat the civilians and the innocent with kindness" (Quran 18:86); "Tell those who believe to forgive those who do not look forward to the days of Allah. It is for Him to recompense each people for what they have earned" (Quran 45:14).

14. "Fight in the cause of God those who fight you, but do not transgress limits, for God loveth not transgressors" (Quran 2:190).

15. See 8:70–71 of the Quran.

16. See Paul Rogers and Sicilla Elworthy, "A Never-Ending War? Consequences of 11 September" (Oxford, UK: Oxford Research Group, Briefing Paper, March 2002), 3.

17. Hirschkorn, Gunaratna, Blanche, and Leader, "Blowback"; UK Government Report, "Responsibility for the Terrorist Atrocities in the United States, 11 September 2001—An Updated Account." A useful source containing a list of Afghan training camps is the South Asia Terrorism Portal, the Institute of Conflict Management, New Delhi, India.

18. UK Government Report, "Responsibility for the Terrorist Atrocities."

19. Hirschkorn, Gunaratna, Blanche, and Leader, "Blowback."

20. UK Government Report, "Responsibility for the Terrorist Atrocities."

21. Ramzi Yusuf had obtained a degree in electronic engineering in Britain before moving to the United States.

22. In 1998, Yusuf was tried in New York and sentenced to 240 years in jail. See Bergen, *Holy War Inc.*, 141; also, Laurie Mylroie, "The World Trade Center Bomb: Who is Ramzi Yousef? And Why It Matters," *The National Interest* (Winter 1995/96).

23. The interview was conducted by a leading Pakistani journalist, Rahimullah Yusufzai, and published in the January 11, 1999, issue of *Time*.

24. See David Nagle, "USS Cole Rejoins the Fleet," Navy.mil, April 19, 2002, http://www.navy.mil/search/display.asp?story_id=1415.

25. See "TERRORISM by Event 1980–2001," (Washington, DC: Federal Bureau

of Investigation, available http://www.fbi.gov/publications/terror/terror2000
_2001.htm).

26. Three aircraft were used as missiles to hit the Twin Towers and the Pentagon. A
fourth plane crashed in a field in Pennsylvania after a group of passengers tried to
overpower the hijackers. All aboard were killed.

27. For one of the most comprehensive lists of casualties, see "September 11, 2001
Victims," http://www.liveindia.com/ladin/wtc.html. For the economic impact,
see "Economic Impact of Terrorist Attack: New York City Fact Sheet," The Century Foundation, http://old.911digitalarchive.org/objects/2.pdf; also, "How much
did the September 11 terrorist attack cost America?" Institute for the Analysis of
Global Security, http://www.iags.org/costof911.html.

28. Remarks by Bush after meeting his National Security Team at the White House
on September 12, 2001. See the document collection titled, "September 11, 2001:
Attack on America" The Avalon Project, Yale Law School, http://avalon.law.yale.
edu/subject_menus/sept_11.asp.

29. News conference by President Bush, CNN, October 11, 2001.

Chapter 15. Conclusion
1. See, for example, Ian Lesser, Bruce Hoffman, John Arquilla, et al., *Countering the
New Terrorism* (Santa Monica, CA: Rand, 1999).

Afterword
1. See "Commander's Initial Assessment," in *Afghanistan Déjà vu? Lessons from the
Soviet Experience*, Electronic Briefing Book No. 292 (Washington, DC: National
Security Archive, October 30, 2009), pp 8–9; also, Patricia Zengerle, "General
Wants 40,000 More US Troops for Afghanistan," *Washington Post*, October 8, 2009.

2. "Commander's Initial Assessment," p 41. "ISAF" stands for the "International
Security Assistance Force," the name for the broader occupation force umbrella.

3. Ibid., 9.

4. See "Colonel Tsagolov Letter to USSR Minister of Defense Dmitry Yazov on the
Situation in Afghanistan," August 13, 1987, in *Afghanistan Déjà vu?*, Electronic
Briefing Book No. 292, National Security Archive.

5. Ibid., 1–2.

6. Ibid., 5.

7. Alison Smale, "A Somber Warning on Afghanistan," *New York Times*, September
13, 2009.

8. "Iranian Commanders Assassinated," BBC News, October 18, 2009.

9. See "Kashmir Militant Extremists," Council for Foreign Relations, http://www.
cfr.org/publication/9135.

10. Declan Walsh, "Taliban Bombs in Pakistan Strike Air Base, Restaurant, and Wed-
ding Party," *Guardian*, October 23, 2009; Karin Brulliyard, "Pakistan Attacks Kill
at Least 39," *Washington Post*, October 16, 2009; Declan Walsh and Adam Gab-
batt, "Dozens Killed As Militants Attack Pakistan Police Buildings," *Guardian*,
October 15, 2009; Lehaz Ali, "Suicide Blast Kills 41 As Pakistan Terror Attacks
Escalate," *National Post*, October 12, 2009.

11. See Hassan Abbas, "A Profile of Tehrik-i-Taliban Pakistan" (Sentinel, Combating Terrorism Center, United States Military Academy, West Point, January 2008).

12. See "Chronology: The Afghanistan War," PBS Frontline, http://www.pbs.org/wgbh/pages/frontline/obamaswar/etc/cron.html. For the frequency of drone attacks and the extent of civilian deaths, see Wajahat Ali, "Acknowledging America's Arrogance," *Guardian*, September 1, 2009.

13. Jayshree Bajoria, "Pakistan's New Generation of Terrorists," Council for Foreign Relations, February 6, 2008, http://www.cfr.org/publication/15422.

14. See Pakistan's English daily, *Dawn*, "Surviving Gunman's Identity Established as Pakistani," January 9, 2009.

15. "Abdullah Pulls Out of Afghan Vote," BBC News, November 1, 2009.

16. Michael Hastings, "The Runaway General," *Rolling Stone*, June 22, 2010, http://www.rollingstone.com/politics/news/17390/119236.

17. David Willis, "U.S. Afghan commander Stanley McChrystal fired by Obama," BBC News, June 23, 2010.

18. Wikileaks.org obtained and released these documents (January 2004–December 2009), which were simultaneously published by the *New York Times*, *The Guardian*, and *Der Spiegel*. See, for example, "Afghanistan: The War Logs," *Guardian*, July 25, 2010, http://www.guardian.co.uk/world/the-war-logs.

BIBLIOGRAPHY

The following material came from the document collection *Soviet Invasion of Afghanistan, Russian and East German Archive,* Washington, DC. The Cold War International History Project, Woodrow Wilson International Center for Scholars.

"Conversation between the Soviet Premier, Alexei Kosygin, and the Afghan leader, Nur Mohammad Taraki." Transcript of the telephone exchanges, March 17 or 18, 1979.

"Meeting of the Soviet Ambassador, Alexander Puzanov, with Nur Mohammad Taraki and Babrak Karmal," June 18, 1978.

"Meeting between the Soviet Ambassador, Alexander Puzanov, and Hafizullah Amin," November 3, 1979.

"Message to the East German leader, Erich Honecker," from the Soviet Communist Party Central Committee, October 13, 1978.

"Message to the East German leader, Erich Honecker," from the Soviet Communist Party Central Committee, September 16, 1979.

"Minutes of the Brezhnev-Honecker Summit in East Berlin," October 4, 1979.

"Minutes of the Soviet Politburo Meeting," September 13, 1979.

"Minutes of the Soviet Politburo Meeting," September 15, 1979.

"Minutes of the Soviet Politburo Meeting," September 20, 1979.

"CPSU CC Politburo Meeting Minutes," November 13, 1986.

"Personal Memorandum Andropov to Brezhnev," December 1, 1979.

Ponomarev, Boris. "Secret Report to Moscow from Kabul on Talks with Amin and Taraki," July 19, 1979.

"Record of the meeting between the Soviet Ambassador Alexander Puzanov and Hafizullah Amin," July 21, 1979.

"Report on Afghanistan" by Andrei Gromyko, Dmitri Ustinov, Yuri Andropov and Boris Ponomarev. Submitted to the Central Committee of the Soviet Communist Party, October 29, 1979.

"Report on Afghanistan" by Eduard Shevardnadze, Dmitri Yazov, V. A. Kryuch-kov et al. Submitted to the Politburo, January 24, 1989.

"Political letter to the Soviet Foreign Ministry from the Soviet Ambassador in Afghanistan," May 31, 1978.

Dobrynin, Anatoly. "Political Letter of Soviet Ambassador to the United States Anatoly F. Dobrynin." Cited in the collection, U.S.-Soviet Relations and the Turn Towards Confrontation. Washington, DC: CWIHP, Woodrow Wilson International Center for Scholars, July 11, 1978.

Mitrokhin, Vasili. *The KGB in Afghanistan.* Washington, DC: The Cold War International History Project, Woodrow Wilson International Center for Scholars, February 2002.

The National Security Archive (Washington, DC)

"Afghan Transport Plane Shot Down by Stinger." Tass, August 13, 1987.

"Afghanistan: Eighteen Months of Occupation." Special Report No. 86. Washington, DC: State Department, August 1981.

Afghanistan: The Making of US Policy, 1973–1990.

"Afghanistan: Two Years of Occupation." Special Report No. 91. Washington, DC: State Department, December 1981.

Buckley, James. "U.S. Cooperation with Pakistan." Statement to the Senate Foreign Relations Committee, November 12, 1981. Current Policy No. 347. Washington, DC: State Department.

"Chemical Warfare in Southeast Asia and Afghanistan: An Update." Report from the U.S. Secretary of State George Shultz to Congress and UN Member States. Special Report No. 104. Washington, DC: State Department, November 1982.

"Chemical Weapons in Afghanistan?" BBC report broadcast at 1500 GMT, April 23, 1980. Cited in U.S. State Department, "Reports of the Use of Chemical Weapons in Afghanistan, Laos and Cambodia," 1980.

"China and the Afghan Resistance." Weekly summary of the U.S. Defense Intelligence Agency, March 6, 1981.

Directorate for Research, U.S. Defense Intelligence Agency. "Afghan Resistance," November 5, 1982.

"Sadat on Arms to Afghan Freedom Fighters." Interview, NBC, September 22, 1981. Washington, DC: Joint Chiefs of Staff Message Center, Defense Department, September 23, 1981.

U.S. Embassy. "Iranian report that Herat has fallen." Intelligence report. Kabul, March 1979.

U.S. Embassy cable. "Afghan coup: Initial assessment." Kabul, July 17, 1973.

———. "An initial evaluation of the Bala Hisar mutiny." Kabul, August 6, 1979.

———. "Khalqis possibly waving olive branch to Washington." Kabul, September 22, 1979.

———. "Policy Review." Kabul, March 1977.

———. "Reflections on the Afghanistan political crisis." Kabul, September 1979.

———. "Senator Charles Percy's meeting with President Daud." Kabul, August 11, 1973.

————. "Soviet airlift to Kabul." Kabul, December 26, 1979.

————. "Soviet Media on Sadat's Statement." Moscow, September 24, 1981.

————. "Taraki's news conference on the effects of the death of Ambassador Adolph Dubs." Kabul, April 30, 1979.

"U.S.-Pakistani Joint Statement," at the end of Under-Secretary of State James Buckley's Islamabad visit, June 15, 1981.

U.S. State Department. "Soviet-Afghan Relations: Is Moscow's Patience Wearing Thin?" Memorandum, May 24, 1979.

————. "The Kidnapping and Death of Adolph Dubs: Summary of Report of Investigation," 1979.

————. "U.S. Response to Soviet Criticism after Sadat Interview: A Summary of the News Briefing." Cable No. 254629 to U.S. Missions, September 23, 1981.

U.S. Central Command. "Stinger: One Year of Combat," October 26, 1987.

"USSR-Afghanistan." U.S. Intelligence Report, March 1, 1980.

"Weekly Summary of the US Defense Intelligence Agency," March 6, 1981.

The Taliban File (NSA Electronic Briefing Book No. 97, September 2003), see http://www.gwu.edu/~nsarchiv/NSAEBB/NSAEBB97/.

"New Fighting and New Forces in Qandahar." Peshawar: American Consulate, November 3, 1994.

U.S. Embassy cable. "Ambassador raises bin Laden with Foreign Secretary, Shamshad Ahmad." Islamabad, October 6, 1998.

————. "Coordinating our efforts and sharpening our message on Osama bin Laden." Islamabad, October 19, 1998.

————. "[Exercised] Pakistan is Backing Taliban." Islamabad, December 6, 1994.

————. "Finally a Talkative Talib: Origins and Membership of the Students' Movement." Islamabad, February 20, 1995.

————. "Osama bin Laden: Charge reiterates US concerns to key Taliban official, who sticks to well-known Taliban positions." Islamabad, December 19, 2000.

————. "The Taliban: What We've Heard." Islamabad, January 26, 1995.

"US Engagement with the Taliban on Osama bin Laden." Secret NDIS, Unclassified, July 16, 2001.

National Security Archive (Other)

"Background Notes on Afghanistan." Washington, DC: U.S. Department of State, March 1977.

Brzezinski, Zbigniew. "Persian Gulf Security Framework." June 3, 1980.

————. "The US response to Afghanistan." Memo. February 12, 1980.

"General Hamid Gul: A Biographic Sketch." Washington, DC: U.S. Defense Intelligence Agency, January 1989.

Kissinger, Henry. "Secretary's Staff Meeting." Held on October 23, 1973.

Other U.S. government sources

"Afghan War Diary, 2004 – 2010," Wikileaks.org.

"Afghanistan: The War Logs." *The Guardian,* July 25, 2010.

Afghanistan: A Country Study. Washington, DC: Federal Research Division, 2002.

"Afghanistan: Soviet Invasion and US Response." Washington, DC: Congressional Research Service, IB 80006, January 10, 1980.

Afghanistan: The State Department Report on Human Rights Practices for 1996.

Afghanistan: The State Department Country Report for 2002.

Bush, President George H. W. "State of the Union Address," January 1991. The American Presidency Speech Archive.

Bush, President George W. News Conference. CNN, October 11, 2001.

Bush, President George W. News Conference with President Chirac of France. CNN, November 6, 2001.

Carter, Jimmy. Briefing to members of the Congress, January 8, 1980.

Carter, Jimmy. "Human Rights and Foreign Policy." Public Papers of the Presidents of the United States, vol. 1, State Department.

————. "State of the Union Address," January 23, 1980. Atlanta, GA: The Carter Library.

"A Cold War Conundrum: The 1983 Soviet War Scare." Washington, DC: Central Intelligence Agency, 1997.

Country Studies: Iran. Washington, DC: Federal Research Division, Library of Congress.

"Gore-Bush Presidential Debates." Commission on Presidential Debates, 2000.

Khalilzad, Zalmay. "Testimony before the U.S. House Subcommittee on Asian and Pacific Affairs," June 14, 1989.

Lake, Anthony. "From Containment to Enlargement." Speech at School of Advanced International Studies, Johns Hopkins University, Washington, DC, September 21, 1993.

Nagle, David. "USS Cole Rejoins the Fleet." Navy.mil, April 19, 2002, http://www.navy.mil/search/display.asp?story_id=1415.

"National Security Decision Directives: Reagan Administration." Washington, DC: Federation of American Scientists.

Pakistan: A Country Study. Washington, DC: Federal Research Division, Library of Congress, 2002.

Profile of Ayman al-Zawahiri. Washington, DC: Federal Bureau of Investigation.

Reagan, Ronald. "'Address to the Nation on National Security' (The SDI Project), March 23, 1983." Washington, DC: Federation of American Scientists.

————. Radio address on defense spending, February 19, 1983.

————. Radio address on foreign policy, October 20, 1984.

————. Remarks Welcoming the British Prime Minister, Margaret Thatcher, in the White House, February 26, 1981. Reagan Presidential Library.

————. Speech at the Presidential Banquet for President Zia-ul Haq of Pakistan, December 7, 1982. Reagan Presidential Library.

————. Speech Welcoming King Fahd of Saudi Arabia in the White House, February 11, 1985. Reagan Presidential Library.

"September 11, 2001: Attack on America." *The Avalon Project.* Yale Law School, http://avalon.law.yale.edu/subject_menus/sept_11.asp.

"September 11, 2001 Victims." http://www.liveindia.com/ladin/wtc.html.

"TERRORISM by Event 1980 – 2001." Washington, DC: Federal Bureau of Investigation, http://www.fbi.gov/publications/terror/terror2000_2001.htm.

"The Development of Soviet Military Power: Trends Since 1965 and Prospects for the 1980s." Washington, DC: Center for the Study of Intelligence, CIA, 2001.

"The Sociology and Psychology of Terrorism: Who Becomes A Terrorist and Why?" Washington, DC: The Federal Research Division, Library of Congress, September 1999.

Truman, President Harry. Address to the U.S. Congress, March 12, 1947.

U.S. Defense Department report. March 21, 2003.

The NATO-Russia Archive. The Berlin Information-Center for Transatlantic Security, http://www.bits.de/.

"Joint Declaration." First U.S.- Russia summit between President Bush and President Yeltsin, Camp David, February 1, 1992.

"Joint Declaration on Common Security Challenges at the Threshold of the Twenty-First Century." Seventh Yeltsin-Clinton summit in Moscow, September 2, 1998.

"Joint Russian-American Declaration on Defense Conversion" after the second Bush-Yeltsin summit, Washington, DC, June 17, 1992.

"Strengthening Transatlantic Security—a U.S. Strategy for the Twenty-First Century." Washington, DC: Department of Defense, December 2000.

"The Vancouver Declaration." First Clinton-Yeltsin summit in Canada, April 3–4, 1993.

Miscellaneous documents

Abbas, Hassan. "A Profile of Tehrik-i-Taliban Pakistan." *CTC Sentinel* 1, no. 2 (January 2008).

"Abdullah Azzam: The Godfather of Jihad." Perspectives on World History and Current Affairs.

"Afghan Constitution: 1963." Afghan Government Online.

"Afghan Constitution of 1990." Afghan Government Online.

"Afghanistan Five Years Later: The Return of the Taliban." London: the Senlis Council, Spring/Summer 2006.

Afridi, Jamal. "Kashmir Militant Extremists." Council for Foreign Relations, July 9, 2009, http://www.cfr.org/publication/9135/kashmir_militant_extremists.html.

Amnesty International. *Amnesty International Report 1997 – Afghanistan*. January 1, 1997. http://www.unhcr.org/refworld/country,,AMNESTY,,AFG,4562d8cf2,3ae6a9fd40,0.htm.

Amnesty International. *Amnesty International Report 1998 – Afghanistan*. January 1, 1998. http://www.unhcr.org/refworld/country,,AMNESTY,,AFG,4562d8cf2,3ae6a9fa54,0.htm.

Arms Control Association. "START 1 at a Glance." *Fact Sheets*.

Bajoria, Jayshree. "Pakistan's New Generation of Terrorists." Council for Foreign Relations, February 6, 2008, http://www.cfr.org/publication/15422/pakistans_new_generation_of_terrorists.html.

bin Laden, Osama, Ayman al-Zawahiri, Rifa'i Ahmad Taha, Sheikh Mir Hamzah, and Fazlul Rahman. Al Qaeda statement. MidEastWeb, February 23, 1998, http://www.mideastweb.org/osamabinladen1.htm.

"China SIGNIT Capabilities." *Weekly Intelligence Notes* #15-01. McLean, VA: Association of Former Intelligence Officers, April 16, 2001.

"Declaration of War against the Americans occupying the Land of the two Holy Places." Al Qaeda statement. MidEastWeb.

Debate in the Sixth Committee of the Sixtieth General Assembly, October 7, 2005.

"Definitions of Terrorism." UN Office on Drugs and Crime.

"Geneva Accords of 1988 on Afghanistan – Agreement between Pakistan's President Zia-ul Haq's government and the Communist government of Dr Najib representing Afghanistan *and* the Accord on International Guarantees between the US and the USSR." Institute of Afghan Studies online.

"Hafizullah Amin." Afghanan.Net, July 23, 2006.

Human Rights Watch. *Human Rights Watch World Report 1999 – Afghanistan.* January 1, 1999, http://www.unhcr.org/refworld/country,,HRW,,AFG,4562d8cf2,3ae6a8b520,0.html.

Information Division. "Covenant of HAMAS: Main Points." Jerusalem: Israel Foreign Ministry. Posted on the Federation of American Scientists website, http://www.fas.org/irp/world/para/docs/880818a.htm.

Project for the New American Century. "Statement of Principles," June 3, 1997.

"Responsibility for the Terrorist Atrocities in the United States, September 11, 2001." UK government report, November 14, 2001.

"A Short History of Threat Reduction." *Arms Control Today,* June 2003.

"South Asia Terrorism Portal." New Delhi: The Institute of Conflict Management.

Unocal. "Statement on the suspension of pipeline." August 21, 1998.

———. Statement on the withdrawal from the pipeline project. December 4, 1998.

Zaida, Mubashir. "Surviving gunman's identity established as Pakistani." Dawn.com, January 8, 2009, http://www.dawn.com/wps/wcm/connect/dawn-content-library/dawn/news/pakistan/surviving-gunmans-identity-established-as-pakistani-ss.

Private Conversations

Asghar, Mohammad, academic and justice minister under King Zahir Shah.

Azimi, Gen. Mohammad Nabi, deputy defense minister and commander of the Kabul garrison.

Baryalai, Mahmood, half-brother of the ousted president Babrak Karmal.

Katawazi, Gen. Abdul Hakim, retired, Kabul Police chief under King Zahir Shah.

Lodin, Gen. Mohammad Afzal, commander of the Eastern Provinces.

Mazdak, Farid, Politburo member.

Najibullah, President.

Plastun, Vladimir, Afghanistan specialist of the Soviet Party organ, *Pravda.*

Tchaikovsky, Yuri, Afghanistan correspondent, Tass News Agency.

Wakil, Abdul, foreign minister and Politburo member in the Communist regime.

Watanjar, Gen. Mohammad Aslam, Politburo and cabinet member.

Articles & Books

Fighel, Jonathan. "The Continuing Threat of Al-Qaida." Herzliya, Israel: Institute for Counter Terrorism, October 5, 2003, http://www.ict.org.il/Articles/tabid/66/Articlsid/586/Default.aspx.

"Al-Qaida." *Guardian*, http://www.guardian.co.uk/world/al-qaida.

Amin, Tahir. "Afghan Resistance: Past, Present and Future." *Asian Survey* 24 (April 1984).

Andrew, Christopher, and Vasili Mitrokhin. *The Sword and the Shield: The Mitrokhin Archive and the Secret History of the KGB.* New York: Basic Books, 2001.

Anwar, Raja. *The Tragedy of Afghanistan: A First-Hand Account.* London: Verso, 1988.

Arnold, Anthony. *Afghanistan: The Soviet Invasion in Perspective.* Stanford, CA: Hoover Institution Press, 1985.

Aston, Clive. "Political Hostage-Taking in Western Europe." In *The New Terrorism*, edited by William Gutteridge. London: Mansell Publishing Ltd., 1986.

Atran, Scott. "Genesis and Future of Suicide Terrorism." *Interdisciplines* (2005).

Azzam, Maha. *al-Qa'ida: the misunderstood Wahhabi connection and the ideology of violence.* Briefing paper no. 1. London: Royal Institute of International Affairs, February 2003.

Bandura, Albert. "Mechanisms of moral disagreement." In *Origins of Terrorism: Psychologies, ideologies, theologies, state of mind*, edited by Walter Reich. Washington, DC: Woodrow Wilson International Center/Cambridge University Press, 1990.

Behera, Ajay "Pakistan's Strategic Vision: With and Without the Taliban." *Asia Times*, March 22, 2002, http://www.brookings.edu/opinions/2002/0322pakistan_behera.aspx.

Beichman, Arnold, *The Long Pretense: Soviet Treaty Diplomacy from Lenin to Gorbachev.* Piscataway, NJ: Transaction, 1991.

Bergen, Peter. *Holy War Inc.: Inside the Secret World of Osama bin Laden.* London: Phoenix, 2002.

Berthold-Bond, Daniel. "The Nature of Dialectic." *Hegel's Grand Synthesis: A Study of Being, Thought and History.* New York: Harper, 1993.

Beschloss, Michael, and Strobe Talbott. *At the Highest Levels: The Inside Story of the End of the Cold War.* Boston: Little, Brown, 1993.

Bjorgo, Tore, "Issues for Discussion." UN conference, Fighting Terrorism for Humanity, New York, September 2003.

Blanche, Ed. "Ayman al-Zawahiri: attention turns to the other suspect." *Jane's Intelligence Review*, October 3, 2001.

Borum, Randy. "Understanding the Terrorist Mind-Set." *The FBI Law Enforcement Bulletin*, July 2003.

Bradsher, Henry. *Afghan Communism and Soviet Intervention.* 2nd ed. Karachi: Oxford University Press, 2000.

———. *Afghanistan and the Soviet Union.* Durham, NC: Duke University Press, 1983.

Brind, Harry. "Soviet Policy in the Horn of Africa." *International Affairs* 60, no. 1 (Winter 1983/84).

Brzezinski, Zbigniew. "CIA's Intervention in Afghanistan." Interview. *Le Nouvel*

Observateur, January 15–21, 1998. English version translated by Bill Blum and posted by the Center for Research on Globalisation on October 15, 2001, http://www.globalresearch.ca/articles/BRZ110A.html.

———. "Peace at an Impasse." Interview by Ghassan Bishara. *Journal of Palestinian Studies* 14 (Autumn 1984).

———. *Power and Principle: Memoirs of the National Security Adviser, 1977–1981.* New York: Farrar, Straus and Giroux, 1983.

Burke, Jason. "The making of the world's most wanted man." *The Observer,* October 28, 2001.

Cheema, Pervaiz Iqbal. "The Afghanistan Crisis and Pakistan's Security Dilemma." *Asian Survey* 23 (March 1983).

"Chronology of China-U.S. Relations." *China Internet Information Center,* http://www.china.org.cn/english/china-us/26890.htm.

Churchill, Winston. "Sinews of Peace (Iron Curtain)." Speech, Westminster College, Fulton, MO, March 5, 1946.

Clarke, Richard. *Against All Enemies: Inside America's War on Terrorism.* New York: Free Press, 2004.

Cooley, John. *Unholy Wars, Inc.: Afghanistan, America and International Terrorism.* London: Pluto Press, 2002.

Cordovez, Diego, and Selig Harrison. *Out of Afghanistan: An Inside Story of the Soviet Withdrawal.* New York: Oxford University Press, 1995.

Crenshaw, Martha. "The Causes of Terrorism." *Comparative Politics* 13 (July 1981).

———. "The logic of terrorism: Terrorist behavior as a product of strategic choice." In *Origins of Terrorism: Psychologies, ideologies, theologies, state of mind,* edited by Walter Reich. Washington, DC: Woodrow Wilson International Center/Cambridge University Press, 1990.

"Culture." College Station, TX: Texas A&M University, http://www.tamu.edu/classes/cosc/choudhury/culture.html.

"Culture Defined." Winston-Salem, NC: Wake Forest University, imej.wfu.edu/articles/1999/1/02/demo/gallery/Literary/defcult.html.

Daley, Tad. "Afghanistan and Gorbachev's Global Foreign Policy." *Asian Survey* 29, no. 5 (May 1989).

Dastarac, Alexander, and M. Levant. "What Went Wrong in Afghanistan?" *Middle East Research and Information Project Report* no. 89, Afghanistan (July–August 1980).

David, Stephen. "Soviet Involvement in Third World Coups." *International Security* 11, no. 1 (Summer 1986).

Davidson, Lawrence. "Terrorism in Context: The Case of the West Bank." *Journal of Palestine Studies* 15, no. 3 (Spring 1986).

de Long, Bradford, Christopher de Long, and Sherman Robinson. "The Case for Mexico's Rescue: The Peso Package Looks Even Better Now." *Foreign Affairs* 75, no. 3 (May–June 1996).

"Directorate for Inter-Services Intelligence (ISI)." Washington, DC: Federation of American Scientists, July 2002.

Dumbrell, John. *American Foreign Policy: Carter to Clinton.* London: Macmillan, 1997.

Eckstein, Harry. "On the Etiology of Internal Wars." *History and Theory* 4, no. 2 (1965).

"Economic Impact of Terrorist Attack: New York Fact Sheet."The Century Foundation, http://old.911digitalarchive.org/objects/2.pdf.

Edwards, David. *Before the Taliban: Genealogies of the Afghan Jihad*. Berkeley: University of California Press, 2002.

Elwell, Frank. "The Sociology of Max Weber." Bartlesville, OK: Rogers States University, http://www.faculty.rsu.edu/~felwell/Theorists/Weber/Whome.htm.

"Exiled Ayatollah Khomeini Returns to Iran." BBC News, February 1, 1979.

Fighel, Jonathan. "Sheikh Abdullah Azzam: Bin Laden's spiritual mentor." Herzliya, Israel: International Policy Institute for Counter-Terrorism, September 27, 2001.

Freedman, Lawrence. "Terrorism and Strategy." In *Terrorism and International Order*, edited by Lawrence Freedman, Christopher Hill, and Adam Roberts, et al. London: RIIA/Routledge, 1986.

Fukuyama, Francis. "The Soviet Threat to the Persian Gulf." Tokyo: Security Conference for Asia and the Pacific, SECAP, 1980.

Gaddis, John Lewis. *The United States and the End of the Cold War: Implications, Reconsiderations, Provocations*. New York: Oxford University Press, 1992.

Gambill, Gary. "The Balance of Terror: War by Other Means in the Contemporary Middle East." *Journal of Palestine Studies* 28, no. 1 (Autumn 1998).

Garthoff, Raymond. "American-Soviet Relations in Perspective." *Political Science Quarterly* 100, no. 4 (Winter 1985/86).

Gates, Robert. *From the Shadows: The Ultimate Insider's Story of Five Presidents and How They Won the Cold War*. New York: Simon & Schuster, 1997.

Ghebhardt, Alexander. "Soviet and US interests in the Indian Ocean." *Asian Survey* 15 (August 1975).

Gibbs, David. "Does the USSR Have a Grand Strategy? Reinterpreting the Invasion of Afghanistan." *Journal of Peace Research* 24 (December 1987).

Gibbs, Jack. "Conceptualization of Terrorism." *American Sociological Journal* 54, no. 3 (June 1989).

Gray, John, *Al-Qaeda and What It Means to Be Modern*. London: Faber and Faber, 2003.

Grinter, Lawrence. "Avoiding the Burden: The Carter Doctrine in Perspective." *Air and Space Power Chronicle* (January–February 1983).

Halliday, Fred. "The Arc of Crisis and the New Cold War." *Middle East Research and Information Project*, Special Anniversary Issue 100–101 (October–December 1981).

———. *Two Hours that Shook the World: September 11, 2001: Causes and Consequences*. London: Saqi Books, 2002.

Halliday, Fred, and Zahir Tanin. "The Communist Regime in Afghanistan, 1978–1992: Institutions and Conflicts." *Europe-Asia Studies* 50 (December 1998).

Hamilton, Lawrence, and James Hamilton. "Dynamics of Terrorism." *International Studies Quarterly* 27 (May 1983).

Harmon, Christopher. "Terrorism: A Matter for Moral Judgement." *Terrorism and Political Violence* 4 (Spring 1992).

Harriman, Pamela. "The True Meaning of the Iron Curtain Speech." Winston Churchill Center, http://www.winstonchurchill.org/learn/biography/in-opposition/qiron-curtainq-fulton-missouri-1946/174-the-true-meaning-of-the-iron-curtain-speech.

Harris, Lillian Craig. "China's Response to Perceived Soviet Gains in the Middle East." *Asian Survey* 20 (April 1980).

Harrison, Mark. "An Economist Looks at Suicide Terrorism." *SecurityManagement Online,* June 5, 2003, www.securitymanagement.com.

Harrison, Selig. "Kashmir issue leading Obama into first tar pit." *Washington Times,* January 6, 2009.

Hastings, Michael, "The Runaway General." *Rolling Stone,* June 22, 2010, http://www.rollingstone.com/politics/news/17390/119236.

"Hegel." Digital Text Projects, Columbia University, New York.

Hirschkorn, Phil, Rohan Gunaratna, Ed Blanche, and Stefan Leader. "Blowback." *Jane's Intelligence Review* 13, no. 8 (August 1, 2001): special report.

Hoffman, Bruce. "Responding to Terrorism Across the Technological Spectrum." *Terrorism and Political Violence* 6 (Autumn 1994).

Holsti, Ole, and James Rosenau. "Consensus Lost, Consensus Regained?: Foreign Policy Beliefs of American Leaders, 1976–1980." *International Studies Quarterly* 30, no. 4 (December 1986).

Horelick, Arnold. "Soviet Policy Dilemmas in Asia." *Asian Survey* 17, no. 6 (June 1977).

———. "The Soviet Union's Asian Collective Security Proposal: A Club in Search of Members." *Pacific Affairs* 47 (Autumn 1974).

"How much did the September 11 terrorist attack cost America?" Institute for the Analysis of Global Security, http://www.iags.org/costof911.html.

Huntington, Samuel. "The Clash of Civilizations?" *Foreign Affairs* (Summer 1993).

Hyman, Anthony. *Afghanistan Under Soviet Domination, 1964–1991.* 3rd ed. London: Macmillan, 1992.

Jalali, Ali Ahmad, and Lester Grau. *The Other Side of the Mountain: Mujahideen Tactics in the Soviet-Afghan War.* 3 vols. Sterling, VA: Military Press, 2000.

Kakar, M. Hasan. *Afghanistan: The Soviet Invasion and the Afghan Response, 1979–1982.* Berkeley: University of California Press, 1995.

Kegley, Charles. "How Did the Cold War Die? Principles for an Autopsy." *Mershon International Studies Review* 38, no. 1 (April 1994).

Khan, Riaz Mohammad. *Untying the Afghan Knot: Negotiating Soviet Withdrawal.* Durham, NC: Duke University Press, 1991.

Kivimaki, Timo, and Liisa Laakso. "Causes of Terrorism." In *Development Cooperation as an Instrument in the Prevention of Terrorism.* Copenhagen: Nordic Institute of Asian Studies, July 2003.

Kober, Stanley, "The Great Game, Round Two," *Foreign Policy Briefing* no. 63 (October 31, 2000).

Koch, Susan. "Cooperative Threat Reduction: Reducing Weapons of Mass Destruction." *USIA Electronic Journal* 3, no. 3 (July 1998), www.usinfo.state.gov/journals/itps0798/ijpe/pj38koch.htm.

Kudlow, Lawrence. "Iraq and al-Qa'ida." www.commentaries.kudlow.com/2002/10/24/kc102402.pdf.

Kuperman, Alan. "Stinging Rebukes." *Foreign Affairs* 81, no. 1 (January–February 2002).

LaFeber, Walter. *America, Russia, and the Cold War, 1945–2000.* 9th ed. New York: McGraw-Hill, 2002.

Lake, David. "Rational Extremism: Understanding Terrorism in the Twenty-first Century." *International Organization* (Spring 2002).

Laqueur, Walter. "Gorbachev and Epimetheus: The Origins of the Russian Crisis." *Journal of Contemporary History* 28, no. 3 (July 1993).

Lenczowski, George. "The Arc of Crisis: Its Central Sector." *Foreign Affairs* (Spring 1979).

Lesser, Ian, Bruce Hoffman, John Arquilla, et al. *Countering the New Terrorism.* Santa Monica, CA: Rand, 1999.

Levitt, Geoffrey. *Democracies against Terror.* Washington, DC: Center for Strategic and International Studies/Praeger, 1988.

Lewis, Bernard. "License to Kill: Osama bin Laden's Declaration of Jihad." *Foreign Affairs* 77, no. 6 (November/December 1998).

——. "The Roots of Muslim Rage." *Atlantic,* September 1990. Reproduced by the Free Republic (online), September 26, 2001.

Maley, William, *The Afghanistan Wars.* Basingstoke, UK: Palgrave Macmillan, 2002.

McCauley, Clark. "The Psychology of Terrorism." Social Science Research Council, http://essays.ssrc.org/sept11/essays/mccauley.htm.

Marsden, Peter. *The Taliban: War, Religion and the New Order in Afghanistan.* Karachi: Oxford University Press, 1998.

Moens, Alexander. "President Carter's Advisers and the Fall of the Shah." *Political Science Quarterly* 106 (Summer 1991).

Muller, Edward, and Erich Weede. "Cross-national Variation of Political Violence: A Rational Action Approach." *Journal of Conflict Resolution* 34, no. 4 (December 1990).

Murphy, Robert. *Culture and Social Anthropology: An Overview.* 2nd ed. Englewood Cliffs, NJ: Prentice Hall, 1986, cited on the website of Malaspina University-College in Nanaimo, BC, Canada, http://www.media-studies.ca/articles/culture.htm.

"Muslim Brotherhood." Washington, DC: The Federation of American Scientists, http://www.fas.org/irp/world/para/mb.htm.

Mylroie, Laurie. "The World Trade Center Bomb: Who is Ramzi Yousef? And Why It Matters." *The National Interest* (Winter 1995/96).

"Najib sufferes major setback in Herat," AFGHANews. 6, no. 8 (April 15, 1990), http://www.scribd.com/doc/29565597/Afgha-Newspaper.

O'Connor, Kim. "dialectic." Chicago: University of Chicago, Winter 2003.

Pape, Robert. "The Strategic Logic of Suicide Terrorism." *American Political Science Review* 97, no. 3 (August 2003).

Pion-Berlin, David, and George Lopez. "Of Victims and Executioners: Argentine State Terror, 1975–1979." *International Studies Quarterly* 35, no. 1 (March 1991).

Post, Jerrold. "Terrorist psycho-logic: Terrorist behavior as a product of psychological forces." In *Origins of Terrorism: Psychologies, ideologies, theologies, state of mind*, edited by Walter Reich. Washington, DC: Woodrow Wilson International Center/Cambridge University Press, 1990.

———. Interview by NBC of Australia, October 22, 2001.

Podhoretz, Norman. "The First Term: The Reagan Road to Détente." *Foreign Affairs* 63, no. 3 (1984).

Qur'an, The. Center for Muslim-Jewish Engagement, University of Southern California online, http://www.usc.edu/schools/college/crcc/engagement/resources/texts/muslim/quran/.

Qutb, Sayed. *Milestones.* English translation available at http://majalla.org/books/2005/qutb-nilestone.pdf.

Rainwater, Janette. *Afghanistan, Terrorism and Blowback: A Chronology.* Progressive Politics Online, September 19, 2002.

Rais, Rasul Bakhsh. "Afghanistan and the Regional Powers." *Asian Survey* 33 (September 1993).

Ranstorp, Magnus. "Hizbollah's Command Leadership: Its Structure, Decision-Making and Relationship with Iranian Clergy and Institutions." *Terrorism and Political Violence* 6 (Autumn 1994).

Raphaeli, Nimrod. "Ayman Mohammad al-Rabi' al-Zawahiri: The Making of an Arch-Terrorist." *Terrorism and Political Violence* 14, no. 4 (Winter 2002).

Rashid, Ahmed. "Afghanistan: Ending the Policy Quagmire." *Journal of International Affairs* 54, no. 2 (Spring 2001).

———. "Afghanistan: Taliban's second-coming," BBC, June 2, 2006.

———. In conversation with Kreisler, Harry. "Islam in Central Asia: Foreign Intervention and Fundamentalism" Berkeley: Institute of International Studies, University of California, March 26, 2002.

———. *Taliban: Militant Islam, Oil, and Fundamentalism in Central Asia.* New Haven, CT: Yale University Press, 2000.

———. *Taliban: The Story of the Afghan Warlords.* London: Pan Books, 2001.

———. "Taliban: Exporting Extremism." *International Affairs* 78, no. 6 (November/December 1999).

Rogers, Paul, and Sicilla Elworthy. "A Never-Ending War? Consequences of 11 September." Briefing paper. Oxford: Oxford Research Group, March 2002.

Ross, Dennis. "Considering Soviet Threats to the Persian Gulf." *International Security* 6, no. 2 (Autumn 1981).

Ross, Geoffrey Ian. "Structural Causes of Oppositional Political Terrorism: Towards a Causal Model." *Journal of Peace Research* 30 (August 1993).

Roy, Olivier. "Has Islamism a future in Afghanistan?" In *Fundamentalism Reborn? Afghanistan and the Taliban*, edited by William Maley. London: Hurst & Company, 2001.

————. Interview, Agence France-Presse, September 27, 1987.

————. *Islam and Resistance in Afghanistan.* 2nd. ed. Cambridge: Cambridge University Press, 1990.

————. "Rivalries and Power Plays in Afghanistan: The Taliban, the Shari'a and the Pipeline." *Middle East Report* no. 202 (Winter 1996).

Rubin, Barnett. *The Fragmentation of Afghanistan: State Formation and Collapse in the International System.* 2nd ed. New Haven, CT: Yale University Press, 2002.

Rubin, Barnett. "Women and Pipelines: Afghanistan's Proxy Wars." *International Affairs* 73, no. 2 (April 1997).

Russian General Staff. *The Soviet-Afghan War: How A Superpower Fought and Lost.* Translated and edited by Lester Grau and Michael Gress. Lawrence: University Press of Kansas, 2002.

Shahar, Yael. "Osama bin Laden: Marketing Terrorism." Herzliya, Israel: International Institute for Counter-Terrorism, August 22, 1998.

Skidmore, David. "Carter's Foreign Policy." *Political Science Quarterly* 108 (Winter 1993/94).

Smyth, Frank. "Jordan Defends Stance in Gulf War." *Christian Science Monitor,* March 6, 1991.

Staten, Cliff. "U.S. Foreign Policy Since World War II." AmericanDiplomacy. Org, July 30, 2005, http://www.unc.edu/depts/diplomat/item/2005/0709/stat/staten_reality.html.

Suliman, Mohamed. "Oil and the Civil War in Sudan." *Institute of African Alternatives,* October 2001, http://www.ifaanet.org/oil_sudan.htm.

Sullivan, Jeremiah. "The Legacy of Nuclear Weapons." *Swords and Ploughshares* 7, no. 2 (Winter 1992).

Swaidan, Ziad, and Mihai Nica. "The 1991 Gulf War and Jordan's Economy." *Middle East Review of International Affairs* 6, no. 2 (June 2002).

Talbott, Strobe. *The Russia Hand: A Memoir of Presidential Diplomacy.* New York: Random House, 2003.

"The Indo-Soviet Treaty of Peace, Friendship and Cooperation." New Delhi: National Security Research Foundation, August 9, 1971.

"The New Pipeline Politics." *New York Times,* November 10, 1997.

"The Story of the (Iranian) Revolution." BBC World Service.

Tripathi, Deepak. *From Our Own Correspondent.* BBC World Service, August 5, 1992.

Vance, Cyrus. *Hard Choices: Critical Years in America's Foreign Policy.* New York: Simon & Schuster, 1983.

Walter, E. V. "Violence and the Process of Terror." *American Sociological Review* 29, no. 2 (April 1964).

Wedgwood, Ruth. "Al-Qa'ida, Terrorism and Military Commissions." *American Journal of International Law* 96 (April 2002).

Weinberg, Leonard. "Turning to Terror: The Conditions Under Which Political Parties Turn to Terrorist Activities." *Comparative Politics* 23, no. 4 (July 1991).

Wilkinson, Paul. *Terrorism & the Liberal State.* London: Macmillan, 1986.

Wilkinson, Paul. "Terrorism: International Dimensions" In *The New Terrorism*, edited by William Gutteridge. London: Mansell Publishing Ltd., 1986.

Wilkinson, Paul. "Trends in International Terrorism and the American Response." In *Terrorism and International Order*, edited by Lawrence Freedman, Christopher Hill, and Adam Roberts, et al. London: RIIA/Routledge, 1986.

Willis, David. "US Afghan commander Stanley McChrystal fired by Obama." *BBC News*, June 23, 2010.

Wirsing, Robert, and James Roherty. "The United States and Pakistan." *International Affairs* 58, no. 4 (Autumn 1982).

Wohlforth, William. "Realism and the End of the Cold War." *International Security* 19, no. 3 (Winter 1994–1995).

Woolf, Amy F. *Nuclear Weapons in the Former Soviet Union: Location, Command and Control.* Issue Brief 91144. Washington, DC: Congressional Research Service, 1996.

World Trade Center Disaster. BBC News, September 11, 2001.

Yankelovich, Daniel, and Larry Kaagan. "Assertive America." *Foreign Affairs* 59, no. 3 (1980).

Yousaf, Mohammad, and Mark Adkin. *Afghanistan: The Bear Trap: The Defeat of a Superpower.* Barnsley, UK: Leo Cooper, 2001.

Yusufzai, Rahimullah. "Interview with Osama bin Laden." *Time*, January 11, 1999.

Zamostny, Thomas. "Moscow and the Third World: Recent Trends in Soviet Thinking." *Soviet Studies* 36, no. 2 (April 1984).

INDEX

Abdullah, Abdullah, 150
Afghan Military Academy, 31
Afghan National Security Forces, 143
Afghan Taliban, 147. *See also* Taliban
Afghanistan, description, xxix, 40
Ahmadzai, Shapur, 36, 195
aid to Afghanistan government
    Iran, 21–22, 33
    Soviet Union, xxi, 27, 31, 33, 36–37, 89, 93
    U.S., xxi, 27, 37
al Qaeda
    about, xxix, 127, 131, 173, 199
    attacks of, 7, 131–133, 145 (*See also*
        specific attacks)
    chronology, 153–54
    grievances, 129
    "new terrorism," 136
    Pakistan, 146–47
    Quran, 129–30
    rise of, 123–29, 130–31
    Taliban, 140–41, 146
al-Azhar Institute, 123
Al-Jazeera, xxix, 161
al-Quds, 129
American Airlines Flight 11, 1, 163
American Airlines Flight 77, 164
Amin, Hafizullah
    conflict within PDPA, 41–45
    coup to oust Taraki, 47–53, 154
    overthrow of, xvii–xviii, 53–56, 154
    rise to power with Taraki, 31–32, 34–36
Andropov, Yuri, xix, 47, 54–55, 157, 185
Angola, 69
Arafat, Yasir, 125
Arc of Crisis, 102–4
Ariana Airlines, 50
armed forces, Afghan, 31, 37–38, 77, 92,
    143, 154

Asghar, Mohammad, 90, 190
Asimov, Isaac, xxix
Atta, Mohammad, 8–9, 163
Azerbaijan, 22, 101, 123, 188, 193
Azhar, Maulana Masood, 147
Azzam, Abdul Rahman, 123
Azzam, Abdullah, 122, 125–26, 198

Babar, Naseerullah, 109, 110, 195
Badakhshan, 40, 196, 198
Badakhshi, Tahir, 52
Baghdad Pact, 28. *See also* Central Treaty
    Organization
Bagram air base, 43, 49, 73, 179
Bali bombings, 146
Baluchistan, 108, 145, 146
Bamiyan Province, 116
Daryalai, Mahmood, 35, 191
Belarus, 98, 99, 193
Bhutto, Benazir, 81, 84, 109–10, 189
Bhutto, Zulfiqar Ali, 23–24, 81, 175
Biao, Geng, 70
bin Laden, Osama
    al Qaeda attacks, 131–33
    background and birth of al Qaeda, xxix,
        121–26, 130
    chronology, 154–55
    statements of, 161–63, 199
    structure and management of al Qaeda,
        127, 131
    Taliban, xxii, 113–14
Borum, Randy, 10
boycott of Moscow Olympics, 62, 183
Brezhnev, Leonid, xix, 33, 36–38, 47, 49,
    55, 185
Bridas, 113
Brown, Harold, 70, 185

Brzezinski, Zbigniew, xxiii, 25, 61, 63–65, 102, 144, 183
Bush, George H.W., xii, 79, 97–98, 100, 157, 188. *See also* Bush administration, G.H.W.
Bush, George W., xiii, 1–2, 102, 106, 133, 162
Bush, Jeb, 105
Bush administration, G.H.W., 79–80, 85, 94, 102, 128, 157

Carter, Jimmy. *See also* Carter administration
    about, 25, 76, 102, 157, 175
    aid to Afghanistan, 37
    aid to Mujahideen, 59, 63, 64, 66, 68–70
    policy on Soviet occupation of Afghanistan, 59–64, 67, 76, 128, 183
Carter administration, 62–66. *See also specific members of*
Casey, William, 68–69, 73–74, 184
Caspian Sea, 101, 196
casualties
    civilian, x, 4, 72, 79, 83, 138
    Soviet, 75, 188
Central Intelligence Agency (CIA). *See* CIA
Central Treaty Organization (CENTO), 25, 28, 175
characteristics of terrorists, 9–10
Chechnya, 7, 123, 131
chemical weapons, 73, 131, 132
Cheney, Dick, 105
China
    as Afghanistan's neighbor, xxix, 21, 24–25, 27, 40
    al Qaeda, 127
    Soviet occupation of Afghanistan, x, xix, 60, 65–66, 68, 70–71, 138
    Soviet Union, 24–25
    U.S., 24–25, 70–71
chronologies, 153–155
CIA (Central Intelligence Agency)
    about, xxix–xxx
    aid to Mujahideen, xix, 59–60, 62–66, 68–69, 73–74, 128, 138
    Iran-contra affair, 184
    ISI alliance, xxx, 64–65, 71, 73–74, 79, 119, 138
    post Soviet withdrawal from Afghanistan, 79
civilians
    casualties, x, 4, 72, 79, 83, 138
    terrorists acts and, 4, 7–8, 115–16
clash of civilizations theories, 102–5, 194
Clinton, Bill, ix, xxii, 100–101, 102, 157. *See also* Clinton administration
Clinton administration, 102, 105, 107, 113, 114, 196. *See also specific members of*
coercion as provocation, 19, 38, 76, 118, 139, 141
Cole, USS, 132

collective leadership resolution of Amin and Taraki, 42
collective rationality, 6
Colonel Imam, 110, 195
communism in Afghanistan
    conflict and collapse of first regime, 18–19, 34–37, 39–45
    Islam and, 117–18
    Najibullah regime, 87–93, 139
    rise of first regime, 17–18, 21, 26, 31–34, 40–41, 133, 137–38, 176
    Soviet occupation, 59–66, 67–70, 76, 79–80, 82, 138
containment, U.S. policy of, 61–62, 183
conventional warfare and terrorism, 4
Cordovez, Diego, 61
corruption and fraud in Muslim countries, x, 103–104, 150
Council for Foreign Relations, 145, 147
counterinsurgency, futility of, ix–x, xi–xii, 149–50
counterterrorism, 141
Crenshaw, Martha, 5–6, 7
Cuba, 60, 69
culture, defined, 17
culture of terror, 13, 19, 76, 95, 137, 138, 139
culture of violence
    dialectics and, 118–19
    overview and definition, xxx, 17–20, 137–38, 143
    Pakistan, 148–50
Czechoslovakia, 55, 78, 94–95, 192

Dar es Salaam, 132, 162
Dari, xxi, 21, 26
Daud Khan, Mohammad
    overthrow and murder of, 18, 21, 26, 33–34, 39, 120, 154
    overthrow of monarchy, 18, 26, 28, 32, 154
    as president, 28–29, 32–34, 119–20, 176
    as prime minister, 27–28
Dawat-i Ittihad-i Islami, 160
"death by a thousand cuts," 73
Delta Oil, 112–13
détente policy, 21, 61, 69, 76
dialectic of Afghan conflict, 117–19, 137, 140, 141, 197
disengagement policies, 94–95, 97, 122
distribution system to Mujahideen, 65, 71, 74, 80–81, 82, 85
Dostum, Abdul Rashid, 107, 110, 191
drones, x, 147, 150
Dubs, Adolph, 37
Durrani Pashtuns, xxxi

East Germany, 78, 94–95, 192
education, xxxi, 108–9, 115, 151
Egypt
    Islamist movements, 120, 121, 123–24, 131, 198

support of Afghan resistance, xix, 60, 65–66, 68–70, 119
   U.S., 104
Egyptian Islamic Jihad, 123
elections
   Afghan, 150
   Pakistani, 23, 24, 81
embassy bombings, U.S., 131, 132, 162
environmental factors as causes of terrorism, 12–14
Etemadi, Nur Ahmad, 52, 181

F-16 aircraft, 68
Faisal, Turki al-, 111
Ford, Gerald, 25, 175
foreign volunteers, 88–89
Foundation, The (Asimov), xxix
France, 60, 91, 153, 175
friendship treaty, 36–37
frustration-aggression mechanism, 8
Fukuyama, Francis, 60–61

Gaddis, John Lewis, 94
Gailani, Pir Ahmad, 159
Gates, Robert, xxiii, 62
Geneva Accords, 76, 82, 87, 154
Germany, 100, 127, 131, 175, 188. *See also* East Germany
Ghilzai Pashtuns, xxxi
glossary, xxix–xxxii
Gorbachev, Mikhail, 154, 157, 185
   disengagement policy, 94, 97
   failed coup against, 92, 98
   Najibullah regime, 88, 92
   nuclear weapons, 99
   Soviet withdrawal from Afghanistan, xix–xx, 75, 91–92, 187
Gore, Al, 106
Great Britain, 27, 60, 78, 91, 110, 131, 175, 188
Gromyko, Andrei, 47, 54
group cohesion, 6, 10–11
group rationality, 6
Guevara, Che, 11, 173–74
Gul, Hamid, 81, 83, 84
Gulabzoi, Sayed Mohammad, 48, 56, 178, 179, 180
Gulf War, 1, 129, 130, 145, 193
Gurr, Ted, 8

Hairaton, 93
HAMAS, xxx, 7, 197
Hanafi school of Islam, xiv, xxxii, 26, 114
Hanbali school of Islam, xxxii
Hanifa, Abu, 26
Harakat-i-Inqilab-i-Islami, 159
Harakat-i-Islami, 160
Harakat-ul-Mujahideen, 147
Harrison, Mark, 5
Hazaras, 26, 38, 115–16, 196
Herat, 21, 37, 51, 91, 107, 194, 195

hijackers of 9/11 attacks, 1, 5, 163–64, 172
Hikmatyar, Gulbuddin
   about, 120, 159, 197
   conflict within resistance groups, 84, 92, 93, 107, 120, 188
   Islamist movement, 32–33
   Pakistan, 80–81, 83, 109–10, 154, 188
   Taliban, 109–10
   U.S. aid to, 187
Hilmand Valley Project, 27
Hizb-i-Islami, 120, 159, 195, 198
Hizb-i-Islami-Rad-i-Afghanistan, 160
Hizbollah, 7
Homeland Party, 90–91, 190
hostages in Iran, U.S., xviii, 60, 182
human rights violations, 84, 116
Hungary, 78, 94–95
Huntington, Samuel, 104–5
Hussein, Saddam, 100, 104, 120, 130, 141

Imam, Colonel, 110, 195
India
   under British rule, 11, 148, 188
   Najibullah, 88, 89
   nuclear weapons, xiv
   Pakistan, xv, 22–24, 68, 112, 148, 175
   terrorism, 7, 145, 147–148
Indian Ocean, 15, 22, 27, 175
institutional breakdown, 19
interim governments, 84, 153–54
Inter-Services Intelligence Directorate (ISI)
   See ISI
Iran
   Afghan oil pipeline, 113
   clash of civilizations, 104
   history with Afghanistan, 21–22, 27, 33, 40, 52–53
   Islamic revolution, 22, 25, 54, 60, 126, 145
   SAVAK, xxx, 22
   Shi'as, xxxi, 40, 82, 84, 109, 120, 160
   Sistan-Baluchistan attack, 145
   Taliban, 109
   U.S., xviii, 2, 22, 25, 38, 60, 61, 113, 184
Iraq
   bin Laden speech, 161, 162
   invasion of Kuwait, 100, 112, 122, 129, 130, 193
   U.S. war in, ix, xiii–xiv, xv, 1
   war with Iran, 104–120, 141, 145, 194
ISAF, x, 143–44
ISI (Inter-Services Intelligence Directorate)
   about, xxx, 186, 188
   CIA alliance, xxx, 64–65, 71, 73–74, 79, 119, 138
   Mujahideen support, post Soviet withdrawal, 79–84, 92, 119, 138, 183
   Najibullah, 190
   Taliban, 109–11, 195
Islam, fundamentalist. *See also specific Islamist organizations and movements*

clash with Western world, 102–5,
128–29
Pashtuns, 80–81
as a political force, 119–21, 148
the Quran, 129–30
rise of, 13, 22, 76, 117, 126, 133, 138–40
schools and sects of, xxxi–xxxii, 26,
109, 114
Soviet Union, 52–54, 65, 79, 133
Islamic Alliance, 32–33
Islamic Jihad, 7, 11, 123, 125, 140
Islamism, 119–21. *See also* Islam, fundamen-
talist
isolationism, Bush policy of, 2
Israel
Egypt, 66, 121
G.W. Bush, xiii
Iran, 22, 174
Islamist movements, xxx, 7, 121, 122, 129
Middle East wars, 68, 174
Palestinians, 103, 161, 172
Italy, 60, 91, 110, 127, 131, 153
Ittihad-i-Islami, 159

Jabha-i-Nejat-i-Melli, 159
Jaish-e-Muhammad, 147
Jalalabad
1979 revolt, 38
cut-off from Kabul, 53
offensives at, 73, 85–84, 89, 111, 189
Jamiat-i-Islami, 120, 140, 159
Jamiat-ul-Ulema-i-Islam (JUI), 108–9, 112,
147, 199
Japan, 100
Jebh-i-Mutahed, 160
Jiddah, 121–22
jihad, xxx, 129–30
Jordan, 68, 104, 123
Jundullah, 145

Kabul, 73
post Soviet withdrawal, 87–88, 89–91,
107
revolts in, 37–38, 42–43, 51–53, 55–56,
71–73, 154
strategic importance of, 79–80
Taliban take-over and retreat, 111–12,
113, 115, 139–40, 153
Kabul Airport, 55, 93
Kabul Radio, 52, 90
Kabul University, 32, 90
Karmal, Babrak, xviii, xxxi, 31–32, 34–35,
55–56, 75, 154
Karzai, Hamid, x, 150, 153–54
Kasab, Ajmal, 148
Kashmir, 7, 111, 131, 145
Kashmiri militants, 6–7, 147
Kazakhstan, 98, 99, 101, 192, 193
Kenya, xxii, 131, 132, 162

KGB
about, xxx
Afghan infiltration, xxii, 18, 31–32
Amin regime, 43–45, 49–50, 54–56
early PDPA regime, xxxi, 31–32, 33,
34, 36
within Soviet Union, 92, 95
KGB in Afghanistan, The (Mitrokhin), xxii
KHAD, xxx–xxxi, 177
Khalil, Farooq Kashmiri, 147
Khalili, Abdul Karim, 160
Khaliqyar, Fazle Haq, 91, 191
Khalis, Yunis, 80, 84, 159, 187, 188
Khalq faction, xxxi, 31–35, 40–41, 49, 56,
90–92, 118, 137, 178
Khalq (newspaper), 32
Khan, Abdul Ghaffar, 148
Khan, Ismail, 81, 107, 110
Khomeini, Ayatollah, 22, 104
Khorram, Ahmad Ali, 33
Khrushchev, Nikita, 28
Khyber, Mir Akbar, 34, 177
Kishtmand, Ali, 36, 52
Kissinger, Henry, 24, 28, 128
Kivimaki, Timo, 13
Kuwait, 33, 100, 112, 122, 193
Kyrgyzstan, 98

Laakso, Liisa, 13
Laden International, 123
Lake, Anthony, 101
Lake, David, 7
land-reform program, Afghan, 36
languages of Afghanistan, xxi, 21, 26
Lashkar-e-Taiba, 147
Law Enforcement Bulletin, 10
law when superseded by violence, 19
leaders, list of Russian/Soviet and U.S., 157
Lewis, Bernard, 102–4
London bombings, 146

madrasah, xxxi, xxxii, 145, 151
Madrid bombings, 146
Mahaz-i-Melli, 159
Maliki, xxxii
Mao Tse-tung, 11, 173
Masood, Ahmad Shah, 72, 81, 92–93, 111,
139, 188, 197
Mazar-i-Sharif, 113, 116, 153
Mazdooryar, Sherjan, 48, 179
McChrystal, Stanley, xvi, 143–44, 151
media coverage of Afghanistan events, xi,
xx, 145
Middle East Wars, 22, 68, 174
militant hideouts, 145–46
military, Afghan, 31, 37–38, 77, 92, 143, 154
Military-Industrial Complex, ix, xi
Mitrokhin, Vasili, xxii
Mohammadi, Mohammad Nabi, 159
Mohsini, Ayotollah, 160

Momin, Abdul, 93
monarchy of Afghanistan, 2, 18, 26, 32, 41
Moscow Olympics, 62, 183
Mujaddidi, Sibghatullah, 159
Mujahideen
    al Qaeda and bin Laden, 122, 147
    Amin regime, 53, 54
    internecine war, 107, 154
    Najibullah regime, xxxi, 83–84, 88–89,
        91–92, 126–27, 154
    Soviet occupation, 59–60, 63–66, 68–70,
        72–76, 80–85, 102, 119
    victory of, 82, 119, 125, 138
Mullah, defined, xxxi
Mumbai attacks, 147–48
Musharraf, Pervez, 146–47
Muslim Brotherhood, 120–22, 123–25, 140,
    197, 198, 199

Nahzat-i-Islami, 160
Naim, Mohammad, 27
Nairobi, U.S. embassy in, 131–32
Najibullah
    about, xxxi, 35, 112, 154–55
    regime of, xxxi, 75, 79, 84, 87–93, 139, 144
Nassery, Zia Khan, 89
national reconciliation policies, 75, 89, 144
National Revolutionary Party, 33
National Salvation Society, 90, 190
NATO, x, xii, 154
NBC reports, 69–70, 185
necessity for creating new strategy, 149–51
neoconservatives, 102–3, 105–6, 128
"new terrorism," 136
Nicaragua, 11, 66, 69, 184
Niru-i-Islami, 160
Nixon, Richard, 21, 25, 128, 175
Niyazov, Saparmurad, 113
Non-Aligned Movement, 28, 47, 89
Non-Proliferation Treaty, 99
Northern Afghanistan, 21, 28, 33, 40, 107
nuclear weapons, xi, xii, 24, 98–100, 193
Nuristanis, 26

Obama, Barack, ix, xv–xvi, 144, 148–49, 151
oil, 21–22, 100–101, 112–14, 196
Oklahoma City bombing, 146
Olympics, boycott of, 62, 183
Omar, Mullah, 108, 110, 113, 155, 194
opposition parties, Afghan, 159–60
organizational cohesion, 6–7, 10
organizations and concept of terror, 6–8,
    10–12, 173
overwhelming power, consequences of,
    144–45

Pahlavi, Shah Reza, 21–22, 174
Pakistan. *See also* ISI
    Afghan refugee camps, 108–9
    Amin coup, 52–53

China, 71
cycle of power, 148–50
history and background, 22–24, 27, 175
India, 23–24, 175
Islamist movements, xiv, 120
Pashtuns, 28–29
Sunnis, 40
support of Mujahideen, 60, 63, 64–65,
    73–74, 79–81, 119
Taliban and al Qaeda, 107–8, 112–13,
    139–40, 146–48, 195
U.S., x–xi, 23–24, 38, 67–68, 177
Paktia Province, 72
Palestinians, 103, 121, 123, 129, 161–62.
    See also HAMAS
Panjshir Valley, 72
Parcham faction, xxxi, 35, 178
    conflict within PDPA, 33, 34–35, 40–41
    formation of PDPA, 31, 177
    member purge and exile, 49, 56
    Najibullah regime, 93, 177
Pasdaran-i-Jihad-i-Islami, 160
Pashto, 26
Pashtunistan, 23, 28–29
Pashtuns
    about, xxxi, 26, 40, 114, 127, 176, 178, 194
    communist factions, 35, 40–41, 137, 190
    Islamist movements, 120
    nationalism, 35, 41–42, 56, 80, 92, 140,
        188
    Pakistan, 23, 28–29, 83, 84, 111, 148
Pavlovsky, Ivan, 43, 48, 179
PDPA (People's Democratic Party of
    Afghanistan)
    conflict within, 34–36, 41–45, 47–53,
        56, 178
    Najibullah regime, 87, 90, 92
    overview, xxxi, 177, 178, 190
    rise of, 32–34, 40–41, 154, 176
Pentagon attack, 132–33, 140, 153, 164, 201
Persian language, 21, 26
Petraeus, David, xv–xvi, 151
pipelines, oil, 101, 112–14, 193
Poland, 67, 94–95, 192
Ponomarev, Boris, 32, 54
poppy crop, 150
Post, Jerrold, 8, 9
power, consequences of overwhelming,
    144–45
Pravda, 70
presidential order to support Afghan insur-
    gency, 63, 64, 183
Project for the New American Century, 105
proliferation of WMD, 98, 99–100
psycho-logic, 8–12
psychological forces for defining terrorism,
    4–5, 8–12, 15, 136
Puzanov, Alexander, 43–44, 47–48, 50–51, 180

Qadir, Abdul, 35–36, 52, 176, 178

Qandahar, 51, 71, 107, 108, 153, 155, 185, 194
Qum, 22
Quran, the, xxxi, 128, 129–30, 200
Qutb, Sayed, 120–21, 197–98

Rabbani, Burhanuddin, 32–33, 107, 109, 111, 120, 159, 187
Rafi, Mohammad, 36, 52, 178, 191
Ratebzad, Anahita, 35
rational choice theory for defining terrorism, 5–8, 11, 12, 13–15, 136
Reagan, Ronald, xviii–xix, 67–68, 74, 76, 128, 186. *See also* Reagan adminis-tration
Reagan administration, 66, 67–71, 73–75, 102, 128
Red Cross, 79, 115
refugees, Afghan, 59, 79, 83, 154
    Iran, 138
    Pakistan, 65, 72–73, 108–9, 138
    Taliban, xxxii, 107–8, 138
Rishkor army base, 51, 52, 181
Romania, 94–95, 192
"Roots of Muslim Rage, The" (Lewis), 102–4
Ross, Jeffrey Ian, 12–13
Rubin, Barnet, 60
Rumsfeld, Donald, 154
Russia, 1, 27, 97–100, 101, 111, 192

Sadat, Anwar El, 66, 69–70, 121, 123–24
Sakharov, Andrei, 95, 192
sanctions, 17, 37, 62
Sarwari, Asadullah, 48, 56, 179, 180
Saudi Arabia
    about, xxxii, 40, 184
    bin Laden, 122–23
    Iran, 22, 33, 82
    Najibullah regime, 18, 89–90
    oil pipeline, 112–13
    support of Mujahideen, xix, 60, 63, 65, 69, 80
    Taliban, 19, 111–12, 139–40
    U.S., 65, 76, 100, 104, 112, 138
SAVAK, xxx, 22
Sayyaf, Abdul Rasool, 32, 80, 84, 159, 187, 188
Sazman-i-Nasr, 160
Scowcroft, Brent, 98
September 11 attacks, xii, 1, 132–33, 140, 153, 163–64, 201
Sevan, Benon, 93, 191
Shafi, xxxii
Shari'ah law, xxxi, 109, 114–15, 116, 126
Shi'as and Shi'a Islam, xxxi, xxxii, 22, 26, 82, 84, 109, 120, 160
Shindand revolt, 71
Sistan-Baluchistan attack, 145
society, Afghan, xxi, 19, 26
    Najibullah regime, 139

as source of conflict, 41–42, 117
    under Soviet rule, 18, 36, 38, 40, 76, 78–79, 118, 137–38
    under Taliban rule, 114–16, 139–40
society, Soviet, 78–79, 95
Solzhenitsyn, Alexandr, 95
Somalia, 131, 175
South-East Asia Treaty Organization (SEATO), 25, 175
Soviet Union
    Afghanistan 1950s through Daud regime, 18, 27–29, 31, 32–34, 41, 175
    Afghanistan under Amin and Taraki, 18, 36–38, 41–45, 47–53
    China, 24–25, 70–71
    economy, 69, 92, 94, 98, 101, 192
    invasion and occupation of Afghanistan, 53–57, 59–66, 67, 71–73, 75–76, 77–79, 119
    Iran, 22
    KGB (*See* KGB)
    leaders' list, 157
    Najibullah regime, 87–89, 91
    political crisis and collapse of, 69, 79, 92–95, 97–99, 185, 188
    withdrawal from Afghanistan, 75–77, 79–80, 82, 84, 91–92, 94, 144
SOVMAT, 68–70
Special Guard, 92
Spin Baldak, battle of, 110, 195
splitting and externalizing, 9
state terror, 13–14, 95, 135
Stinger missiles, 74–75, 122, 187
Strategic Arms Limitation Treaties, 61, 62
Strategic Arms Reduction Treaty (START 1), 100, 193
strategic choice theory for defining terrorism, 5–8, 11, 12, 13–15, 136
strategic partnership of U.S. and Russia, 97–100, 101, 192
structural analysis for defining terrorism, 12–14, 15, 136–37
Sudan, 123, 131
suicide terrorism, 5, 7, 133, 140, 145
Sunnis, xxxii, 26, 40, 114, 120, 139, 145, 159
Syria, 68

Tajikistan, 22, 78, 131
Tajiks, 26, 38, 40, 92–93, 109, 116, 120
Taliban
    al Qaeda, 127–28
    background, xxxii, 107–9, 121, 145, 153–55
    Najibullah, 93
    Pakistan, 109–11, 112–13, 149, 195
    rise and rule of, 19, 114–16, 128–29, 139–40
    Saudi Arabia, 111–112
    U.S. and, x, 112–14, 133, 140, 197
Tamil Tigers, 7

Tanai, Shah Nawaz, 90, 92, 154, 188, 190
Taraki, Nur Mohammad, xxxi, 31–32,
    34–38, 41–45, 47–50, 56, 154
Tehrik-i-Taliban Pakistan, 146–47
terror, culture of, 13, 19, 76, 95, 137, 138, 139
terrorism, defining, xxxii, 3–5, 8–15, 135–
    37, 171
terrorist constituency, 13, 174
tetonic forces of history, 94
Time interview of bin Laden, 132
Tolstoy, Leo, 151
trade routes through Afghanistan, 89, 109,
    110, 113
training
    Afghans by Pakistan, 52, 65, 73–74,
        119, 183
    Afghans by Soviets, 31
    bin Laden and al Qaeda, 122, 123, 131, 132
troop levels, U.S., 143
Tsagolov, K., 144
Tudeh party, 54
Turabi, Hassan al-, 123, 198
Turkmen, 26, 38, 40
Turkmenistan, 101, 110–11, 112–13, 196
Turner, Stansfield, 64
Tylor, E. B., 17

Ukraine, 98, 99, 188
United Airlines Flight 93, 164
United Airlines Flight 175, 163
United Arab Emirates, 60
United Nations, 3, 33, 61, 93, 100, 113, 115
United States. *See also specific presidents and*
    administrations
    Afghanistan 1950s through Daud regime,
        27–29, 176
    al Qaeda and bin Laden, 130–33, 161–62
    China, 24–25, 70–71
    CIA (*See* CIA)
    first Afghan communist regime, 18, 25,
        37, 50, 51–52
    invasion and occupation of Afghanistan,
        140–41, 143–45
    Iran, 22
    leaders list, 157
    Pakistan, 23–24, 67–68, 149–51 (*See also*
        ISI alliance *under* CIA)
    policy post Soviet collapse, 97, 99–100,
        128, 146
    policy post Soviet withdrawal from
        Afghanistan, 84–85, 91

Russia and, 97–100, 101
    Soviet occupation of Afghanistan, 59–66,
        68–70, 73–76, 128, 138
    Taliban, 112–14
unmanned aircraft attacks, x, 147, 150
UNOCAL, 112–14
Uruzgan Province, 108
Ustinov, Dmitri, 47, 54
Uzbekistan, 78, 88, 153
Uzbeks, 24, 26, 38, 40, 93

Vance, Cyrus, 25, 61
Velayati, Ali Akbar, 113
Vietnam War, xi, xii
violence, culture. *See* culture of violence
volunteers, foreign, 88–89

Wahhab, Mohammad Ibn Abd al-, xxxii
Wahhabism, xxxii
Wakil, Abdul, xx
Watan Party, 90–91, 190
Watanjar, Aslam, 42, 48, 56, 176, 179, 180,
    181, 191
Wazarat-e Amancyat-e Dawlati (WAD), xxxi
weapons depot destruction, ISI's, 80
Weinberger/Powell doctrine, xii
women, treatment of, xxii, 84, 109, 114,
    115–16, 139–40
World Bank, 37
World Islamic Front for Jihad, 129
World Trade Center bombings, 131, 132–33,
    140, 153, 163, 201

Xinjiang, 24, 40, 70, 127

Yazov, Dmitry, 144, 191
Yeltsin, Boris, 97–98, 99, 101, 157
Yemen, 66, 175
Yousaf, Mohammad, 60, 184
Yusuf, Ramzi, 131–32, 200

Zahir Shah, xxi, 18, 26, 39, 182
Zawahiri, Ayman al-, 123–26, 199
Zawahiri, Rabia'a al-, 123
Zia-ul Haq
    alliance with U.S. to support
        Mujahideen, 60, 64–65, 74, 81,
        119, 148
    military regime and Islamic agenda of,
        23–24, 52–53

ABOUT THE AUTHOR

Deepak Tripathi is a former BBC correspondent and editor (1977–2000). During this period, he set up the BBC office in Kabul, served as the corporation's resident correspondent in Afghanistan, and reported from Pakistan, Syria, Sri Lanka, and India. He is the author of *Overcoming the Bush Legacy in Iraq and Afghanistan* (Potomac Books, 2010) and *Sri Lanka's Foreign Policy Dilemmas* (Chatham House, 1989). His articles have appeared in publications such as the *Economist* and the *Daily Telegraph* of London, and he continues to write for journals and newspapers such as *Al-Ahram Weekly*, *CounterPunch*, *History News Network* (George Mason University, Virginia), *Informed Comment*, the *Palestine Chronicle*, and *ZNet*. In the 1970s, he worked for the federal government in Washington, D.C., and has taken a keen interest in U.S. foreign policy and great power rivalries in South and West Asia for more than thirty years. He currently lives near London.